C
WELSH HISTORIC MO...

A Guide to Ancient and Historic Wales

Gwynedd

Frances Lynch

London: HMSO

ISBN 0 11 701574 1

Front cover: Harlech Castle (no. 132) by Henry Gastineau (*c.*1820). By kind permission of the National Library of Wales.
Back cover: Tan y Muriau Neolithic burial chamber (no. 21)

Other volumes in the series:
Dyfed
Glamorgan and Gwent

Forthcoming:
Clwyd and Powys

Series Editor: Sian E Rees

HMSO publications are available from:

HMSO Publications Centre
(Mail, fax and telephone orders only)
PO Box 276, London, SW8 5DT
Telephone orders 0171-873 9090
General enquiries 0171-873 0011
(queuing system in operation for both numbers)
Fax orders 0171-873 8200

HMSO Bookshops
49 High Holborn, London, WC1V 6HB
(counter service only)
0171 873 0011 Fax 0171 831 1326
68–69 Bull Street, Birmingham, B4 6AD
0121 236 9696 Fax 0121 236 9699
33 Wine Street, Bristol, BS1 2BQ
0117 926 4306 Fax 0117 929 4515
9–21 Princess Street, Manchester, M60 8AS
0161 834 7201 Fax 0161 833 0634
16 Arthur Street, Belfast, BT1 4GD
01232 238451 Fax 01232 235401
71 Lothian Road, Edinburgh, EH3 9AZ
0131 228 4181 Fax 0131 229 2734
The HMSO Oriel Bookshop
The Friary, Cardiff CF1 4AA
01222 395548 Fax 01222 384347

HMSO's Accredited Agents
(see Yellow Pages)

and through good booksellers

Printed in the United Kingdom for HMSO
Dd297408 6/95 C40 G3397 10170

Contents

Editor's Foreword

As an archaeologist working with the preservation of our historic monuments, I have come to the firm conclusion that one of the best methods of conservation is to awaken in people an awareness of the unique contribution that ancient sites make, enriching our landscape by their quiet presence. With that aim in mind, this series of four regional guides was conceived, covering, in turn: Dyfed; Glamorgan and Gwent; Gwynedd; and Clwyd and Powys. Each volume describes 150 well preserved monuments which are accessible to the public. The volume on Gwynedd covers the area roughly equivalent to the old counties of Anglesey, Caernarfonshire and Meirionnydd.

The time-span covered by the volumes is from the first appearance of man in the Old Stone Age to the 16th century AD. The 16th century heralded many changes which suggested it as an appropriate termination point for a guide devoted to ancient monuments rather than to townscapes and general landscapes. Speaking somewhat casually, it marked the end of serious use of the castle in Wales, the end of the monasteries and, with the Act of Union of 1536, the political merging of Wales with England.

Inevitably there are many omissions from the book, sometimes made very reluctantly. Churches in use are not included as, despite their obvious interest and appeal, they are neither ruins nor monuments, and their very number is such that they need a guide of their own. The remains of industrial sites are a particular casualty of the cut-off date, as the vast majority of the more spectacular date from later than the 15th century. There are other sites of which the very fragility of the archaeological remains, or of the wildlife within them, render visits inadvisable. Yet more sites were left out because they were remote and difficult of access. The main omissions, however, were the many monuments which lie inaccessible to the public on private land, many of which are very fine. For this reason, an appendix has been added, listing well preserved sites for which special permission must be obtained before visiting.

Ancient sites are a tangible link with our past; they are our only link with the remotest past before literacy gave us a written history. And for the events of that written history, later sites are the stage, scenery and backdrop to the action that took place. To see these monuments makes our past come alive, if we can only clothe their stones and earthworks, battlemented walls and traceried windows with our imaginations. If this book helps the visitor to do this, its main objective will have been achieved.

Sian E Rees
Series Editor

How to Use the Book

The introduction gives an outline of the physical shape and the nature of Gwynedd. The main gazetteer is then ordered in period-based chapters, so that monuments of a class fall together, and each chapter is preceded by a brief discussion of the history and the type of monuments of that period in Gwynedd. Each site is given a number to aid identification on the maps at the end of the book.

Location

The monuments are ordered numerically in the gazetteer, and each is given the name by which it is commonly known. The nearest identifiable village or town is also given, from which the access directions usually start. Where several monuments occur nearby, directions are cross-referenced to link them into a longer guided walk. The site type, a rough indication of its date, the Ordnance Survey 1:50,000 map number and the site's six-figure national grid reference are also given. It is hoped that the directions alone will enable those without the 1:50,000 map to find the sites, but the enjoyment and interest of travelling is so much enhanced by maps that everyone should carry one. In addition to the 1:50,000 series, the Snowdonia National Park (virtually all of Gwynedd except Anglesey and Lleyn) is covered by three Outdoor Leisure maps at 1:25,000 (nos 16, 17, 18 and 23). These mark all the footpaths and almost every monument, and are invaluable to those who want to take the longer walks described in this guide.

To locate a site on an Ordnance Survey map, first get the appropriate 1:50,000 map, the number of which is given on each entry (e.g., OS 157). Then look at the grid reference for the site, which consists of two letters and six figures (e.g., SM 750255). The letters at the beginning of the reference can usually be ignored as long as the correct map is being used, as they are a large-scale reference for the appropriate 100km grid square. Then take the first three numbers, which refer to the numbers on the top or bottom of the map: the first two of these will indicate the western line of the 1km square in which the site lies; the third will measure in tenths how far eastward within that square the site lies. Repeat the procedure with the second group of three numbers, which refer to the numbers on the right or left side of the map and increase in value northwards. Although this may sound complicated, after doing a few trial searches there should be no problem with easily locating any given site.

Accessibility

A guide to the accessibility of each site is given by the following:

U Unrestricted, i.e., access at any reasonable time free of charge.

R Restricted, i.e., access is restricted by opening hours, entry charge or the requirement to obtain permission before going onto private land. If this symbol is used, an explanation is usually given at the end of the access direction.

The upland appears to be open land but much of it is privately owned and in agricultural use. Many owners are willing to allow access and, in these cases, the monuments on their land have been included here. But their kindness must not be abused. Particular care must be taken during the lambing season.

Cadw standard hours

Several monuments maintained by Cadw are unrestricted, while a few operate under the 'key keeper' system by which the key may be collected from a nearby farm or shop. The major castles, however, all operate on 'Cadw standard hours' – they are open from Monday to Saturday and often part of Sunday during main daylight hours, except for Christmas Eve, Christmas Day, Boxing Day and New Year's Day. Full details of opening hours may be obtained from Cadw on request (Brunel House, 2 Fitzalan Road, Cardiff CF2 1UY, tel: 01222 465511).

Churches are very often kept locked. The entries indicate where the keys may be obtained if this is the case, but it may be necessary to make arrangements some days in advance in order to avoid disappointment.

Disabled visitors

An attempt has been made to estimate how accessible each monument may be for disabled visitors. The entries are rated 1 to 4, this number appearing directly after the U or R at the head of each entry.

1 Easy access for all, including wheelchairs.

2 Easy access (short walk) for pedestrians but limited for wheelchairs.

3 Restricted access for disabled, but site visible from road or car park.

4 Access for able-bodied only – quite a long or steep walk.

Where bracken is liable to obscure the site in high summer this has been indicated.

Abbreviations

These occur especially in the access directions:

km	kilometre	PO	Post Office
L, LHS	left, left-hand side	R, RHS	right, right-hand side
m	metre	tel	telephone
ml	mile	trig. point	trigonometrical survey station (concrete pillar on hilltop)
NT	National Trust		
OS	Ordnance Survey		
persevere	continue along a road, ignoring turnings to R and L		

Welsh Place-names

Any visitor to Wales will soon realise that the spelling of Welsh place-names can vary considerably, different versions of the same name being found on maps, road signs and in publications. Compounds of two or more elements may be found separated, hyphenated or run together. This series has tried to use the most commonly found versions, but has avoided using hyphens wherever possible.

Safety

Ancient monuments are often hazardous, and all visitors must take sensible precautions. Ruins, however carefully looked after, can present dangers for the unwary, and especially for children, who should be supervised at all times and warned very seriously against climbing on walls. Loose stones, on cairns or ramparts for example, can cause twisted ankles – a major problem if you are far from the road.

Many of the walks described in this guide are in remote upland areas. Wear appropriate shoes and always carry a waterproof and some warm clothing, for the weather can change very quickly and alarming mists can descend. Always take a map and a compass, and tell someone where you are going and when you expect to return.

Monuments in categories 1–3 are suitable for all ages. Adults accompanying children will need to assess the suitability of category 4 sites according to the tastes and abilities of the individual child, but there will normally be a natural history or aesthetic appeal to the walk, or even a picnic, in addition to its historical attraction.

Country Code

It is, of course, most important to observe the Country Code, especially when visiting the monuments in the book which are situated on public footpaths through private land, or on private land itself. Keep dogs on leads, always shut gates securely, and open and shut them rather than climbing over. Do not attempt to climb a stone wall unless there is a stile. Keep to paths, do not drop litter, and avoid any action which might start a fire. If you keep to these rules, monuments in private hands will continue to be cherished and visitors welcomed.

Further Information and Useful Addresses

A number of the monuments described in the gazetteer are 'Guardianship Sites', owned or maintained by Cadw: Welsh Historic Monuments, a body set up in 1984 with the statutory responsibility for protecting, conserving and presenting the 'built heritage' of Wales on behalf of the Secretary of State. Many more of the sites listed in the book are privately owned but have been 'scheduled', or given statutory protection by the Secretary of State. Lists and maps of scheduled ancient monuments are produced by Cadw, and a series of guidebooks provide detailed descriptions of the monuments it maintains. Further information can be obtained by contacting Cadw at: Brunel House, 2 Fitzalan Road, Cardiff CF2 1UY, tel: 01222 465511.

Much of Gwynedd is within the Snowdonia National Park, and the Park Authority also has a duty to conserve and protect monuments within its area, although it does not directly own or manage any. There are several information centres run by the Park Authority, which can provide help with accommodation and also information on the man-made and natural heritage of the area. The Study Centre (Plas Tan y Bwlch, Maentwrog, Blaenau Ffestiniog, Gwynedd LL41 3YU, tel: 01766 85324) runs residential courses on the archaeology and history of the area. The headquarters' address is Snowdonia National Park Offices, Penrhyndeudraeth, Gwynedd LL48 6LS, tel: 01766 770274. The borough councils also play a role in the conservation and management of monuments and areas of natural beauty: Ynys Môn (Anglesey) maintains a coastal footpath around much of the island, and Aberconwy manages the summit of the Great Orme at Llandudno as a Country Park.

The National Trust has substantial landholdings in north Wales, and many of these upland areas contain notable concentrations of monuments, mainly of the prehistoric period. Areas such as the Carneddi above Bethesda and Gregennan on Cadair Idris provide wonderful walks, combining beautiful scenery with historical interest of a very high order. The Trust is also the owner of the Roman fort at Segontium (no. 92). Their north Wales headquarters are at: Trinity Square, Llandudno, Gwynedd LL30 2DE, tel: 01492 860123.

The Gwynedd Archaeological Trust is the body responsible for maintaining a Sites and Monuments Record, a list of all known monuments in Gwynedd. It carries out rescue excavation and survey work on sites which are threatened with development or erosion. The Trust may be contacted at: Garth Road, Bangor LL57 2RP, tel: 01248 352535.

The following museums have material from ancient sites in Gwynedd:

The National Museum of Wales, Cathays Park, Cardiff (with illustrated archaeological guidebooks).

Bangor Museum, Ffordd Gwynedd, Bangor (with illustrated archaeological guidebooks).

Oriel Ynys Môn, Rhosmeirch, Llangefni, Anglesey (with interpretative displays).

Grosvenor Museum, Grosvenor Road, Chester.

While all attempts have been made to ensure that the accessibility of monuments is as described, unforeseen circumstances can alter access quite suddenly; monuments may sometimes have to be closed for short periods for repair and, sadly, footpaths do disappear from time to time and owners change, or change their attitude to visitors. Discretion must therefore be exercised during visits and no liability can be accepted for errors in the information supplied.

Introduction

The county of Gwynedd epitomises the classic idea of Welshness. It was the heart of the last surviving independent principality in Wales, and the Welsh language and cultural traditions in this region have resisted the inroads of English and international uniformity longer than anywhere else in the country. The image of a mountain fastness conjured by the name Eryri (Snowdonia) is appropriate, for much of the region is remote, rocky and sparsely inhabited. However, the glaciated landscapes around the great mountain of Snowdon, so famous in the annals of geology, geomorphology and the Wales Tourist Board, are not characteristic of the whole of the county.

Anglesey, in particular, is an area of accessible lowland. On a base of some of the oldest rocks in Britain lies a softened but complex landscape which has for centuries provided the main 'food basket' for the region. For this reason it has always been well populated and, at the centre of the Irish Sea trade routes, always open to contacts and ideas from the wider world.

The Lleyn peninsula shares with Anglesey a mild maritime climate similar to the former county of Pembrokeshire in south-west Wales, and seldom suffers severe winters. But this narrow western plateau with its striking line of extinct volcanoes has remained far more isolated than Anglesey, since its coastline of beautiful steep cliffs has few good harbours.

The high ground of Ardudwy and southern Meirionnydd surrounding Cardigan Bay drops down to a narrow coastal strip into which most modern development is concentrated, but earlier settlement extended to the higher land, leaving an unparalleled record of ancient landscapes surviving virtually intact. Those exploring these hills will encounter monuments, fields and settlements of several different periods, and some of the most worthwhile walks have been given a grouped entry in this book, rather than being separated chronologically, to ease appreciation of the richness and depth of this historical palimpsest.

The same is true of the high ground of Arllechwedd, the region between Bangor and Conwy. Being outside the Snowdonia massif, these hills enjoy a better climate, making them an attractive agricultural area at periods of warmer weather or high population pressure, such as the earlier Bronze Age. Remains of this period, and huts and fields of Roman and medieval date, are easily seen at many points on these hills, especially on the south-facing slopes above Rowen, in the sheltered Conwy valley. This is an area of exceptional richness and fertility with noticeably fine and fruitful gardens. The deep valley gives access to the heart of Gwynedd at Betws y Coed, the centre of several modern lines of communication.

These steep, wooded headwater valleys did not, however, provide easy routes before Telford's engineering skill opened up the region at the beginning of the 19th century. The earlier routes avoided the mountainous centre, making greater use of the sea and of the wide fault valley in which lie Bala Lake and the Mawddach estuary. The prehistoric distributions, however, suggest that upland tracks may have linked Bala with the coastal concentration of population in Ardudwy, implying that the valley bottom was choked with marsh and forest during this period. But forts near Bala (see Caer Gai, Appendix) and at Brithdir confirm that the valley was clear and well-used by Roman times, and its importance was consolidated by the building of medieval mottes at several of the same sites. Edward I, however, turned again to sea routes, and the distribution of his famous series of castles reflects a different strategic thinking.

Because only a few areas of Gwynedd are agriculturally fertile, the region as a whole has never been rich in any absolute sense. But it is not without natural resources, which at various times have been exploited to great effect by the local population and – in later centuries – by outsiders. The earliest large-scale exploitation was the Neolithic use of volcanic rock, notably from Graig Lwyd above Penmaenmawr (no. 18), to fashion stone axe-heads which were dispersed all over Britain. When copper, and later bronze, became the essential materials for tool-making, the minerals of north Wales were mined on a surprisingly large scale, creating a local industry which, for some centuries during the middle Bronze Age, was in the forefront of development (see no. 34). Recent excavation in Meirionnydd has shown that iron-making was well established in the 1st century AD. In the absence of ironstone, this industry was based upon the exploitation of bog-ores. The arrival of the Roman army and access to the imperial market must have led to an intensification of much of this industrial activity, and an increase in agricultural production, shown by the development of terraced fields around early farms.

The record of industrial economy is virtually blank in the post-Roman and early medieval periods. Archaeology and the scant historical documents suggest a rural, agricultural society of scattered farmsteads with only very small centres of population based on royal courts and monasteries. Towns, in any true sense, were virtually unknown until the 13th century, when Edward I planned to consolidate his rule by founding boroughs alongside, and under the protection of, each of his great castles. Although Welsh burgesses were fairly soon holding office in these originally 'English-only' towns, the boroughs were slow to develop and expand. Indeed some, like Newborough on Anglesey, are today no more than villages.

Because the single farmstead is Wales's natural settlement unit, the towns and villages in this region of quite exceptional natural beauty are often rather disappointing. Most of them date from the 19th century, and they tend to straggle along the road without a centre or visual focus. However, the record of earlier human activity in this splendid landscape can bear comparison with that of any other region in these islands and, because of the use of stone and the pastoral nature of later agriculture, it is far better preserved than in many other parts of Britain. It is this wealth of visible, tangible history in a landscape of surpassing beauty which this guidebook aims to present.

1
Early Hunters

The earliest evidence of man in north Wales does not come from Gwynedd, but from Clwyd. Human bones and stone hand-axes which had been swept by a flood into the back of a narrow cave at Pontnewydd, near St Asaph, testify to man's presence here a quarter of a million years ago. However, this camp site is unlikely to have been unique: more than one family group would have been hunting the tundra territory of north Wales, but all evidence for Old Stone Age or Palaeolithic activities would have been swept away by the readvance of glaciers in the last Ice Age. Only where it has been protected, as in the cave at Pontnewydd, has information about their tools (mainly hand-axes), and about the large animals they hunted, been discovered.

Caves provided ready-made shelters for people and animals, and frequently contain the bones of those who died there. The limestone headlands above Llandudno – the Great and Little Ormes – contain many caves. Several have yielded animal bones from the interglacial periods, but no evidence for human occupation at that date. The earliest artefacts from Gwynedd are the decorated deer teeth and carved horse jaw from Kendrick's Cave on the east face of the Great Orme (see Appendix). This jawbone, decorated with a sharply cut zigzag pattern, is a unique piece; its authenticity has been doubted, but modern opinion would accept its antiquity at about 30,000 BC, just before the worsening climate drove people from the region for some 15,000 years.

The record of continuous human occupation in Gwynedd begins after the last Ice Age, in the context of a warmer climate and an increasingly thick deciduous woodland housing a range of animals still familiar to us. Because of the change in environment and the food it provided, tools became more specialised, and spear and arrow tips smaller. These stone or flint tools are usually the only evidence of man's presence. Small, mobile hunting groups moved between inland and coastal camps to exploit a seasonal diversity of food resources. Consequently, houses were flimsy, and perhaps little more than windbreaks.

Most sites in Gwynedd where Middle Stone Age (Mesolithic) stone tools have been found are close to the present coast, but it should be remembered that the sea level was a good deal lower then than it is today. Many sites have been lost beneath the sea, but the inland camps have survived where hunters exploited woodland environments but also enjoyed access to coastal marshes and their rich resources of

Artist's impression of a hunters' camp like that at Aberffraw (no. 1)

wildfowl. Unfortunately the acid soils have destroyed the bones of their prey, so we cannot reconstruct a very full picture of their life and economy. However, where circumstances are more favourable to survival, as at Star Carr in Yorkshire, we can see that these hunters made effective use of all manner of plants and trees, and animals were valued not only for meat but for bone and antler for use in making pins, needles, fish-hooks, harpoons and all sorts of tools and equipment. Nearly every poaching device known today was used by Mesolithic hunters.

Characteristic flint tools, tiny arrow tips (microliths) and round scrapers for cleaning skins have been found, with waste chips from their manufacture, at a number of sites along the southern shore of the Lleyn peninsula, from Aberdaron to Pwllheli. Finds have also been made on similar clifftops in Anglesey, but nothing reveals the presence of these sites today save a scatter of flint flakes in the soil. Such flint scatters may be discovered during modern building or agricultural activity or, occasionally, during archaeological excavation. It was such an excavation which revealed the Mesolithic camp at Trwyn Du, Aberffraw (no. 1), which was overlain by an early Bronze Age burial monument which is still visible. Recent building works in the village revealed that a number of other hunting camps had been established along the banks of the river in the centuries around 7000 BC.

1
Trwyn Du, Aberffraw

Middle Stone Age site and round cairn

c.7000 BC and late 3rd millennium BC

OS 114 SH 353679 U4

Park in Aberffraw, go to old bridge and walk 0.7ml (1.1km) along river on W (easy at low tide, more awkward at high tide). The headland, Trwyn Du, projects across estuary, but path continues straight ahead through kissing gate on to summit (with stone seat). Looking seaward, cairn stands at 10 o'clock

White 1978

This is the only extensive Middle Stone Age site excavated in Gwynedd. The excavation in 1974, necessitated by erosion on the site, revealed a scatter of worked and waste flint chips, the residue of tool manufacture on the spot. The camp site, on which no evidence of structures was found, would have looked out over a river valley but not an estuary, since the sea level was then lower. The tools included small arrow tips, skin preparation tools, and two small stone axes suggesting some tree-cutting and wood-working. Charcoal from a camp fire produced a radiocarbon date of about 7000 BC.

About five thousand years later a burial monument was built on the spot, partly covering the remains of the earlier settlement. This cairn was built over a narrow grave surrounded by an elaborate pattern of stones, and was retained within a kerb of large slabs, alternately tall and low. Six of the tall ones, spaced at regular intervals, can still be seen projecting through the grass.

Between the kissing gate and the stone seat is the foundation of a small, rectangular building and the base of a field-wall – presumably the remains of a medieval or later cottage.

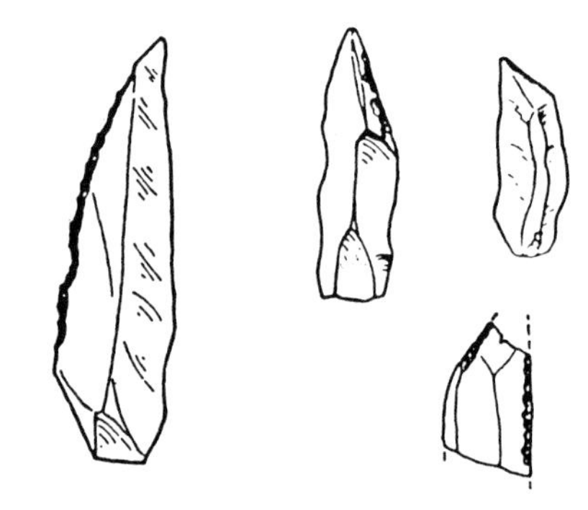

Flint arrow tips (microliths) from Aberffraw

2

The First Farmers

The change from a hunting to a farming economy is one of the most momentous in human history, but the process by which it was effected in various areas of the world is difficult to pin down. In Britain the native hunting societies had developed woodland and animal management to some extent, but the appearance of new crops and animals – such as sheep and goats, which are native to the eastern Mediterranean – must indicate the arrival of some colonists from the Continent.

The development of agriculture enabled man to live a more settled life, with the consequence that we can still recognise signs of ancient human presence in our modern landscape. Botanical research has shown that the first inroads on the dense primeval woodland of these islands was being made in the 4th millennium BC to clear land for fields and pasture.

More dramatic links with this past are the great stone tombs which still stand in our fields today. These tombs, like those in many other parts of western Europe, are family vaults used over many centuries. It is thought that they symbolise permanence and continuity for the community who built them and whose ancestral bones they contained. These tombs take various forms, all of them monumental, and all originally covered by mounds of earth or stone. Most have been robbed by now, leaving the impressive stone chambers exposed.

Twenty such tombs still stand in Anglesey, and there are several in Ardudwy, Lleyn and the Conwy valley. The Anglesey tombs are very varied in design, suggesting that farming groups with rather diverse ancestry had settled in that fertile and accessible island. Several are small passage graves (nos 5, 7 and 10) akin to those in Brittany, Ireland and Scotland; others are box-like structures similar to those in the Clyde region (nos 2 and 6); one (no. 4) is a smaller version of Newgrange in Ireland, and a few defy classification.

The tombs in Ardudwy and Lleyn are more uniform. They belong to a group known as portal dolmens, characterised by tall entrance stones fronting a small, rectangular chamber which was often covered by an exceptionally large capstone. Tombs of this design are also to be found on the east coast of Ireland, reminding us that early man was a competent sailor for whom the sea provided easier travelling than the trackless inland forests.

Each tomb was used over a long period, and might remain a focus for the identity of its community for a thousand years or more. During this time some might be

Artist's impression of the funeral ceremonies in the central chamber of Barclodiad y Gawres (no. 4)

quite radically altered or enlarged, a process exceptionally well illustrated at Trefignath (no. 2) and at Dyffryn Ardudwy (no. 23). It is thought that most of the tombs were built in the earlier Neolithic, around 3000 BC, but some, such as the semi-subterranean one at Lligwy (no. 13) and the well-known monument, Bryn Celli Ddu (no. 8), may have been constructed much later, perhaps closer to 2000 BC, when new burial traditions were beginning to be adopted in other parts of the country.

The houses of the living are much more elusive than the houses of the dead; they were made of wood, and the only evidence of their presence is the pattern of holes in which the posts had been set. Such discoveries are very rare and only made by chance, but one has been found at Llandegai, near Bangor. It was a large house (13m by 6m) divided into three 'rooms', of which the central one is believed to have been the main living area. This style of house is common in Europe and has been found in Ireland. In Europe they are grouped into large villages which may be surrounded by a defensive palisade. In Ireland, and at Llandegai, they occur as single farmsteads and any enclosure or defence of the site is rare. In fact, the impression given by the settlements and artefacts of the period is one of a peaceful and egalitarian society, though not without organisation and control, as their ability to build such large communal monuments demonstrates.

One of the most characteristic artefacts of the period is the stone axe-head, used to fell trees and build houses: the essential tool of the farmer. These axes may be made from chipped and polished flint where that is available, or from igneous rocks. The igneous axes are rather tougher than the flint ones, and the rocks are so distinctive that they can be traced to their point of origin. This work has revealed that many axes were made at what may be called 'factories', where particularly suitable rocks were quarried on a surprisingly large scale. Two such sites exist in Gwynedd, at Graig Lwyd, Penmaenmawr (no. 18) – where quarrying still continues – and on the northern end of Mynydd Rhiw (no. 22). Graig Lwyd was a very important site and its products have been found all over Britain, demonstrating the extent of trade or exchange, and showing that contacts of some kind were maintained between communities in all parts of the country.

This contact may explain some of the changes which we can see affecting north Wales in the late Neolithic (around 2500 BC). In the earlier Neolithic all the comparable sites, in tomb design, house building, pottery, etc., had lain to the west, and had been related to movement across and up and down the Irish Sea. Later there is a change, and many aspects of life seem to be affected by ideas which emanate from the south and east, suggesting much more traffic along inland routes.

The appearance of henge monuments at Llandegai (now covered by an industrial estate) and at Bryn Celli Ddu (no. 8) in the later Neolithic indicates a shift in religious thinking, for it is believed that these open, circular bank and ditch enclosures were designed for some religious or social ceremonial which was much less intimately connected with death and burial than the religion of the megalithic tombs. The change from anonymous communal burial in such tombs, to individual graves furnished with goods which reflect the personality and status of the occupant, is another social trend which appears to emanate from the south-east.

This latter trend, which is associated with the appearance of Beaker pottery (a particularly finely made drinking cup of a type found in many parts of Europe as well as in Britain), was thought to result from a large-scale invasion of Britain by continental people with a different, more aggressive and hierarchical form of society. The reality of such an invasion is now doubted, but the changes to society were real and, in some parts of Britain, fundamental. In Wales they did not take such deep root, but even here the Bronze Age had a different atmosphere, not just as a result of the new technology, but also due to different attitudes to life.

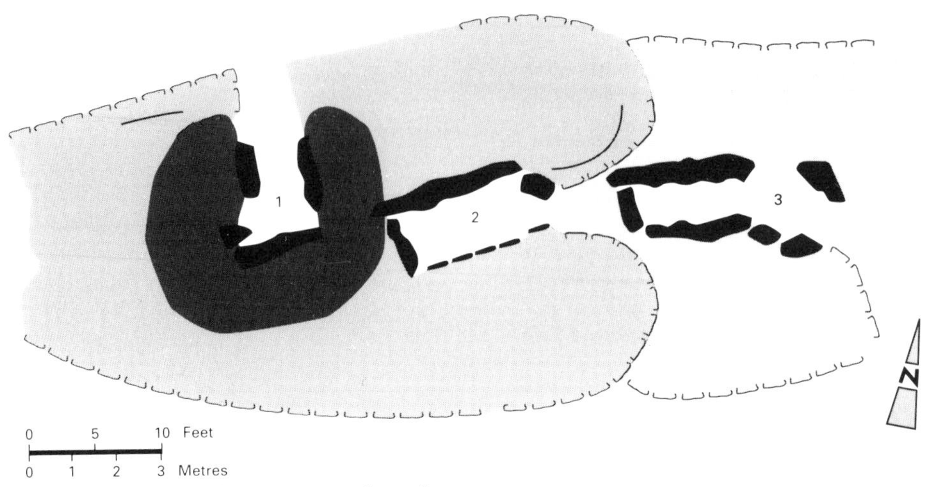

The sequence of development at Trefignath

2
Trefignath, Holyhead

Neolithic burial chamber

4th/early 3rd millennium BC

OS 114 SH 259805 U2 Cadw

Approaching Holyhead from E, 1.4ml (2.25km) after end of embankment turn L off A5 to Trearddur, L at small crossroads (by school), continue for 0.6ml (1km), passing a fine standing stone (Cadw); park on L where road widens. Tomb (signposted) is 50m further on (room for 1 car)

Smith and Lynch 1987

This impressive monument has recently been excavated and now provides some of the best evidence for multi-period construction in Britain. It was originally believed that these great 'family tombs' were built at one period and remained unaltered throughout their history of use. It is now realised that they might be quite radically changed, just as parish churches have evolved over the centuries. The timescale, too, is comparable, with tombs in use for up to a thousand years. During this time changes in design of burial chambers or covering cairns may suggest that some communities adopted religious ideas from elsewhere. The concept of the 'multi-period tomb', therefore, has greatly helped our understanding of the interaction of the first farming communities in the Irish Sea region and elsewhere.

People had been living on this rocky knoll before any of the burial chambers were built, but the evidence is meagre, no houses were found, only the remains of hearths and broken early Neolithic pottery. The contrasting record of pollen from under the earliest cairn and the later additions showed that the original woodlands were felled and grass and agricultural plants came to dominate the landscape.

The first tomb to be built was at the western end of the rock, a simple, square structure with a narrowed entrance facing north (1). It was covered by a circular cairn and may be interpreted as a passage grave, a type of tomb found in several regions of Europe. A better example may be seen at Bodowyr (no. 7).

The next burial chamber to be built represents a change of design, perhaps due to a new population, or perhaps new contacts with the south-west of Scotland. It was a rectangular chamber with two stones marking the entrance from a narrow forecourt (2). The sidestones have not been re-erected and the broken capstone lies over them, so the plan is not clear, but the neat drywalling which marked the edge of its long cairn is easy to see if you look below the upper (protective) layer of stones.

Finally, the eastern chamber with its dramatic entrance stones was added in front (3). It was designed in the same tradition as the central chamber, which it rendered inaccessible. The long cairn was extended to cover the new chamber, and the revetment wall abuts against the front of the earlier cairn. The junction can be clearly seen on the ground (look at the lowest course of stone in the outer wall), and the chronological relationship of the two phases is indisputable. This last addition is dated by late Neolithic pottery of southern English type left as offerings at the entrance.

There was some renewed interest in the tomb in the Iron Age, when a pit was dug at the east end, but it remained essentially intact until the 19th century, when most of the stones of the cairn were removed for wall-building and the contents were rifled.

3
Presaddfed, Bodedern

Neolithic burial chamber

4th/early 3rd millennium BC

OS 114 SH 347809 U3 Cadw

From Bodedern, take B5109 E for 0.5ml (0.75km), turn L then 1st R through lodge gates; car park 300m up drive

This monument consists of two structures set in line some 1.5m apart. The southern one is a standing chamber, polygonal in plan, about 3m across by 1.3m high, with its capstone still in place. The northern structure has largely collapsed; what must have been the capstone is leaning against two supporters.

Its position in the bottom of the valley is unusual and early accounts of it are confusing, so it is difficult to be certain of the original design. Following the excavation of Trefignath one might suggest that it was a pair of closed chambers, built in succession and unified under a single (destroyed) cairn.

There is a local tradition that, in 1801, the southern chamber was lived in by a family evicted from a nearby cottage.

Nineteenth-century drawing of Presaddfed

4
Barclodiad y Gawres, Llanfaelog

Neolithic decorated passage grave

3rd millennium BC

OS 114 SH 329707 R2 Cadw

From Aberffaw, take A4080 NW for 1.75ml (2.75km). Park in car park at beach; take path through kissing gate to end of headland. Tomb is locked but key may be obtained (£5 deposit) from Coastal Heritage Centre in Aberffraw (winter weekends excepted). Take a good torch

Powell and Daniel 1956

This important site is a cruciform passage grave related to the famous tombs of the Boyne valley in Ireland: Newgrange, Knowth and Dowth. Like them it had a long, narrow passage leading to a vaulted central chamber with three lower side-chambers, the whole covered with a large, circular mound of earth and stones. Several of the wall stones are decorated with lightly pecked abstract designs featuring spirals, zigzags and lozenges.

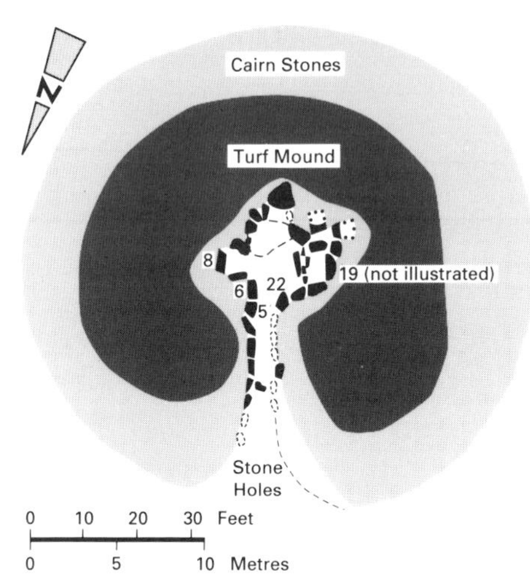

Barclodiad y Gawres (numbers show the locations of decorated stones)

The tomb has been partly restored and re-roofed, making it difficult to appreciate the original plan; the entrance appears wide and the interior is dominated by a modern circular wall. Ignore these features and look at the ground-plan of the large boulders.

The left side of the passage is intact, but only stone-holes mark the position of the right side. The central chamber is 2.5m across, and one slab of its corbelled roof survives; beneath it is the back chamber; to the left is a relatively intact side-chamber, only lacking a capstone which would have rested directly on the side-slabs. The chamber on the right is more complex. It is separated from the central chamber by blocking stones, and the fallen stones beyond it mark an annexe or additional compartment in which the cremated bones of two individuals were found during the excavation of 1952–3.

This excavation revealed a very intriguing aspect of funerary ritual. In the centre there had been a fire which was quenched by throwing over it a stew containing all sorts of reptiles, fish and small animals – a real witch's brew. It was then carefully covered with limpet shells, so all the bones survived.

There are five decorated stones. The clearest is that on the right as you enter the central chamber, where one pattern of zigzags and lozenges is sharply cut. The decoration on the two stones immediately opposite to it and on the back stone of the left side-chamber is less easy to make out without a torch. The back stone of the right side-chamber has only a single small spiral. The decoration on the stones was never emphasised by chalk or charcoal, but it could be summoned up in the dark centre of the tomb by the light of moving torches.

5

6

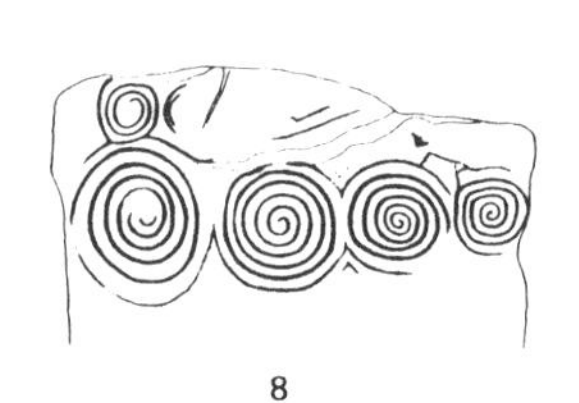
8

22

Decorated stones in the chamber at Barclodiad y Gawres

Revd John Skinner's sketch of Tŷ Newydd, 1802

5
Tŷ Newydd, Llanfaelog

Neolithic burial chamber

4th/early 3rd millennium BC

OS 114 SH 344738 U3 Cadw

From Llanfaelog railway bridge, drive NE on A4080 for 0.5ml (0.75km), turn L and persevere for 0.4ml (0.65km) (past 1 R turn) to corner where tomb is signposted. Climb stile and walk along edge of field

Phillips 1936

This tomb is badly damaged and has had to be supported by a stone column and concrete plinth, but early records and the results of excavation in 1935 suggest that it is a small, early passage grave, set in a typically prominent position and originally covered by a round cairn. The few finds from the excavation suggest that, though the tomb was probably built early in the Neolithic era, it continued long in use.

Only the chamber area now survives, but stones from the passage to the south-east were present in the early 19th century. The sketch by Revd J Skinner also shows the fallen half of the capstone, now obviously too narrow. It was reported that this stone was split when a fire was lit on top of it to celebrate a birthday at the neighbouring farm.

6
Din Dryfol, near Aberffraw

Neolithic burial chamber

4th/early 3rd millennium BC

OS 114 SH 395724 U2 Cadw

From junction of A5 and A5114 S of Llangefni, go NW on A5 for 2.5ml (4km) then turn L (signposted Tregof caravan site); continue beyond caravans; bear R at T-junction and R again at next, then 1st L towards Soar. 1.1ml (1.8km) from last junction turn 1st L after double bend (Fferam Rhosydd); tomb is signposted. Park carefully in farm lane and follow signs across two fields, through kissing gates on to rocky hill on which tomb stands

Smith and Lynch 1987

This tomb has been badly damaged, a process beginning in the Roman period and continuing to early in the 20th century. This means that the remains are impressive but not easily intelligible.

Recent excavation revealed that the tomb had a history similar to that of Trefignath (no. 2); the monument had been built in two or three stages, starting with the rectangular chamber at the west end. Its north side and entrance stones are still standing. East of this, represented now only by a fallen sidestone, was another rectangular chamber which once had wooden entrance posts – a very unusual combination of building materials. The

Din Dryfol, chambers from the west

chambers had been covered by a long, narrow cairn laid between rock outcrops. This cairn once had a low stone facade running up to the wooden portal.

At a later date the whole tomb – cairn and chambers – was extended eastward, but nothing remains of that structure except the huge 3m-high portal stone which looms above you as you approach the site. Pottery accompanying some cremated bones suggested that the tomb was built at the same time as Trefignath, but it probably had a shorter period of use.

Bracken is tall in high summer but the vegetation and butterflies on the hill and around the stream just behind are a great part of the attraction of this visit.

7
Bodowyr, Brynsiencyn

Neolithic burial chamber

4th/early 3rd millennium BC

OS 114 SH 463682 U3 Cadw

From Brynsiencyn, go W on A4080 and take 1st R after sharp bend; continue down hill (past Caer Lêb, no. 81), over river to offset crossroads. Turn L, then immediately R. Tomb is signposted 200m on R but this marker can be hidden by hedge. Room for 2 cars

This is a very attractive monument, everybody's ideal of a dolmen. It has not been excavated, but its size, shape and prominent position suggest that it is a small, early passage grave, one of a group of four of this type in Anglesey, and part of a scatter of such tombs reaching from Brittany to the Northern Isles.

A passage grave would originally be covered by a circular cairn and have a polygonal chamber approached by a lower passage. Both the cairn (recorded in early descriptions) and the passage have been removed by agricultural activity, but three stones supporting a mushroom-shaped capstone still define a polygonal chamber

Nineteenth-century drawing of Bodowyr burial chamber

1.4m across by 1.3m high. At the east side is a lower stone which formed a sill between the burial chamber and the lost passage.

8
Bryn Celli Ddu, Llanddaniel Fab

Neolithic burial chamber overlying henge monument

Late 3rd millennium BC

OS 114 SH 507702 U2 Cadw

From Llanfairpwll take A4080 SW for 2ml (3.5km) and turn R at 1st crossroads. Tomb is signposted. Cars may not be taken up farm road, so park where road widens just beyond school and walk from there (c.5 mins and 3 kissing gates)

Hemp 1930; Lynch 1991, pp 91–101

This is one of the best-known monuments in Wales; the burial chamber is accessible and atmospheric, and the history of excavation, interpretation and reinterpretation makes it a particularly interesting site to visit.

The visible features of the monument are: the burial chamber (1) entered by a long narrow passage (7.5m long, 1m wide) and containing a rounded pillar whose purpose is very problematical; the cairn (2), which is restored (2a) only around the chamber, bounded by a stone kerb; the ditch in which the kerbstones stand (3); three stones (4) set within the area enclosed by the ditch; a cast of a decorated stone now standing behind the chamber (5); the site of a pit (6) immediately behind the chamber (the walling here is modern, revetting the cairn and allowing sight of the old ground surface on which the stone covering the pit lay); an enclosure of small stones (7) in front of the entrance. It surrounded an ox burial of rather uncertain date.

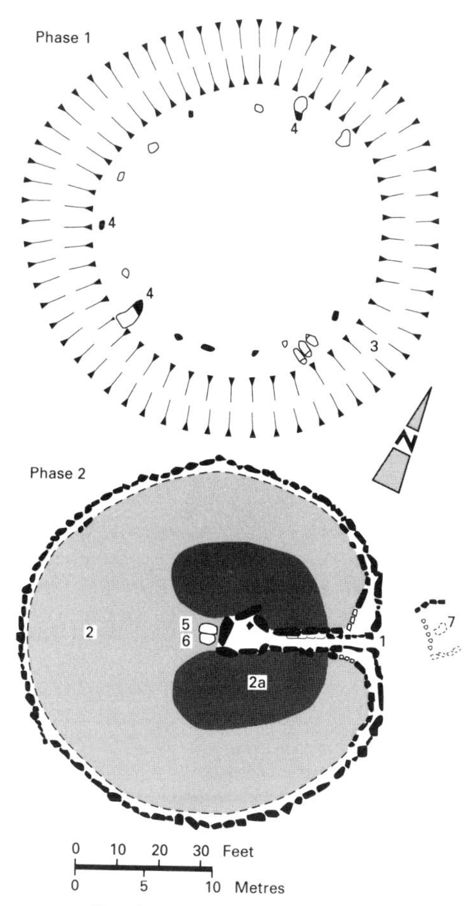

Bryn Celli Ddu at two stages in its history

The site had been known and visited since 1699, when men with lanterns broke in and crept along the passage to the chamber where the pillar, standing like a ghost, terrified them out of their wits. But courage returned, and it was frequently visited in the following centuries until it became very dilapidated. The site was excavated and restored in 1927–31 by W J Hemp, who believed that all the features listed above were of one date. Since then his evidence has been reassessed and the history of the monument revised. It is now thought to be the product of two different religious systems – one new and perhaps alien, and the other a reaffirmation of older traditions long-established on Anglesey.

The Phase 1 monument is a henge, an open-air sanctuary for religious ceremonies less closely connected with death and burial than the megalithic tombs. The origin of these ideas lies to the east, somewhere in central England during the late Neolithic. The ditch (3), originally with a bank outside it, the ring of stones (4), and possibly some central feature belong to this first monument. A purple clay found over the interior and on the inner slope of the ditch was thought to be a 'ritual floor' but is now known to be a decayed turf surface, which demonstrates that the ditch was already silted and grass-grown before the passage grave with its cairn and kerb was built.

The status of the pit dug through the purple clay just behind the site of the chamber and of the decorated stone which was found lying beside it are a little uncertain. The stratigraphy and the style of decoration, which belongs best with the passage grave, suggest that these features (5 and 6) relate to the second phase. They may result from a 'rededication' of the site when the tomb was built, because the juxtaposition of the monuments – the passage grave obliterating the henge – suggests a certain antagonism between the two religious systems.

The burial chamber (1) is a classic passage

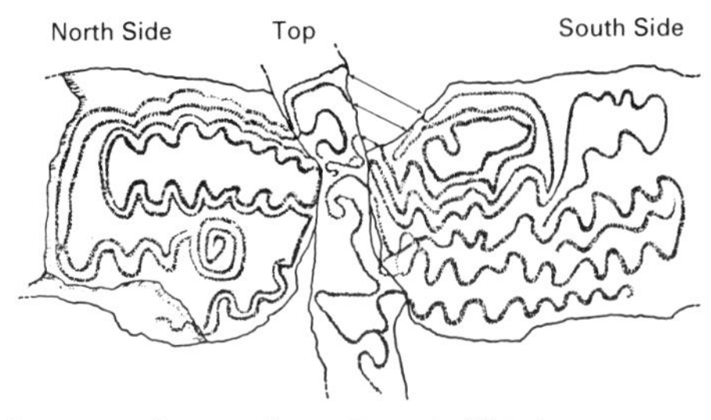

Decorated stone from Bryn Celli Ddu

grave with a high, polygonal chamber clearly differentiated from the lower entrance passage. It must be one of the latest of this style to be built in Britain. Because it had been exposed for so long it is not surprising that no bones or other artefacts were found in the chamber during the excavation. There is a rough spiral cut on the first stone on the left as you enter the chamber, but its authenticity has been doubted.

A tall standing stone can be seen on the ridge to the north of the tomb (on the right of the lane as you return). At present this is surrounded by a cairn of stones, the result of recent field clearance. There has been no excavation to elucidate the date and purpose of the stone, but it may be assumed to be a Bronze Age monument, testimony to the continuing significance of this valley.

9

Plas Newydd, Llanfairpwll

Neolithic burial chamber

3rd millennium BC

OS 114   519697   R3

Site is on lawns behind Plas Newydd (NT) on A4080 1.2ml (2km) SW of Llanfairpwll. This area is private but monument can be seen from NT path to house

The monument is impressive but difficult to classify and – were this not Anglesey, which retains so many tombs – one might be

Nineteenth-century view of Plas Newydd burial chamber

tempted to think that it was a fake, a product of 18th-century romanticism. It consists of a larger and smaller element – either a chamber and passage or a chamber and side-chamber – but, without excavation, it is impossible to be dogmatic about the original design, nor about the shape of the now-vanished covering cairn.

There is another tomb, Bryn yr Hen Bobl ('Hill of the Old People'), in this parkland (see Appendix).

Nineteenth-century drawing of Tŷ Mawr burial chamber

10
Tŷ Mawr, Llanfairpwll

Neolithic burial chamber

4th/early 3rd millennium BC

OS 114 SH 539721 U1

From A5 (Llanfairpwll by-pass) take A5025 N towards Amlwch. Tomb is visible in 2nd field on L after by-pass bridge. Land is private, but view from road or top of Marquis's Column is adequate

This small chamber collapsed some time in the 19th century, and the capstone still lies on the splayed supporters as it did in 1873. When standing, the chamber would have been 1.38m high and, like Bodowyr (no. 7), it had a sill stone on the east between the lost passage and the burial chamber. You can see this unbroken stone still standing beneath the capstone, and its presence allows this badly damaged monument to be classified as a small passage grave, probably one of the earlier tombs on Anglesey.

Remains of Hendrefor burial chamber

11
Hendrefor, Beaumaris

Neolithic burial chamber

4th/early 3rd millennium BC

OS 114 SH 551773 U1

From Beaumaris, take B5109 Pentraeth road W for 5ml (8km). 1ml (1.6km) beyond Llansadwrn junction, site is visible on LHS. Field is private but view from road adequate. Field sometimes under crop in summer

The tomb consists of two groups of stones: a tall portal at the east, with a capstone and supporter lying behind it; 6m to the west are three more fallen stones. Both groups were standing in the early 19th century, but there is no record of any structure between them. They may be the remains of a single long chamber, or of two separate chambers. The evidence from Trefignath (no. 2) would suggest that they were both eventually covered by one long cairn, but they might have been built at different times – perhaps another complex, 'multi-period' monument. There has been no excavation.

Pant y Saer from the north-west (the pole stands against the front of the burial chamber)

12
Pant y Saer, Benllech

Neolithic burial chamber

3rd millennium BC

OS 114 SH 509824 U2

Off B5108 (Benllech–Brynteg road) 0.5ml (0.8km) from crossroads in centre of Benllech. Take marked, raised footpath to L, beside terrace of houses, cross stile at end, turn R, cross 2nd stile, go diagonally across field to 3rd stile, go ahead 50m, tomb visible on L among gorse (5 mins walk)

Scott 1933

This is a well-known but rather sad monument – modern rubbish is frequently thrown into it, and the limestone of which it is built is beginning to crumble. It was excavated in 1875, and again in 1932.

The small, square burial chamber is built over a pit in the limestone and surrounded by the remains of a kidney-shaped cairn. The capstone has tilted to the east, and the western sidestone is missing. The front was formally closed by the large slab (on the left as you look into the chamber) and the forecourt area focuses upon this. The forecourt walls, and other walling within the cairn discovered in 1932, are now covered. All in all, the impact of the tomb today is very different from its original appearance.

Fifty-four persons, men, women and children (including nine full-term foetuses) were originally buried in the chamber with a few broken scraps of pottery. This large number suggests a long period of use of this small tomb. Offerings of pottery placed against the front of the chamber suggested that ceremonies of remembrance or funeral feasts had taken place in the forecourt. Long after it was closed, in the 2nd millennium BC, a stone cist with a beaker and two inhumations was inserted into the chamber. It is possible that these mourners used the west sidestone to cover the cist.

13
Lligwy Tomb, Moelfre

Neolithic burial chamber

Later 3rd millennium BC

OS 114 SH 501860 U1 Cadw

From roundabout on A5025 just SW of Moelfre, take narrow road signposted Din Lligwy (no. 79). Tomb is c.0.5ml (1km) along road on L. Kissing gate into field but monument visible from road. Room for 2 cars on verge

Baynes 1909

The main feature of this monument is the huge capstone (5.5m by 4.8m and over 1m thick) which appears to be lying on the ground. In fact it covers quite a high chamber, mainly dug into the rock, and surrounded by a number of rough supporters which raise the cover only about 0.5m above the ground. The entrance was probably through the widest gap, on the east.

The monument was excavated in 1909 and was found to contain two groups of unburnt burials separated by a paving of flat stones. Between 15 and 30 individuals were represented, and pieces of broken Beaker and grooved ware pottery with the bones suggested that the monument had been built towards the end of the Neolithic period, when the tradition of this kind of burial was on the wane and less trouble was taken with the architectural details of the burial chamber.

Lligwy burial chamber

14
Lletty'r Filiast, Llandudno

Neolithic burial chamber
3rd millennium BC
OS 115 SH 772829 U3

On Great Orme, Llandudno. Visible from copper mines site (no. 34) and reached by going up towards Tea Gardens and walking back along path to Cromlech Road (5 mins). Alternatively, reach Cromlech Road via St Beunos Road as you enter Orme Country Park

This is one of the few north Welsh tombs to have a folk name. Llety'r Filiast means 'The Lair of the Greyhound Bitch', a name which, with variation, has been applied to several other tombs elsewhere in Wales. Unfortunately no story survives to explain it.

The chamber has been damaged but it seems to have been rectangular, 2m by 1.6m and 1.25m high. What remains is not very distinctive, but it probably belongs to the portal dolmen class, a type of monument which is normally rather more impressive! Dyffryn Ardudwy (no. 23) is a classic example.

Lletty'r Filiast burial chamber

The chamber stands at the east end of an oval mound which incorporates both a natural outcrop of rock and the remains of the cairn which would have originally covered it.

The position of this early monument indicates the ground level on this side of the Pwllau valley before the Bronze Age miners began their exploration of the important copper ores in the cliffs opposite.

15
Maen y Bardd, Rowen

Neolithic burial chamber
4th/early 3rd millennium BC
OS 115 SH 740717 U4

Beside Roman road above (W of) Rowen. Best approached as part of a longer archaeological walk (see map with no. 37), it lies in a landscape of many varied monuments. Leave car in Rowen village, take RH turn (YHA sign) in centre and walk up steep hill past Youth Hostel on to Roman road (no. 91). Alternatively drive through village bearing L up very narrow road for 1.1ml (1.75km) to T-junction, turn R and leave car at corner where Roman road (track on R) joins modern one. Walk E 0.6ml (1km) down Roman road, past settlements (no. 82)

Maen y Bardd ('Stone of the Bard') is an attractive monument in a magnificent site surrounded by later sites and features of

Maen y Bardd, looking towards the portal

interest – definitely worth the walk! The tomb is never obscured by bracken, but other monuments here can be.

It is an intact box-like structure, 1.1m square by 1.2m high. On the west the sidestones and the capstone project to form a portal area, though this 'entrance' does not have the extra height which is normal in portal dolmens, the class of tomb to which this monument almost certainly belongs. The shape of the cairn around it has been confused by a later field-wall and by a stream which cuts it on the east.

On the open hillside 100m north-east of the tomb is another square, cist-like monument which has been considered contemporary with Maen y Bardd, but it is probably a grave belonging to the Bronze Age, some 1200 years later. The two fine standing stones, one just below the road 200m west of Maen y Bardd, the other above the road 300m further on, belong to the 2nd millennium BC and demonstrate that this route was in use long before it was formalised by the Roman army.

16
Hendre Waelod, Llansanffraid Glan Conwy

Neolithic burial chamber

4th/early 3rd millennium BC

OS 115/116 SH 793747 U2

From Llansanffraid Glan Conwy, take A470 S and turn L at angled crossroads at top of hill 1.25ml (2km) S of village (the Bodnant turning is too far). Persevere for 0.6ml (1km); turn L down hill; at bottom leave car with care where footpath is signposted (room for 1 car only). Follow path, keeping to lower side of hedge, go through narrow wood; tomb is on fence line at edge of wood

This is the only one of the Conwy valley portal dolmens with the traditional high portal stones – in this case, originally 3m high and probably covered by a separate lintel, now lost. The chamber behind is large but rather

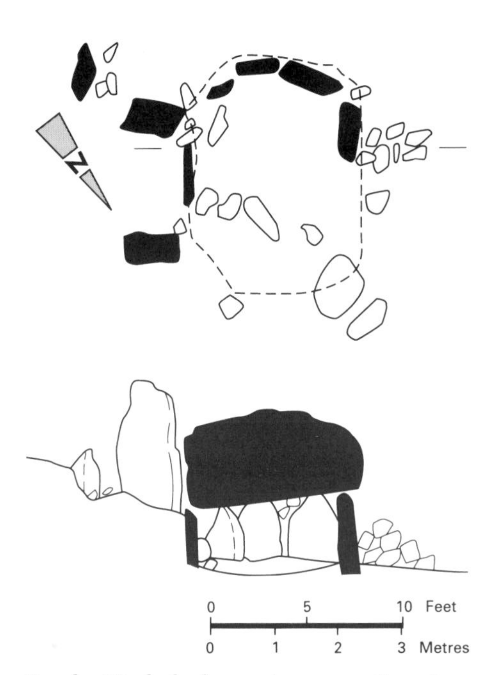

Hendre Waelod, plan and cross-section of burial chamber

low, covered by an enormous capstone which has slipped to the north. Access from the portal to the chamber is blocked by a low slab which can be seen by crawling under the capstone (not for the squeamish!).

The tomb stands on a sloping site, and soil has engulfed the bottom of the portal stones and filled the forecourt area. One stone of a possible facade flanking the entrance is visible on the south. The remains of a long cairn can be traced by the line of stones in the footing of the fence.

17

Capel Garmon, Betws y Coed

Neolithic burial chamber

3rd millennium BC

OS 116 SH 818543 U2 Cadw

From Betws y Coed, take A5 E for 2.6ml (4.5km) and turn R at crossroads (signposted Capel Garmon). Persevere for 1.5ml (2.4km); tomb signposted on L. Leave car where road widens by farm gate and walk to tomb (signposted, c.5 mins)

Hemp 1927

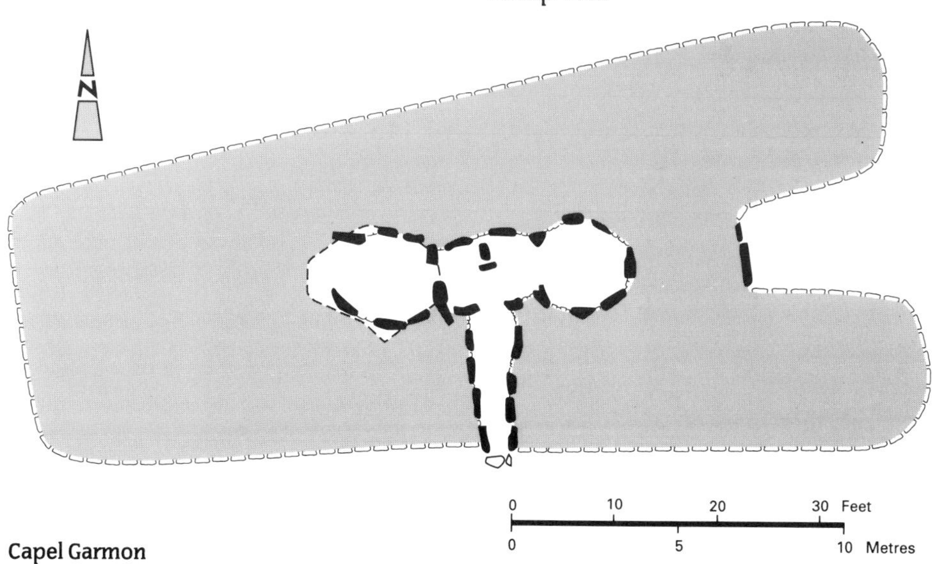

Capel Garmon

This is a major site, well laid out in a position commanding magnificent views of Snowdonia. The tomb is especially interesting because it belongs to the Severn-Cotswold group, a type unusual in north Wales, but common in southern Powys. Its presence here is an indication that prehistoric populations moved and brought with them traditions from their homelands; it is more difficult to say why they might have come north, but perhaps they might have been involved in the trading of stone axes from Graig Lwyd (no. 18).

The cairn survives well, and its outline is indicated on the surface by a line of small stones. These are not original but simply mark the position of the drywalled edge of the cairn located by excavation in 1925. The high quality of this wall can be seen at the south side, where a space has been cleared at the entrance to the passage. This passage opened on to the side of the cairn, not the front which has a 'false portal' – two stones, apparently a door, but leading nowhere. They formed the backdrop to ceremonies in this narrow forecourt. This arrangement is found at a number of long cairns in Powys and the Cotswolds, and suggests that interments were being separated and distinguished from other ceremonies at the tombs.

The chamber (which you enter through a break in the western end caused by the use of the tomb as a stable in the last century) is of complex design. The passage led to a divided rectangular space off which branched two circular burial chambers. Only one capstone survives, but otherwise the monument is well preserved, built in a 'post and panel' technique with very fine drywalling typical of the Cotswold area. This has been restored quite extensively, but in the eastern chamber the original can be seen in the lower courses. Look hard for a line of three very small drill marks which indicates the junction of new and old work.

Because of 19th-century disturbance, not many bones were found during the excavation, but some came from the side of the passage and some sherds of late Neolithic (Beaker) pottery were found, suggesting that the tomb remained in use into the beginning of the 2nd millennium.

Stone axeheads from Graig Lwyd, sequence of manufacture from rough-out to polished axe

18
Graig Lwyd, Penmaenmawr

Neolithic axe factory

3rd millennium BC

OS 115 SH 717749 U4

Various footpaths from Penmaenmawr town. Most direct (but steep) is from Graig Lwyd Farm on SW side of town (c.45 mins walk). By car from Penmaenmawr take road towards Sychnant Pass, turn R into Graig Lwyd Road at Catholic church; go round sharp bend and turn up 1st L (Mountain Lane, signposted Druid's Circle, no. 35) and persevere for 1ml (1.6km). Leave car at large gateposts (Jubilee Walk); walk SE up hill; on saddle bear R and continue past farm (Bryn Derwydd) and onto open land (signposted Druid's Circle); 40 mins, walk not so steep

Warren 1922; Clough and Cummins 1988, p 271

Graig Lwyd is the great extinct volcano which dominates the town of Penmaenmawr on the south side. It is still being actively quarried and much of it is inaccessible. The Neolithic quarries were mainly at the edge of the volcanic plug, where the hard igneous rock (an augite granophyre or microdiorite) bursts through the softer laminated shales and forms a series of low cliffs. Because it has always been a commercially useful rock it is difficult to be certain of the date of small quarries and worked areas, but excavations in 1993 have identified a line of small quarries on the eastern summit. On the low cliffs facing the stone circles and cairns it is possible to see other early working areas and to appreciate the sudden change in geology.

The system of working at this site was to strike a block of a suitable size from the cliff, flake it roughly to shape, then work on it more carefully to straighten the edges and provide an even cross-section, all by flaking with a hammerstone in the technique best known in flint. These waste flakes, hammerstones and broken, unfinished axes have been found at the quarry sites. The Graig Lwyd stone has the same quality of concoidal fracture as flint but it is a great deal stronger. The 'rough-outs' were taken down the hill to more comfortable surroundings for the longer process of polishing. The flaking might take no more than half an hour, but the polishing could take from two to four days. When the axe was polished it would be set into a long wooden handle, very like the felling axe of today.

The finished products found their way all over Britain. Their origin at Penmaenmawr can be confirmed by petrological analysis, and this work has revealed a great network of trade routes from these large-scale production centres or 'factories'. Graig Lwyd was the third largest in the country. Bangor Museum has a map of the distribution of the Graig Lwyd products, and a display of the various stages of manufacture.

19
Bachwen, Clynnog

Neolithic burial chamber

4th/early 3rd millennium BC

OS 123 SH 407495 U4

Footpath just S of Clynnog church (no. 145) towards sea, at T-junction turn L, into field at end (10 mins walk); kissing gates and stiles. Public path leads to tomb, but not beyond

This small tomb stands in the centre of a field overlooking the sea. A thin, slightly wedge-shaped capstone is supported on four widely spaced stones (the southern one was moved slightly when the chamber was excavated in 1876). Nothing of interest was recorded during that excavation, and the design of the chamber is undistinctive, but its topographical position, wedge capstone and rectangular shape suggest that it is a portal dolmen, but without many of the really characteristic features.

The monument is best known for its decorated capstone, whose upper surface is covered with 110 cup-marks and two shallow grooves. Eight other cups occur on the east side of the capstone. Nobody knows the true meaning or purpose of these cups, which are often assumed to have had some magical role. It is interesting that they are found most frequently on portal dolmens or close to them. These ones are larger and deeper than those at Cist Cerrig (see Appendix), which occur on the natural rock, not the tomb itself.

Nineteenth-century drawing of Bachwen burial chamber

Burial chamber on Mynydd Cefn Amwlch

20
Mynydd Cefn Amwlch, Tudweiliog

Neolithic burial chamber

4th/early 3rd millennium BC

OS 123 SH 229345 U3

From Tudweiliog, take B4417 S for 1.4ml (2.25km) and turn L towards Sarn Meyllteyrn. Tomb is 0.3ml (0.5km) from junction, in field on R. Footpath through private field to tomb. Close gates

This is a very attractive monument, a ridged capstone supported on three stones some 1.5m high. Fallen stones which may have been part of the chamber lie nearby. However, they are possibly rather too big to fit, and the original shape of the chamber and its cairn is uncertain, which makes it difficult to classify the tomb.

A rather charming legend exists which says that the chamber was once demolished by the farmer and the stones carted away, but the cows grazing in the field were so distressed by this vandalism that they bellowed incessantly until the tomb was rebuilt.

21
Tan y Muriau, Rhiw
Neolithic burial chamber
4th/early 3rd millennium BC

OS 123 SH 238288 U2

On minor Mynytho–Aberdaron road 5ml (8km) SW of Mynytho, halfway up steep slope of Mynydd Rhiw, turn R (N) to Plas yn Rhiw (NT). Continue beyond NT house to top of road where 1 car can be tucked into RHS of a very sharp bend. Walk through gate and up to farm. Just through farm gate cross stone stile on L and cross two small fields. Tomb is on private land but owner allows access as long as no damage is caused

This is a particularly interesting monument because a very impressive portal dolmen stands at the west end of a long cairn with a low lateral chamber which may be a later addition. This represents, perhaps, the adoption of new ideas about the design of burial chambers by this remote but not isolated community.

The portal dolmen at the upper, west, end is covered by an enormous wedge-shaped capstone, beneath which is a classic H-shaped portal, now obscured by the field bank built against it. It can be seen by crawling under the capstone, which is supported by a low backstone. The sidestones have gone, as have the stones of the upper cairn which must have lain in the angle of the field-wall.

By contrast, the long tail of the lower cairn (perhaps an addition) has survived quite well against the field-wall. At its west end is a much slimmer capstone lying at a tilt, having slipped from its narrow chamber which opened on to the south side of the cairn. A third chamber once existed in the lower end of the cairn.

Plan and cross-section of chambers at Tan y Muriau

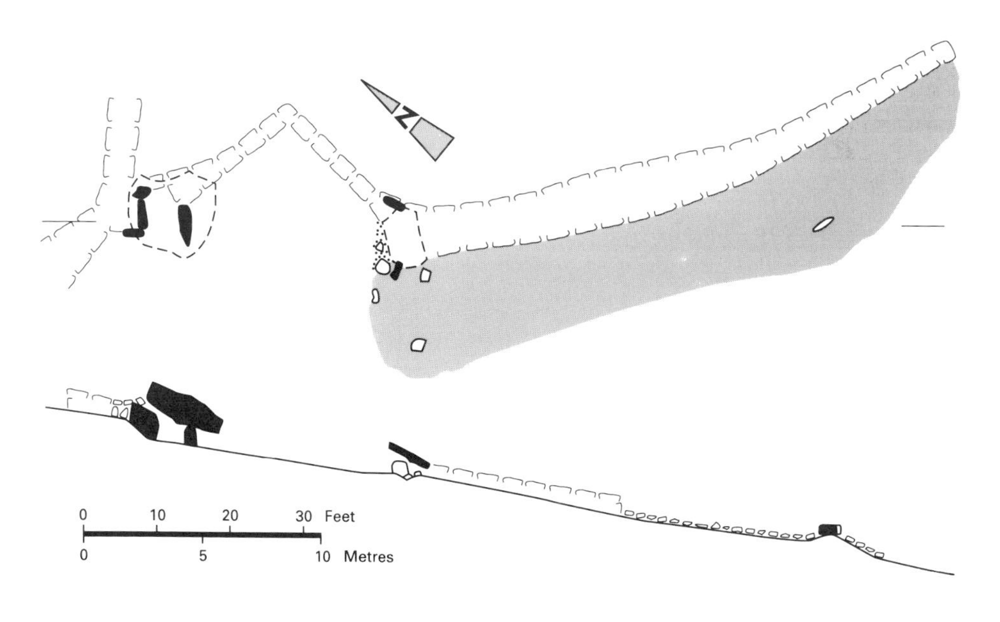

22
Mynydd Rhiw, Aberdaron

Neolithic axe factory

5th/3rd millennium BC

OS 123 SH 234299 U1

From Tan y Muriau (no. 21), return to road, continue up hill and bear R around church. Continue along narrow road till just past block of NT land on L. Leave car where common land starts and follow main track to brow of hill. Refilled quarry pits are just discernible to R of track as it rounds hill

Houlder 1961; Clough and Cummins 1988, p 282

Like Graig Lwyd (no. 18) Mynydd Rhiw is a volcanic plug, but the stone used for axes here is not the volcanic material but a narrow band of altered shale around it. A further contrast is that the rock was mined, with impressive accuracy, in a series of shallow pits which overlie the band of fused shale. As each pit got dangerously deep it was abandoned and another one dug, the spoil being used to fill the old quarry, which also formed a convenient working hollow for those roughing out the axes in this windswept spot.

The site was excavated in 1959, and the pits used to be quite easy to identify; it was also possible to see a good many of the sharp, smooth, concoidially struck flakes lying around them. But in recent years the vegetation has grown back and they are more difficult to recognise. Searching can still produce some samples of the rock, which should *not* be taken from the site.

Some of this rock has been found in Mesolithic contexts in Anglesey, so its 'trade' pre-dates that of Graig Lwyd, but it was never such an important production centre; less than 20 axes have been found, none further away than Gwent. Because of limitations of the raw material, the axes produced are usually thin and narrow, more like chisels, but very finely worked and polished.

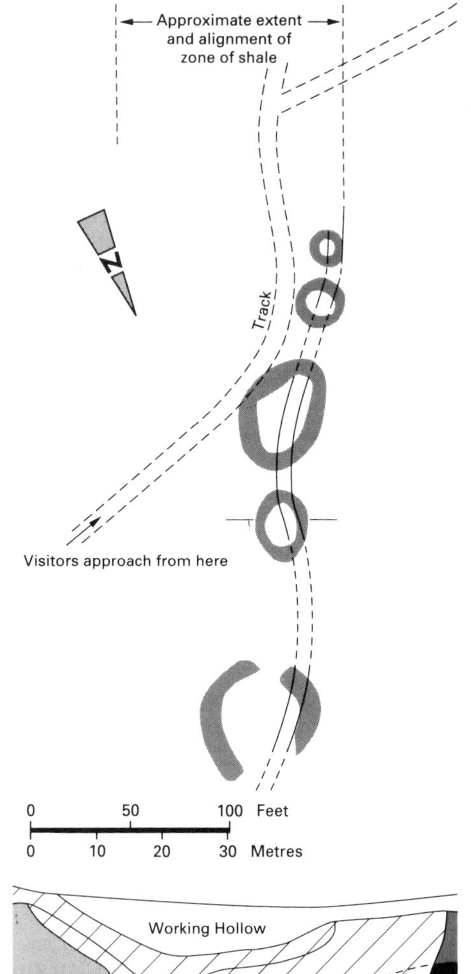

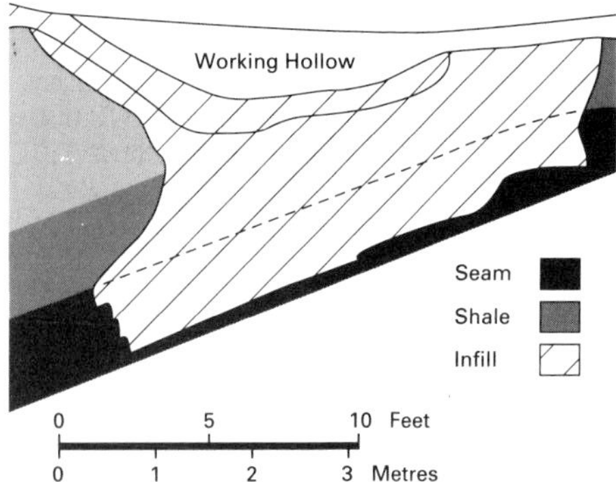

Neolithic quarries on Mynydd Rhiw, with a cross-section of a quarry pit

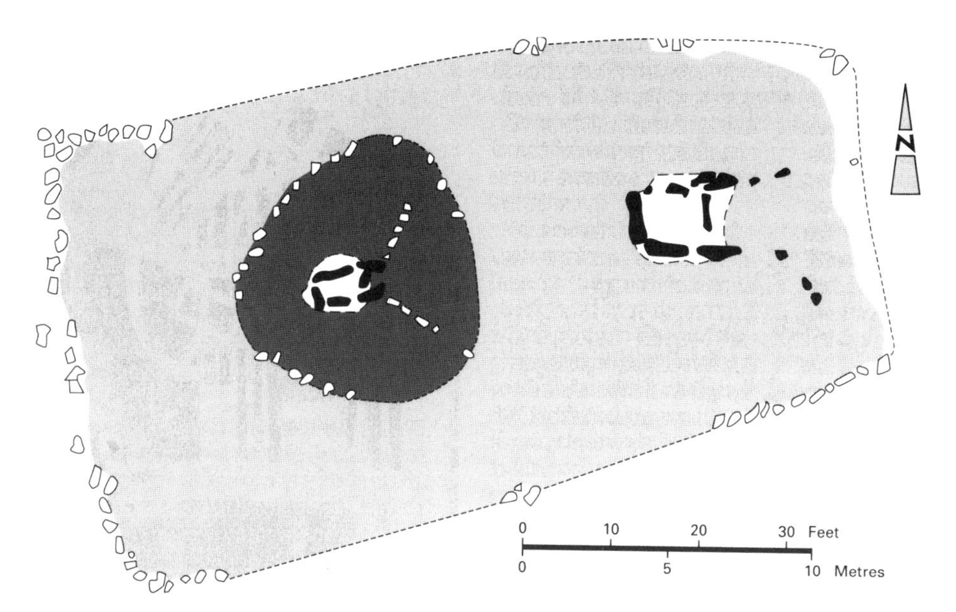

Burial chambers at Dyffryn Ardudwy

23
Dyffryn Ardudwy Cairn, Dyffryn Ardudwy

Neolithic burial chamber

4th/early 3rd millennium BC

OS 124 SH 588228 U2 Cadw

Site is at S end of Dyffryn Ardudwy village, signposted on L just before school. Leave car carefully in cul-de-sac on L before site. Site is up short footpath with kissing gates. Guidebook available in village shops

Powell 1973

This monument, excavated in 1960, was one of the first sites where multi-period building was recognised (see no. 2), and has become central to the understanding of the portal dolmen group in this country and in Ireland.

Portal dolmens form the most common type of tomb in this region. They stood at the centre of the farmed land, a focus for the community like a modern parish church, and many of them are very striking and daring examples of architecture and engineering. Although the largest and most impressive ones, Cist Cerrig and Gwern Einion, are not generally accessible (see Appendix), the western chamber here is a beautiful monument and one of the most classic in design. The current belief that they are amongst the earliest tombs built in these islands is largely the result of the excavations here at Dyffryn.

The monument consists of a roughly rectangular cairn containing two chambers facing up the hill. These are delineated in solid black on the plan. The western (lower) one is the earlier of the two. It is a small structure with an H-shaped portal with high closing slab, a rectangular chamber and sloping capstone – all typical features of the portal dolmen. It was covered by a small, circular cairn held back from the forecourt area by drystone walls running up to the entrance stones. The base of the cairn and these forecourt walls can be easily seen. Within the forecourt was a pit containing deliberately broken pottery, a ceremonial offering in front of the tomb. This pottery, like the design of the tomb itself, showed many similarities to contemporary Irish material. There is a cup-mark on the inner face of the north portal stone.

The later eastern chamber is much larger but less classic in design. It does not have the high entrance stones, but the front has a portal area defined by projecting sidestones and a low (broken) closing slab. In front of this was a squarish forecourt which had been carefully blocked or filled in by pitched stones set against the closing slab and by a low bank built across it further out. This blocking covered offerings of pottery in a slightly later style than those from the western chamber. When the eastern chamber was built, the large rectangular cairn which covered it engulfed the western chamber and its round cairn.

There were no bones surviving in the western chamber, and those in the eastern chamber came from a Bronze Age cremation burial put into the chamber at a later date. Two small finely polished plaques made from Mynydd Rhiw stone (see no. 22) were found in the eastern chamber; their purpose is unknown.

24

Bron y Foel Isaf, Dyffryn Ardudwy

Neolithic burial chamber

4th/3rd millennium BC

OS 124 SH 607246 U1

From Dyffryn Ardudwy village, go N on A496 and turn R after hotel; persevere up hill for 1.3ml (2.1km); at complex crossroads take RH road to Bron y Foel. Turn R just before farm; tomb is in roadside wall, 160m on R. Turn car higher up

Remains of burial chamber at Bron y Foel, from the lane

This is a badly damaged tomb, almost certainly the remains of a portal dolmen. One sidestone, a low backstone and the large slipped capstone survive. A curving bank to the east may represent blocking of the forecourt (like Dyffryn Ardudwy's eastern chamber, no. 23).

Although it is so badly damaged, it is worth a visit because the view is magnificent and the capstone is impressive.

Nineteenth-century drawing of Cors y Gedol burial chamber

25
Cors y Gedol, Tal y Bont

Neolithic burial chamber

4th/3rd millennium BC

OS 124 SH 603228 U1

From Dyffryn Ardudwy village, go S on A496 and take 1st turn L after village, up through lodge gates to Cors y Gedol gates. Bear R, skirt farm buildings and turn R up hill. Almost immediately turn R through gate; tomb is 0.2ml (320m) on R. Turn car further along road, near café, which is open in summer (once a drovers' gathering place above Pont Fadog pack-horse bridge). Bracken can be a problem in high summer

This is a badly damaged monument, like Bron y Foel Isaf (no. 24), but it is easy to get to by car and is surrounded by a particularly well preserved field system (of later date, see no. 86), so the area is worth visiting.

The tomb now consists of only three stones: a large capstone lying against two small uprights. It is not clear whether these are the remains of the back or the front of the chamber. Early drawings are no help; they show it in the same condition as today. The base of a rectangular cairn 30m long can be recognised fairly easily around the chamber when the bracken has died back.

26
Carneddau Hengwm, Tal y Bont

Neolithic burial chambers

3rd millennium BC

OS 124 SH 613205 U4

From Tal y Bont, go S on A496 for 1ml (1.7km) to Egryn Abbey (4th farm on L). Leave car at roadside. Walk to farmyard then follow marked track up hillside. See map with no. 133. Steep walk (c.45 mins–1hr) but several monuments here (nos 47 and 133). Where slope levels off continue E towards old aerial ropeway. Go through gate and proceed across rough wet land to corner of wall to R of ropeway. At corner, turn L, along wall to first tomb. There is a stone stile just beyond. W end of S cairn and all of N cairn are in a field which is private land, but access is allowed. Keep dogs on leads, shut all gates

These two monuments are of exceptional interest; the southern one is arguably of multi-period construction and the other is a laterally chambered cairn of Severn-Cotswold type, more commonly found in south Wales. Moreover, the cairn material is unusually well preserved and both monuments feature in 17th- and 18th-century writings since, though they appear so remote today, they were then quite close to the main road which ran through Bwlch y Rhiwgyr (no. 47).

The southern cairn (46m long) is the larger of the two, and is divided by the field-wall. At the east end is what must have been a very

Ruined portal dolmen, at the east end of the southern cairn at Carneddau Hengwm

impressive portal dolmen. One side is intact, with the closing slab still standing, but the backstone and second sidestone lie under the fallen capstone. The smaller slab lying to the south may have been a capstone over the portal area, for the antiquary Thomas Pennant, who saw the tomb in 1780 before it was damaged, says it had two overlapping capstones (*Tours in Wales*, 1783). The cairn belonging to this tomb may have been about 20m long, incorporating some coarse drywalling, still visible, towards its end.

The continuation of the cairn westwards is probably an addition built to cover a very different chamber entered by a passage from the north side. It has been modified by use as a shepherd's hut (there was a fireplace in it when Pennant saw it) but can be reasonably confidently identified as a Severn-Cotswold lateral chamber, representing the grafting of new ideas on to the longer-established portal dolmen tradition.

This same southern tradition lies behind the design of the northern cairn. This has been more seriously disturbed, and the nature of the chamber under the capstone at the west end cannot be determined. The east end, however, clearly contains two opposed lateral chambers, the southern one 4m long by 1m wide, the northern one now incomplete. Early drawings hint at a 'false portal' (see no. 17) at this east end, and later workers have observed a very characteristic fine drystone wall edging the cairn at certain points. This tomb, therefore, reflects the wholesale introduction of new religious and architectural ideas to this long-established community in Ardudwy.

3
The Bronze Age

In terms of the monuments which survive today, one of the most significant differences between the Neolithic and the Bronze Age lies in distribution. Neolithic activity was centred on the lowlands; in the early Bronze Age man expanded into the uplands, where his tombs and religious centres survive in profusion. Circular stone huts, much smaller than the preceding Neolithic long houses, may also be found there amongst low-walled fields and clearance cairns – heaps of stone cleared from the land. In many parts of Britain, notably Dartmoor and the Cheviots, such settlements can be dated to the Bronze Age; in Wales they remain undated, but one may suspect that many of the smaller huts, such as those in Cwm Ffrydlas above Bethesda (no. 40), do date from this period. This settlement shift is due to three factors: an increase in population after a thousand years of agriculture; some exhaustion of lowland soils; and an improvement of climate which provided an opportunity for the exploitation of higher ground.

Whereas the farms and fields are elusive and difficult to date, the burial monuments of the period are quite clear. These are the round stone cairns or earthen barrows built of turves which are to be seen on many hilltops, prominently sited on ridges or aligned along mountain trackways like those in Ardudwy (nos 43–46) or on Cadair Idris (nos 49–52). The burials that they cover are individual, each person potentially identifiable and sometimes accompanied by their own prized possessions. In Wales, and in western Britain generally, the family traditions of earlier centuries are at least partially maintained, for each mound normally covers a number of burials. Bodies were laid on the surface or in dug graves at the beginning of the period, but by about 1600 BC cremation had become the norm, the burnt bones usually placed in a bag or pottery urn for final burial. Outwardly these monuments are quite simple – a heap of stones often edged by a kerb of larger boulders, or a mound of turves originally encircled by a wooden kerb – but excavation often reveals underlying circles of hurdles or stones which hint at quite complex rituals accompanying funerals at this date.

In the Neolithic there seems to have been a single religious focus: the monumental tomb frequented for centuries for ceremonies, not necessarily always funerals. In the Bronze Age it would seem that religious practice involved a wider range of monuments, all of them linked by the circular plan which begins with the late Neolithic henge monuments. At one end of the spectrum are the round burial

Artist's impression of ritual ceremonies performed in a Bronze Age ring cairn

cairns, at the other the stone circles – rings of upright stones providing no evidence of their purpose. In between are a variety of ring cairns – sometimes with upright stones, sometimes just a circular bank of stone – within the centre of which may be human burials, pits with charcoal, token deposits of reburied bones, all indicating ancillary ceremonies whose meaning we cannot guess. The religion of the Bronze Age, therefore, is less closely tied to the rituals of death, and may have extended to an interest in the movement of sun, moon and stars, although sophisticated modern 'proofs' of such observations should be treated with caution.

Ceremonial circles are common on the uplands of Arllechwedd and Meirionnydd, where a great variety of types may be found. None survive in Lleyn and Anglesey, where the Bronze Age monuments are all burial mounds (only a few, such as the fabled Bedd Branwen (no. 29), being well preserved) or standing stones. The standing stones are enigmatic memorials; they seldom mark a burial but may commemorate events or agreements which have left no archaeological record. Where dating evidence survives, it suggests erection in the first half of the 2nd millennium BC.

Excavation in Gwynedd barrows has shown them to be cemeteries of small but prosperous communities whose choice of pottery and personal finery demonstrates contacts with Ireland, Scotland and the rich centres of international trade in the south of England. There is very little sign of a formal social hierarchy, though differences of personal wealth obviously existed. The virtual absence of weapons contrasts with graves in some other parts of Britain and Europe, and suggests that the warrior ideal was less warmly admired here.

The introduction of copper- and bronze-working is a crucial but ill-documented stage in man's development. Copper objects first appear in the graves of the wealthy in the south of England at the end of the 3rd millennium BC, but these people were obviously consumers and not producers. The early copper industry of Ireland is less well dated, but may have been more influential in Wales since the Irish were manufacturers, and the first Welsh metal axes are very like Irish products. Normally the industrial prehistory of an area is written through artefacts and museum exhibits, not field monuments, but in north Wales it is now possible to visit extensive mine workings on the Great Orme (no. 34) which have been reliably dated to this period. The technical skill that they represent is matched during the middle Bronze Age by metallurgical expertise, for the contemporary metal tools from Wales are made from an exceptionally well mixed lead-bronze of unique composition.

Artist's impression of Early Bronze Age metalworkers at work

It is difficult to know where to place the burnt stone mounds (nos 46 and 84) in any discussion of the Bronze Age since, although their date is well established by radiocarbon dating, their purpose is uncertain and, indeed, may vary from one example to another. The mounds are relatively easy to recognise; they occur beside streams and are composed entirely of burnt stone, often dolerite, which has been used to heat water in a trough or other large container. The mounds are often horseshoe-shaped, the trough being in the centre. The hot water thus produced may have been used for cooking or some other, perhaps industrial, purpose.

After 1200 BC, in the late Bronze Age, much of Europe and the eastern Mediterranean was in turmoil, and many tribes were on the move. Britain at this time was in close contact with northern and western France, and adopted new weapons and styles of fighting – perhaps in response to minor invasions, perhaps simply through trade. Regardless of foreign stimuli, significant stresses were developing internally. A worsening climate was destroying upland agriculture (its decline accelerated by man's over-exploitation of fragile soils), and the scattered, open settlements of the early and middle Bronze Age were abandoned as larger, enclosed sites were established at the fringe of the encroaching moorland.

This trend towards a more concentrated pattern of settlement – the new sites protected by palisades, and later by more substantial defences – is one that can be seen in many parts of the country. In north-east Wales several hillforts demonstrate a sequence from palisades in the late Bronze Age to massive ramparts in the Iron Age. One excavated site in Gwynedd, Castell Odo, near Aberdaron (no. 70), provides evidence of this, but an early foundation date may be expected at many other hillforts which, until recently, were believed to belong entirely to the Iron Age.

27
Penrhos Feilw, Holyhead

Standing stones

2nd millennium BC

OS 114 SH 227809 U3 Cadw

From Trearddur Bay, take coast road W past Porth Dafarch (no. 78); 1ml (1.6km) on, just past large chapel, turn R; sign 300m on L; pull-in for car, stones visible from road

These are fine slabs of writhing Holyhead schist, standing stark against the backdrop of the mountain. Both are almost 3m high and stand 3.3m apart. Such pairing of stones is relatively rare in Anglesey, but more common in south Wales. There is an unsubstantiated tradition that they formed part of a more complex monument, standing at the centre of a stone circle with a burial cist between them. On the whole, this seems unlikely to be true.

Penrhos Feilw standing stones

28
Soar Stone, Llanfaethlu

Standing stone

2nd millennium BC

OS 114 SH 319863 U1

Stone stands beside A5025, 0.4ml (0.75km) SE of Llanfaethlu, on L (E) just beyond Soar chapel, shortly after sharp bend

Almost 3m high and over 2m wide, this is a particularly impressive example of the type of Bronze Age memorial whose *raison d'être* is very poorly understood. A few mark burials, but this is not normally the case. There has been no excavation here.

29
Bedd Branwen, Llanddeusant

Round barrow

Mid-2nd millennium BC

OS 114 SH 361849 U3

From Llanddeusant church (2.2ml, 3.5km, SE of Llanfaethlu) drive NE 0.4ml (0.75km) to crossroads with chapel, turn R; take 2nd farm road on L (Glanalaw) opposite water installation. Go down lane (public footpath) for 0.4ml (0.75km) to field gate on RHS just short of wood. Electricity pole where power line changes direction is at edge of barrow. Field is private, but owner allows access to monument except when field is under hay or crop

Lynch 1971

This is a monument chiefly famous for its literary associations: the fabled grave of Branwen, daughter of Llŷr, who in the *Mabinogion* story died of a broken heart here beside the river Alaw, lamenting the trouble she had unwittingly caused between the warriors of Wales and Ireland.

The descriptive detail in the text suggests that this was indeed the mound the author envisaged, but the monument is much older than any known version of the story. The central stone was erected at the end of the 3rd millennium BC, and the burial mound was built around it in the 2nd millennium BC to form a cemetery for up to a dozen individuals evidently wealthy enough to import exotic materials from distant regions. The pottery and grave goods are on exhibition in Bangor Museum.

Excavation in 1966 showed that the mound was of complex construction. Radiocarbon dating suggested that the stone at the centre had stood as an independent monument for some centuries before the site became a burial ground. Three urns with cremated bones, accompanying pots and other goods were buried; then a broad ring of stone was built over them, and the area between the ring and the central stone was filled with overlapping slabs pitched towards the centre. Finally, it was all covered with turves and soil extending to a kerb of boulders, some of which are visible at the edge of the mound. A

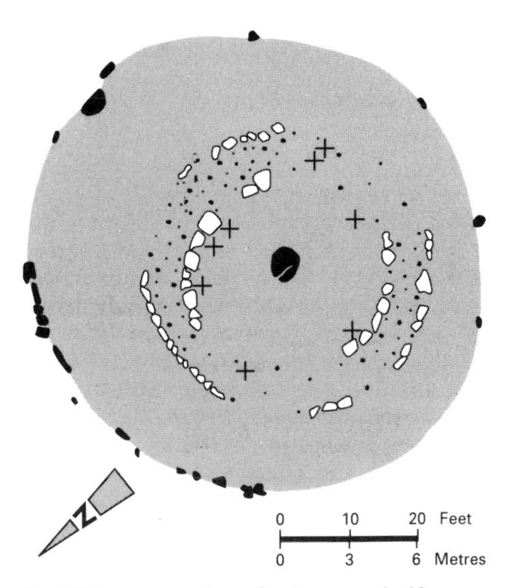

Bedd Branwen, plan of cairn revealed by excavation

further group of at least four cremated burials in urns was added to the mound after it was complete. The similarity of the urns in the two groups suggested that the interval between these events was not long.

The arrangement of burials in this barrow, and the personal belongings chosen to accompany the dead, have some interesting social implications. Unlike contemporary burial monuments in some other parts of Britain, no one individual is afforded a position of primacy in the cemetery. The burials were placed in apparent equality around the stone ring, even though their personal belongings suggest variation in wealth. One man had a fine necklace of imported beads, amber and carved jet; another wore only one jet bead. No one was buried with a dagger, another contrast with other regions of Britain where the warrior was the admired ideal. The impression of Anglesey society gained from Bedd Branwen is repeated in the other contemporary monuments on the island, but few provide so full a picture.

The separate burial of infant earbones, an unexplained ritual practice found several times in north Wales, is especially evident here. On three occasions a pair of petrous temporal bones from a new-born child was placed in a smaller pot and buried beside the urn containing adult bones. Such things give us a glimpse of darker worlds.

30
Llanfechell Triangle, Llanfechell

Standing stones

?2nd millennium BC

OS 114 SH 364916 U4

Site is on hilltop just N of Llanfechell village, 1ml (1.6km) S of Cemaes on the N coast; can be reached by footpaths from four directions. Easiest approach is from NE, from Cemaes–Llanfechell road, 0.6ml (1km) SW of Cemaes roundabout; near sharp bend leave car and take unmarked footpath (steps over wall) beside cottage (Tyddyn Paul). Keep to R of wall until stones come in sight (5–10 mins)

Llanfechell triangle

The three stones, all over 2m high, stand in a unique triangular arrangement about 3m apart. Only excavation could demonstrate a date and suggest a purpose for them. Strangely, no legends have been woven around them. The view, however, is worth the walk!

A more traditional single standing stone can be seen in the fields behind the church at SH 370917. It is on private land, but is visible at a distance.

31
Maenaddwyn, Llannerchymedd

Standing stone

2nd millennium BC

OS 114 SH 460833 U1

Stone stands beside road from Maenaddwyn (2.2ml, 3.5km, E of Llanerchymedd) to Tregaian, on L (E) 0.4ml (0.75km) S of Maenaddwyn crossroads

A substantial stone over 3m high. Recent excavation during roadworks demonstrated

Maenaddwyn

no obvious reason for its erection, and no grave or offering was found at its foot. In the 18th and 19th centuries several standing stones are recorded in this area, so this surviving one may not be the one which originally gave its name to the village at the crossroads, Maenaddwyn ('Addwyn's Stone').

32
Llanddyfnan Cemetery, Pentraeth

Standing stone and round barrows

2nd millennium BC

OS 114 SH 501785 U1

Stone is visible from B5109 Pentraeth–Llangefni road, on R (N), 1.3ml (2.25km) W of Pentraeth. Largest barrow is visible on L (S) 0.4ml (0.75km) back down road. A gentle rise in the field, it is best seen from W against sky. Monuments are all on private land, but can be seen adequately from road

Baynes 1909a

Although there is no detail to examine here, the group is interesting because of the juxtaposition of the standing stone and the barrows, which originally formed a line of four running east from it. Only the largest mound can now be seen. A similar juxtaposition is seen at Graeanog (no. 42) but, though both types of monument belong to the Bronze Age, this combination is surprisingly rare. The stone has not been excavated but it was recently straightened, having stood at a tilt for many decades.

The large barrow was excavated at the beginning of the 20th century, and seven Bronze Age cremation burials were found. As at Bedd Branwen (no. 29), there was no central burial, although one individual appeared to be rather wealthier than the others. The pottery and some of the grave goods (a razor and a decorated bronze bracelet) suggest contacts with Scotland and Ireland, whereas the axe and knife from the wealthiest burial came from the south of England. All are now in the National Museum of Wales in Cardiff.

Food vessel and grave goods from Llanddyfnan barrow

At a much later date, probably the 5th or 6th century AD, another body was buried in the top of the mound: a man laid out on his back without any grave goods. This may be a Christian burial; there are several examples of such reuse of old burial places, though it was by then more normal to be buried at a church.

Another barrow in this group, just east of the large one but much more difficult to see, was excavated in 1908. It covered a single inhumation in a boat-shaped pit grave. The burial rite and the shape of the grave suggest that it may pre-date the main barrow by 300–400 years, and might belong to the 'founding father' of this community.

33
Bryn Gwyn Stones, near Brynsiencyn

Bronze Age standing stones or stone circle

2nd millennium BC

OS 114 SH 462669 U3

Stones are visible from A4080 1.25ml (2km) W of sharp corner at NW end of Brynsiencyn, opposite Bryn Gwyn Hall. Footpath leads along hedge to stones and on to Castell Bryn Gwyn (no. 80) (c.10 mins)

The present remains consist of two huge stones (4m by 3m and 3m by 3m respectively) on either side of a field gate, between two large trees. The thinner stone once formed the wall of a small cottage, and the notches cut for the purlins can still be seen in its top.

In the 18th century more stones existed, and they were said to form part of a very large stone circle surrounded, some claimed, by an even larger ditch and bank. This would have been the largest circle in Wales, but unfortunately the early records are confused and the ditch has not been confirmed by aerial photography, so the question remains open.

Revd John Skinner's sketch of the Bryn Gwyn stones incorporated into a cottage, 1802

Entrance to Bronze Age mines on the Great Orme

34
Great Orme Mines, Llandudno

Bronze Age mining site
2nd millennium BC
OS 115 SH 770831 R3

Site is on Great Orme, close to Halfway tramway station. Free coach service operates from Prince Edward Square near Llandudno pier, and from summit car park. Open 10am–5pm every day, Mar–Nov. Admission charge. No underground access for the disabled

Crew and Crew 1990

This is a unique and exceptionally important site, the only Bronze Age copper mine in Europe which can be visited by the public. Visitors can penetrate deep into the hillside along specially heightened galleries which cross the terrifyingly cramped Bronze Age working areas, and can see the surface trench mines and the opencast workings, as yet not fully excavated. An evocative video is shown, and visitors are encouraged to talk to excavators exposing more of the early workings next to the main exhibition area.

Until a few years ago it was believed that all evidence of Bronze Age mining would have been removed by subsequent work at those ore sources accessible to primitive technology. But new research in those mines – like the Great Orme, where 19th-century miners had recorded cutting through earlier galleries – allied with the use of radiocarbon dating, has shown that this was an over-pessimistic view.

In Wales alone, four Bronze Age mines have been identified. The evidence results from the practice of 'firesetting' – weakening the parent rock by lighting a huge fire against the face and then breaking it by simply hitting it with large hammerstones. This slow and exhausting process produces two by-products of great archaeological value: charcoal, which can be radiocarbon dated, and broken hammerstones – large, rounded pebbles which can be easily recognised among the angular mine debris. Several of these tools can be seen at the Great Orme, together with the bone tools which were used to scrape away the soft dolomitised limestone from around the ore-body. The geology of the Orme mines is rather exceptional in that the parent rock – both limestone and shales – is, in many parts, unusually soft, which may explain the scale of work here. The early miners had to rely on the most simple of tools, but clearly their geological knowledge and operational experience of mine design was very sophisticated.

The tour starts in the Visitor Centre, which has good explanatory boards, then visitors are encouraged to see the video before emerging in front of the limestone cliffs in which vertical and horizontal veins of green malachite and blue azurite can still be seen. At the base of the cliff are several gallery entrances; two were reworked in the 19th century and consequently are of sufficient size to walk into. During the guided tour underground it is possible to see untouched Bronze Age galleries and to appreciate the appalling difficulties of working in them, especially when firesetting became necessary at the numerous points where the rock hardens. The galleries descend steeply, and even lower levels can be glimpsed beneath the final viewing platform. On the return, visitors pass an enormous underground chamber entirely excavated in the Bronze Age.

After the underground tour, visitors should see the open trench mines which were driven into the cliff at a higher level. Radiocarbon dating suggests, not surprisingly, that these surface mines are rather older (with dates around 1600 BC) than the deep galleries which were being opened up at the very end of the Bronze Age. When excavation began, it was thought that these trench mines would continue into the cliff as underground galleries but, as the vast mass of 19th-century spoil was removed, it became apparent that a huge opencast area existed behind them. The full extent of this has not yet been revealed, but already it is possible to appreciate the enormous scale of the prehistoric workings. Features of the 19th-century mine are also being exposed on the cliff above.

The bulk of the prehistoric mining probably belongs to the middle Bronze Age, a period when the other side of the archaeological evidence – the products, the bronze tools – suggest that Welsh industry was flourishing and was at the forefront of British manufacturing.

The summit of the Orme preserves a very interesting historical landscape (examine the aerial photograph in the Country Park Visitor Centre). There is a Neolithic tomb (no. 14), a small hillfort on the east side, and an area of medieval farmland (no. 116) near the early church of St Tudno, as well as a mass of possibly ancient shafts just north of the tramway, reworked in 1849, when Llandudno became known as the Welsh California. The modern town of Llandudno on the sand spit is entirely a product of the 19th century, while all the early history, from the Palaeolithic onwards, is concentrated on the two great limestone headlands, and chiefly on the larger one.

35
Druids' Circle Sanctuary, Penmaenmawr

Bronze Age ritual and burial monuments

2nd millennium BC

OS 115 SH 722746 (Druid's Circle) U4

See Graig Lwyd axe factory (no. 18). From N ('Bryn Derwydd' route) as you come in sight of sea, stones of circle are visible on skyline to L. This raised plateau is the 'sanctuary', but other monuments are below it, both E and W. Route from Graig Lwyd Farm: bear L at top, through gate, bear L to saddle of hill

Griffiths 1960

The Druids' Circle is a famous monument, sketched by many 18th-century travellers enjoying a welcome respite from the rigours of the horse-drawn coach journey over the mountains. The kerb of this road, which avoided the notorious headlands but was itself a rather hazardous route, can be seen on a lower shelf. A swathe of contrasting vegetation signals the presence of the underground Shell Oil pipeline (1974), which took the same route.

The circle itself is famous, but it is only one of a group of interesting monuments which in the Bronze Age may each have had a specific, inter-related role in ceremony. There are two circular monuments of differing but standard designs which are likely to have been used for recurrent rituals throughout the early Bronze Age, eventually having burials placed within them. There are also smaller rings and groups of stones whose roles are less well understood. Clustered around the plateau are burial monuments, burial and rebirth remaining a central tenet in Bronze Age religious thinking. One such, a barrow on the approach route, is topped by an electricity pole.

Below the main group is a small ring of five boulders. Excavation in 1957 revealed a central pit filled with small pieces of quartz, a stone often used in the Bronze Age to emphasise important features of a monument. Although presumably important, the purpose of the pit is obscure.

The Druids' Circle consists of a ring of large stones set on the inner edge of a low stone bank, 23m in diameter, with an entrance on the west side. It is a classic example of what is called an embanked stone circle. Excavation in 1957 revealed a group of cremation burials in the centre, set into three pits but otherwise unmarked. The identifiable bones were of young children and it was suggested that these might have been sacrificial victims – a theory very difficult to prove! The ring is not an exact circle; it is flattened on the north-east where a track cuts across the plateau. It can be argued that the circle may have been flattened to avoid covering the track, which must, therefore, be older. Perhaps the stone axes were taken from the nearby axe factory (no. 18) by this route.

Whereas the Druids' Circle is visible from afar, the ring cairn is virtually hidden; it lies behind a fold in the hill, at 10 o'clock as you stand in the circle looking westward and 150m away. It consists of a low bank of stone without tall uprights, but with larger stones set at fairly regular intervals around the inner edge of the 15m diameter bank. Nothing was found in the centre here; all the features of interest were at the foot of the bank. Excavation in 1957 revealed scorched earth in front of a very long stone on the south-east, implying that a fire had been burning there. Directly opposite, another fire had been lit over a pit where soil and charcoal had been buried in an urn. Burials of charcoal and burnt

The Druid's Circle

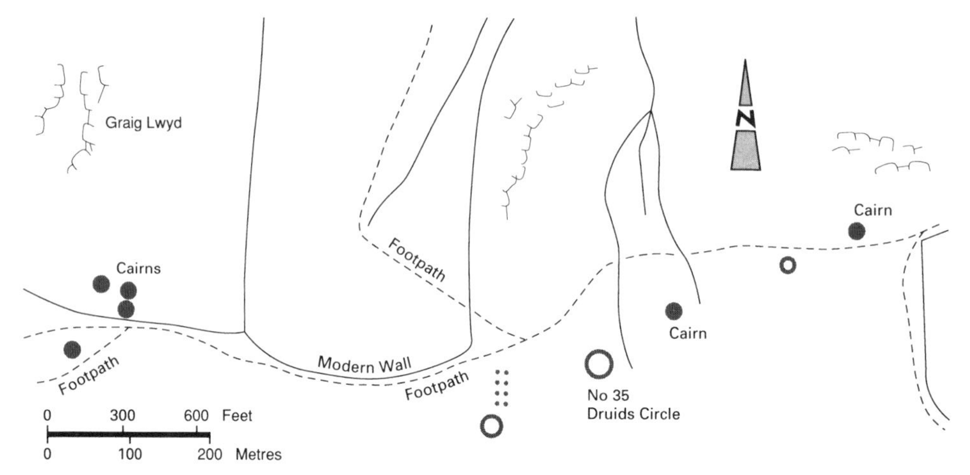

Map of monuments on Penmaenmawr

soil are often found in ring cairns, which seem to have been used for ceremonies which must have been ancillary to funerals. Where human bones are found at these sites (as here, tucked behind the long south-east stone) they usually belong to a late stage in the history of the monument.

From the ring cairn, go back over the hump to a double line of 1m-high stones crossing a hollow. They may have formed a barrier across the entrance to the sanctuary. However, stones to the west of them surrounded a late cremation burial. Had they marked the edge of the sacred area, this should perhaps have been on the other side. Several have obviously been over-turned and interpretation is difficult.

Walk down off the plateau towards the saddle between Moelfre and Graig Lwyd, where there is a group of three cairns and an arc of boulders, perhaps the remains of another stone circle. The largest but simplest cairn (20m diameter by 2.4m high) stands on the open moor. It has been robbed and a large crater dug in the top. The other cairns are on the other side of the wall; one has been robbed to build the wall, but large kerbstones remain on the north side. The other, beside an electricity pole, is a very good example of a kerb cairn – a very small mound (3m diameter) enclosed by a kerb of disproportionately large stones.

36

Maen Penddu, above Henryd/Rowen

Standing stone and stone circle

2nd millennium BC

OS 115 SH 739735 U4/U2

Continue SE across moor from Druid's Circle (no. 35), on reasonably clear but wet path. Maen Penddu stands just over summit of ridge. Alternatively, drive from Henryd (off B5106 1.8ml, 3km, S of Conwy) to Llangelynin Old Church (see no. 142) and walk 0.6ml (1km) W up track, following stream in NW corner of 1st field

Maen Penddu ('Black-headed Stone'), though not itself visible from afar, commands a truly magnificent view. It stands almost 2m high, a neat, flat-topped stone. Just above, across the

Maen Penddu

track, is an almost buried stone circle. It is not large in diameter, and the stones are low; four or five can still be seen just emerging through the peat and bilberries. The two monuments were almost certainly related in their use, and they stand on a saddle beside a track which must be ancient, a position often chosen for ceremonial sites of this type.

The degraded bank of a later enclosure on the south side of the track can just be seen running up to the stone.

37
Bwlch y Ddeufaen, Rowen
Standing stones and cairns
2nd millennium BC
OS 115 SH 716718 U2/U4

See Maen y Bardd (no. 15). Bwlch y Ddeufaen is pass at W end of Rowen valley. It can form part of a longer walk or can be approached by car, going W straight through Rowen and turning R at first T-junction and continuing to end of tarmac (car park). This is 0.4ml (0.6km) E of stones

The pass is marked by two very fine standing stones (3m and 2m high respectively) on either side of the road. There are two smaller uprights close to the northern stone, and a series of small stones emerging from the peat a short distance east of the southern one. These are reminiscent of the stone setting near Bryn Cader Faner (no. 45), but the

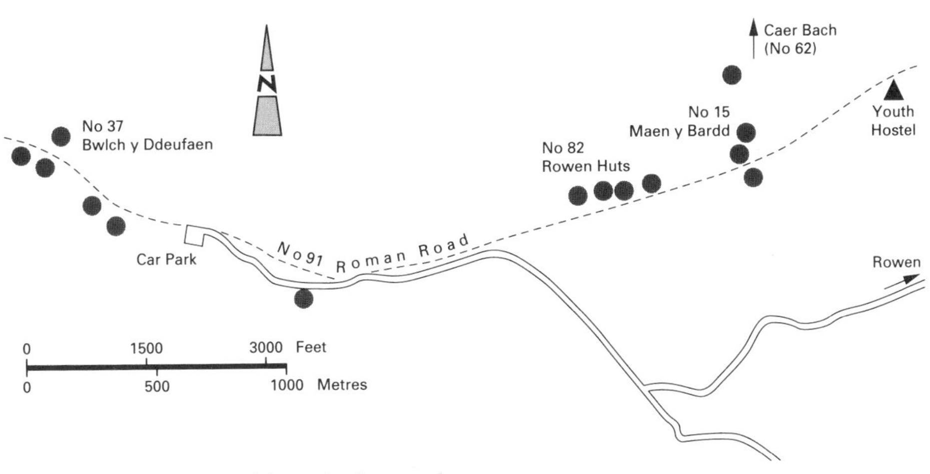

Map of monuments in Bwlch y Ddeufaen and along the Roman road above Rowen

pattern is less clear and they are not certainly Bronze Age.

A large cairn, Barclodiad y Gawres ('Apronful of the Giantess'), lies 250m east of the south stone, a little below the track. A very large stone grave, which should normally be in the centre, is exposed close to the north side. The surrounding stones may have been moved quite extensively. Another good cairn can be recognised a short way away.

On returning to the car park it is possible to see the Roman road (no. 91) forming a shelf above the modern one.

Walk eastward down the road for 450m to a stone stile in the south wall to view a stone circle standing on a prominent rocky shelf. Few of the stones are taller than 0.5m but they are set in a very accurate circle, 23m in diameter, and the monument has a certain elegance. Two stones standing to the west may be significant outliers.

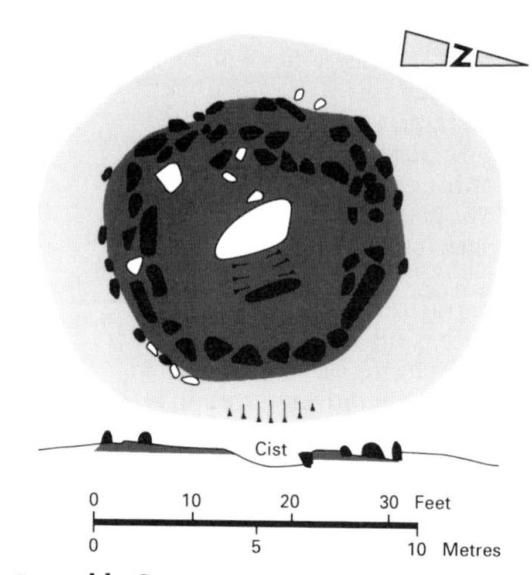

Carnedd y Saeson

38

Carnedd y Saeson, Abergwyngregyn

Round cairn

2nd millennium BC

OS 115 SH 678717 U2

From Abergwyngregyn (on A55, 2.2ml, 3.5km, W of Llanfairfechan) go S on road up valley for 0.6ml (1km) to bridge; cross bridge, continue up hill for 0.8ml (1.2km) to end of road, and park. Walk through gate and up hollow way. Cairns are close to top, above track to Anafon valley. Consult map (see no. 83) for location of monuments on slope

Carnedd y Saeson ('Cairn of the Englishman') is the largest of the cairns on this slope. It is about 10m across, with a large stone cist or grave exposed at its centre. This would have held an unburnt body, perhaps accompanied by personal belongings for the afterlife. The edge of the cairn is marked by several rings of large stones, more elaborate than the normal kerb and probably originally concealed, like the cist itself, beneath a heap of stones which have been removed over the years.

Further up the slope are several more round cairns, but none has a grave exposed and many of them may be simply field clearance heaps, for the summit of the hill is covered with cultivation ridges, probably medieval in date and connected with several rectangular huts in the vicinity (see no. 83).

39

Cairn on Meuryn Isaf, Abergwyngregyn

Round cairn

2nd millennium BC

OS 115 SH 671709 U4

Go up valley road to bridge (see no. 38). Park in Forestry Commission car park just over bridge. Cross river, take FC path to L up N side of ridge, persevere to top, bearing R towards nose of ridge. Continue up beyond cleared area; cairn is at junction with path on R. 3/4hr walk

This is a fine burial cairn, even though it has been disturbed. A very good length of the well-built encircling kerb survives on the north side. The large stone in the centre must have formed part of the grave or cist.

It stands in what would have been a truly dramatic position before the forest was planted, looking right down the valley to the sea. The path up affords a very good view of the cairns and fields on the north side of the valley (nos 38 and 83). The southern valley leading up to the Aber Falls also contains evidence of settlement, the best hut group being just by the last fence before the falls. Vegetation tends to obscure it in summer.

40
Cwm Ffrydlas, Bethesda

Settlement

2nd millennium BC

OS 115 SH 644684 U4

See no. 84. From E side of Moel Faban walk NE along well-made track towards quarry on Y Gyrn; shortly after sheepfold comes in sight take sheep track on R down towards small upright stone with white quartz block on top. Walk towards second sheepfold, keeping the mine on other side of the valley in line with it

Griffiths 1950, p 45

These very ephemeral huts and fields are difficult to recognise on the ground, but are worth the effort of identification because they are one of the most characteristic and accessible of Griffiths's 'Class II settlements' – groups of very small huts set within irregular, non-terraced fields. Such settlements are believed to be early Bronze Age in date.

The group consists of six small and very poorly built huts, most of them on the lines of the field-walls. The visible stones may never have been structural walls, but simply, as excavation on Arran has recently shown, a stone skin piled against a wooden wall. The fields are of irregular, rounded shape and variable size. Heaps of stone cleared from the surface also lie along the line of the walls, and the easiest way of orientating yourself with the plan is to find the largest of these clearance cairns, which is on the east side of the settlement, covered in reeds.

A number of other clearance cairns, without field-walls, may be seen on the slopes above the track to the north-west, suggesting quite an extensive area of cultivation spreading out from this small settlement. Because of the altitude, it is assumed that this period of intensive agricultural use occurred during the period of better weather in the earlier Bronze Age, but there has been no excavation to confirm this.

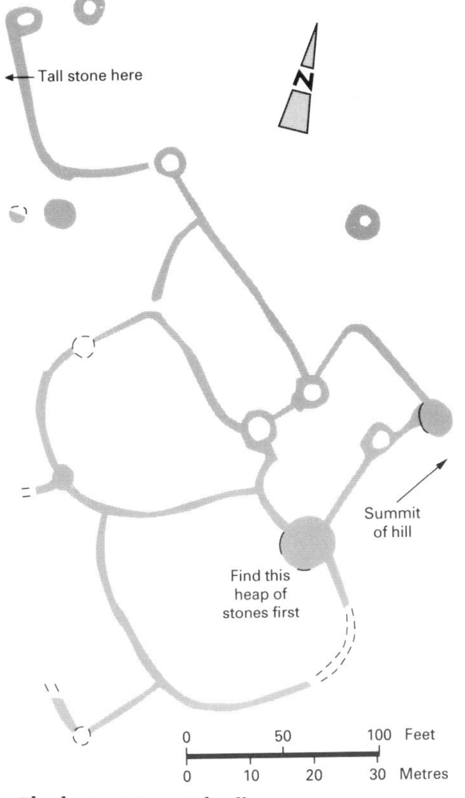

The huts at Cwm Ffrydlas

The largest cairn on Drosgl

41
Cairns on Drosgl, Bethesda

Round cairns

2nd millennium BC

OS 115 SH 663680 U4

See no. 40. Continue up Cwm Ffrydlas path to saddle, take RH path straight up to summit (steep walk, 1.5ml, 2.5km, from no. 40)

Crew 1985

Many mountaintops are crowned by cairns; most of the larger ones are ancient but some are walkers' cairns or survey markers, so a Bronze Age date should not be automatically assumed. This summit has four cairns: the largest one and the small one just to the north are ancient; another small one to the south is a geological feature, and a fourth small cairn is a walkers' cairn – the full range conveniently gathered for comparison!

The group was excavated in 1976. The larger cairn was structurally quite complex, but very little of the burial had survived later disturbance. There were two cists in the centre, both about 0.5m square. One had been robbed, but a little cremated bone and a whetstone were found at the very bottom; the other appeared to be undisturbed, but the bone inside had decayed. The overlying cairn was enclosed within three concentric kerbs, probably all built at the same time (compare no. 38). Only the outermost wall would have been visible, creating a drum-like profile to the mound.

The small cairn was simpler, just a central cist and a single kerb. However, a good deal of cremated bone was found here, the remains of a young woman.

42
Graeanog Cairns and Standing Stone, Llanllyfni

Bronze Age burial and ritual monuments

2nd millennium BC

OS 115 SH 455492 U2

From Penygroes (5.3ml, 8.5km, S of Caernarfon on A487), continue S for 1.5ml (2.4km) and turn R (signposted Tai Lon/Capel Uchaf/ Clynnog). Persevere over humped bridge for 1.3ml (2.1km). Park carefully near sharp RH corner outside Bwythen Graianog. Go through a wide white gate and keep to LH edge of field; standing stone will come into view. Land is private, but owner allows access to monuments

The standing stone is a very impressive monument, a well-formed pillar, 3m high. It

Graeanog cairn and standing stone

stands close to two round cairns, one of which is partly embedded in the field-wall. Some of the large kerbstones which marked its edge can still be recognised. Although unexcavated, this is an interesting group because of the juxtaposition of the burial monuments (cairns) and the stone. The purpose of standing stones is very uncertain, and their relationship to burial rituals is debatable since it is rare to find them so close.

Graeanog is a gravel island surrounded by marsh; settlement has been concentrated here for centuries, and several late prehistoric and early medieval farmsteads have been excavated recently in advance of quarrying. A particularly clear and well preserved series of early terraced fields can be seen on the slopes to the south-east, just north of Caerau (see Appendix).

43
Llanbedr Stones, Llanbedr

Standing stones

2nd millennium BC

OS 124 SH 583270 U3

Site is just N of Llanbedr village (3ml, 4.8km, S of Harlech on A496), on L (W) just beyond garage. On private land, but visible from road and nearby public footpath

Two tall stones stand beneath a tree near the mouth of the river Artro. One, a fine, rectangular, tapering column, 3.3m high, is too large for a cattle rubbing stone. There is some doubt, however, about the antiquity of the smaller one. Their lowland position is unusual, but they may mark the starting point of the great Bronze Age trackway leading to Moel Goedog (no. 44), Bryn Cader Faner (no. 45) and over to Trawsfynydd and beyond.

Carreg standing stone, near Llanbedr

This route has many such tall stones along it: memorials placed where travellers would be sure to see them. From here the track skirted the marsh and headed for the higher ground behind Llanfair.

To rejoin the track near Rhiwgoch, take the main road north to Llanfair and, just after the by-pass, turn right (unsignposted road opposite road to beach), then left at the T-junction and right (1st through road) up the hill. Persevere upwards for 1.1ml (1.8km), straight through the crossroads for another 0.6ml (1km) till Carreg – a standing stone with a ruined cairn just behind it – appears on the right; 500m up the road, just beyond a cattle grid, is another, taller stone on the left. Another 500m further on is a small stone on the right, and yet another on the left where the road levels out.

All the stones are believed to have been erected in the Bronze Age, and they indicate the route up on to the higher ground which provided the easiest passage, before modern drainage of the lowland. This prehistoric route was the road taken by Giraldus Cambrensis in 1188, and continued to be the main road until the beginning of the 19th century.

44
Moel Goedog Circles, Harlech

Ceremonial and burial monuments

2nd millennium BC

OS 124   SH 610324   U2

Continue from no. 43 where the road levels out. It may be difficult to park; do not block any tracks. Take track bearing R from road, then L, continue ahead through two field gates. Circles are 0.3ml (0.5km) from road. Above to R is Moel Goedog hillfort (no. 73). Track is public footpath; fields are private land but owner allows access to monuments. Track continues NW to Bryn Cader Faner (no. 45) but there are few monuments for next 1.8ml (3km) except cultivation ridges, a large burnt mound and a small slate quarry

Lynch 1984

Upper ring cairn, Moel Goedog

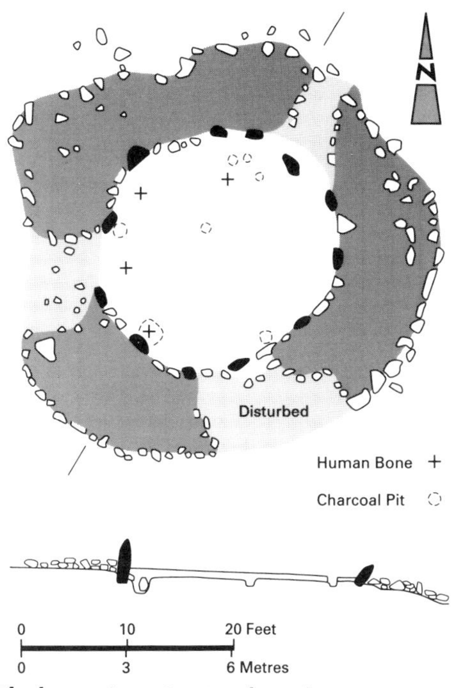

The lower ring cairn, Moel Goedog

The circles form a pair on either side of the track; they seem to mark a climax to the group of standing stones placed with increasing frequency on the approach (see no. 43). First there is a massive, squat boulder on the left and then a slightly smaller one on the right. At this point the upper circle can be seen on a slight ledge on the hillside.

A ring of large boulders set on the inner edge of a low, grass-grown stone bank forms a circle 6.5m in diameter. The centre is hollowed and probably artificially levelled. There has been no excavation here, so one cannot tell what or who was buried, nor whether it was built at exactly the same time as the lower circle. However, the circles' complementary setting in the landscape – one being visible from the south, the other from the north – would suggest that they were designed as a pair. The very large stone on the south side may be an earthfast boulder; the incorporation of a natural feature is quite common in monuments of this kind (see no. 56).

Return to the track and continue to the lower circle, which is just below on the left. It is a ring cairn, similar in design to the upper circle but with taller stones set at regular intervals on the inner edge of its low stone bank. Four of these stones had been missing since the 17th century, so new ones were placed in the original stone-holes when the monument was excavated and restored in 1979. These added stones have been marked with a deep T cut into the back.

The interior had been levelled into the slope and several pits had been dug before it was covered with a thin layer of stones (only surviving in the northern quarter). Some of the pits had been dug close to the inner edge of the bank, others were in the centre of the ring. The pits contained various deposits – charcoal alone, charcoal with scraps of burnt human bone, and burnt bone alone, the product of a 'normal' cremation burial. In one case the scraps of bone had been previously buried near the coast (to judge by the soil around them) and had been reburied up here. Some of the bone and charcoal was in pots typical of the early Bronze Age, some just poured directly into the pits.

This evidence indicates that a variety of activities had taken place within the circle. Some of them are matched at other ring cairns in the region (nos 35 and 56); others – the reburial of bone for instance – were unknown before this excavation, but have since been recorded in south Wales. There was evidence to show that the various pits had been dug at different times, and radiocarbon dates suggest that the circle was in use between 1700 and 1400 BC.

Bryn Cader Faner

45

Trackway to Bryn Cader Faner, above Talsarnau

Cairn circle, cairns and settlement

2nd millennium BC and 1st millennium BC/AD

OS 124 SH 629343–647354 (Bryn Cader Faner) U4 (map and compass essential)

Track continues from Moel Goedog (no. 44) joining another (see below) at SH 631338. To walk only this N section drive S from Talsarnau on A496; 0.3ml (0.5km) after Harlech junction turn L (signposted Maes y Neuadd Hotel). At top, turn L then R (back of hotel) and persevere up very narrow steep road to end (Moel y Geifr) where 1 or 2 cars can be parked. Follow Welsh Water track on R for 0.75ml (1.25km). Shortly after 3rd gate track bears R to lakes. Leave track here (this is a crucial point) and continue straight ahead through boggy patch, skirting wall to L of rocky knoll. Time: 2½–3 hours, either to Bryn Cader Faner and back, or on to Y Gyrn (no. 46)

Beyond the knoll the track bears right on to a plateau, a patch of relatively good land with signs of occupation and use – a 'cairnfield' (small heaps of stone resulting from field clearance) and a rather tenuous enclosure and two round hut foundations. These are on the rocky slope to the left of the track; the huts can be seen best from the top of the rise. Further on, on the right, is a ruined cairn with upright stones on the south-west side, suggesting quite a complex structure, now too ruined for confident interpretation.

Continue along the track for about 250m. Below, on the right, are several small, upright stones set in the ground. One small circle with a 'robber pit' in the centre can be recognised; the design of other lines and rings is more problematic. Nearby is the base of a large robbed cairn incorporating a lot of white quartz. Undoubtedly the whole complex represents Bronze Age ritual activity of some kind, but the small upright stones are an unusual component.

The cairn was probably robbed in the 17th or 18th century, when the track was rebuilt as a well-engineered road with a kerb that is still visible, despite the growth of bog which can make the route very wet.

About 500m beyond the cairn the track cuts across an older wall. This wall belongs to a settlement of later prehistoric date with at least two good round huts overlaid by a recent sheepfold. It lies in a sheltered fold of the hill about 120m to the left of the track. Return to the track before it swings north around the rocky boss.

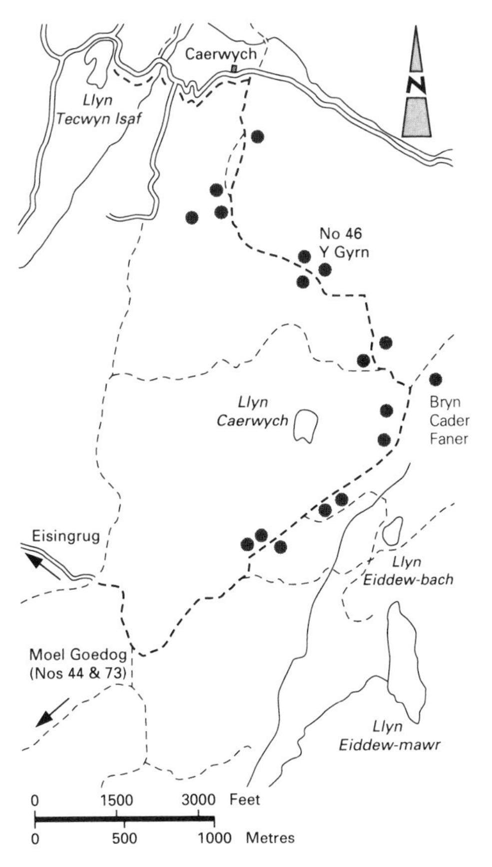

Map of monuments near Bryn Cader Faner and Y Gyrn

From here Bryn Cader Faner itself is visible standing on an isolated rocky eminence (SH 647354). It is a monument of simple but brilliantly effective design, placed with sophisticated precision in its dramatic setting so as to achieve maximum impact on travellers approaching from the south. It is arguably the most beautiful Bronze Age monument in Britain.

It is a small cairn, 8m across and less than 1m high, but around the edge is a ring of tall, thin slabs set at an angle, projecting from the mass of the cairn like the rays of the sun. The monument may be classified as a cairn circle, and was probably a site of burial rather than ceremonial function. It has been disturbed, and a hole in the centre no doubt indicates the position of a cist or grave, the content of which is unknown. The army, on manoeuvres before the Second World War, pulled out stones on the east side but, miraculously, the striking silhouette remained intact.

From Bryn Cader Faner, either return to Moel y Geifr or, if you leave a car at each end, go down by Y Gyrn (no. 46) and Caerwych to Llyn Tecwyn Isaf (SH 630370). For this route, descend the west side of Bryn Cader Faner ridge, turn left, then branch right along a track overwhelmed by bog, but drier and more easily visible on the other side of the valley. There is another group of huts under a modern sheepfold in the end of this valley, and old walls can be traced on the hillside opposite. A small mine adit, a circular foundation (a ring cairn or perhaps a large hut) and another pair of similar stone rings may be seen to left and right of the track as you descend – as well as a spectacular mountain panorama.

At the bottom, follow the track round to the left, cross a stream and keep close to the base (south side) of the next rocky hill.

46

Y Gyrn and Maes y Caerau, Llandecwyn

Burial and ceremonial sites, burnt mound, concentric circle settlement and round huts

2nd and 1st millennium BC

OS 124   SH 641358 (cairns)
SH 635362 (Maes y Caerau)   U4
(map essential)

To approach from below, leave A496 at Talsarnau (N end) and go E on Llandecwyn road, and be sure not to miss the sharp LH turn 100m after main road junction; 0.9ml (1.5km) from Talsarnau turn L at T-junction, then bear R at chapel and leave car by lake (small charge) or beyond at 1st RH turn. Do not attempt to drive up to Caerwych Farm. Walk up and through farmyard, turn R up track behind last barn. Track is clear but there is a stiff climb to Y Gyrn. Better to approach from Bryn Cader Faner (no. 45) and come down via this route (as in the description below). The lower sites can be slightly obscured by bracken

There are three sites below Y Gyrn: two burial or ceremonial monuments and a burnt mound. The cairns lie on level ground just east of the point where the stream drops out of the hanging valley. The burial cairn lies on the south side of the stream and to the left of a reasonable track, which you reach after crossing boggy ground. A central cist, clearly recognisable though recently collapsed, probably held a crouched inhumation burial. The cairn around it was built with two concentric rings of large boulders, but these were probably concealed within the mass of the stone (see nos 38 and 41).

The second mound is to the right of the track, close beside the stream a little to the east of the burial cairn. It is a good example of a burnt stone mound or cooking site. Characteristically sited close to water, it is composed of burnt dolerite and has a slight hollow in the side facing the stream. This may indicate the position of a trough in which water was heated by throwing in hot stones. When the trough was used again, these stones were shovelled out – hence the development of the large mound. Dolerite was the preferred stone because it could be

Ring cairn below Y Gyrn

reheated and reused more often than other rocks.

The third monument in this group is a ring cairn without upright stones in its bank, and with an earth-filled centre. It is about 12m across and 1m high. It lies on the north side of the stream, just below the west end of the ridge of projecting rock, from which it is easy to see.

From here, follow the track which keeps to the north of the stream and descends steeply through a gate below the crags. Continue to the next wall where, if the sun is low, a well preserved area of cultivation ridges may be seen. There is a medieval or later ruin just before the gate. It was probably a *hafod* or summer grazing base.

Go through the gate and turn left over the brow of the ridge to look down on to the concentric circle farmstead, Maes y Caerau. The settlement consists of a single very large (over 12m diameter) stone house surrounded by two circular enclosures or yards. The double enclosure is rather unusual, but the concentric arrangement is characteristic of the area, and this type of farm has recently been dated to the earlier Iron Age (600–200 BC) (see Erw Wen, Appendix). The fields are private land, so wandering from the public footpath should be kept to a minimum.

Return to the path which, below the gate, cuts through a small rectangular enclosure, a yard containing two round houses, one on either side of the track. This is a much less distinctive type of settlement than the concentric circles, and it could belong to either the prehistoric or the Romano-British period – or both. A single hut stands on a shelf just above the next gate. Across the next field and just through the gate there is another burnt stone mound on the right with a stream curving around it.

Return to the road through Caerwych Farm.

Ruined cairn Bwlch y Rhiwgyr. The people are standing on the surviving rim of stone

47

Hengwm Ring Cairn and Bwlch y Rhiwgyr, Tal y Bont

Settlement and ceremonial and burial monuments

2nd millennium BC

OS 124 SH 617203 (Hengwm), SH 627200 (Bwlch y Rhiwgyr)
U4 (map essential)

From Carneddau Hengwm (no. 26), walk c.400m E towards foot of central E–W wall on hillside; ring cairn ('Cairn Circle' on OS map) is on 3rd shelf of raised promontory, in line with N corner of field abutting central E–W wall. To continue to Bwlch y Rhiwgyr, cross stile behind ring cairn; follow track for 0.6ml (1km) past remains of manganese mines, into narrow defile. Cairn is at very top, bisected by boundary wall. Path continues S towards Barmouth

Crawford 1920

The ring cairn is a low monument, but quite elaborately designed and carefully sited to appear on a false crest when seen from below. It was excavated in 1919, when nothing was found within the hollow central area. The circle is formed with small, upright slabs and, rather unusually, the outer edge is marked by the highest ring, with stones set at an angle, like those at Bryn Cader Faner (no. 45).

Just east of the ring cairn are the remains of a settlement enclosure: three round huts and two field clearance cairns on the line of the walls of a small oval 'field'. The huts have been damaged by use as lambing shelters, but they are of a size and construction which might suggest a Bronze Age date, contemporary with the ring cairn.

The cairn at Bwlch y Rhiwgyr is most dramatically sited, but it has been badly damaged through use as a quarry by the builders of the later wall. At present it looks like a ring cairn, but originally it was probably a high mound of stone because the bank has a very ragged inner edge and stone can be felt beneath the grass in the centre. The pass and the view from it are exciting; the track beyond is rather less rewarding archaeologically, but passes Cerrig Arthur (see Appendix) and provides a good walk down to Barmouth.

48
Llech Idris, Trawsfynydd

Standing stone

2nd millennium BC

OS 124 SH 731311 U2

From Trawsfynydd, go S on A470 and take 2nd road on L (signposted Abergeirw), after 2.2ml (3.5km) take LH fork, continue for 500m then take RH fork; leave car (plenty of space). Walk down track on R for 350m. Stone is in field below, on L

Llech Idris

This well-known stone may mark an inland stage of the Bronze Age track which started at the coast at Llanbedr (see no. 43). It is a very fine pointed slab standing over 3m high. The name was current before the 17th century, Idris being the legendary giant of Cadair Idris.

A Roman tile kiln has been found beneath the bank a few metres to the north of the stone. Earthworks visible beyond it to the north-east are rifle butts for military training. All this area was an army training ground from the Boer War until the 1960s and there is a wide variety of military structures and features in the vicinity.

49
Llyn Gregennan Walk, Cadair Idris

Ceremonial and burial monuments and settlement

2nd millennium BC and 1st millennium AD

OS 124 SH 657142 (NT Car Park) U4/U2 (map advisable)

Circular walk of about 2.5ml (4km) starts at NT car park at Llynnau Gregennan. From centre of Dolgellau take road towards W, then fork L (signposted Cadair Idris) and persevere on this road for 4.4ml (7.5km) until lakes and car park are signposted to R. Bracken can obscure parts of Llys Bradwen in summer

This walk includes Llys Bradwen and the Arthog Circle. From the car park, return along the road passing a small mine adit, a sheep-fold and a tall stone, Carreg y Big, standing in an unusual position beneath a rocky knoll. On the eastern ridge, in a patch of rougher grass, is a Bronze Age cairn 'excavated' in the last century, when a cist was found. The south-facing slopes beyond are covered with cultivation ridges and field clearance cairns,

Standing stone on the slopes of Cadair Idris

and there is a settlement, probably medieval, beneath the ruined sheepfold just over the brow. The foundation of a curving enclosure wall and two (?semi-detached) platform houses can be seen beneath the more recent walling.

Turning west, examine the remains of a large cairn beside the wall of the road. Like that in Bwlch y Rhiwgyr (see no. 47) it looks like a ring cairn, but its sharp, ragged rim is the result of damage, not design. A large, high cairn in this position would have provided a dramatic focus at the head of the valley. It is recorded that the remains of the cairn were used as an amphitheatre for cock-fighting.

From here, walk along the road past a modern ruin and through a gate. Take the left fork up a track towards an impressive standing stone on top of a rounded hill. This track, known as Ffordd Ddu ('Black Road') is an old road over the shoulder of Cadair Idris, but most of the Bronze Age monuments stand beside the lower (asphalted) road which skirts the slope (see no. 50). Return to this lower road and, beyond the next gate, turn right towards Arthog. After about 500m turn right, down to a clapper bridge over the river.

Llys Bradwen ('Court of Bradwen') lies on flat land immediately across the river. The site consists of two conjoined square enclosures cut into the hillslope. The larger one is about 30m square, and the other, on the upper right-hand side, is some 13m across. Both are enclosed by large stone-faced banks, but no buildings are visible in either. The original entrance is on the south; the northern gap is recent. Legendary and place-name evidence hints at an early medieval date for this establishment, which is not defensive in any true sense, though its hidden position might be suitable for the court of a minor chieftain. Roman pottery found here recently suggests that the settlement may have had a long history.

Continue up the track to the left and, where it turns right at the top, notice cultivation ridges overlying an earlier lynchet. A broad bank delimits the cultivation and runs under the modern wall on the right. This evidence of earlier agriculture has been destroyed in the more intensively farmed fields to the right, but the Arthog Circle has survived in the second field. This is on private land, but visible over the wall.

The circle is probably the remains of a Bronze Age burial monument rather than a ceremonial circle, but so little remains that certainty is impossible. Four stones less than 1m high still stand on the arc of a circle 4m in diameter, and two stones outside the arc may have been moved when the monument was incorporated into a field-wall (now largely removed). The large block of quartz on the north-east is of uncertain date.

Follow the footpath sign up the hill beneath two small abortive gold-mining adits. Follow the path over the hill, cross two stiles and bear left to return to the car park, or continue on the level through two gates to rejoin the road.

50

Bedd y Brenin, Cadair Idris

Round cairn and settlement

2nd millennium BC and later

OS 124 SH 634115 U4 (map advisable)

Proceed W on asphalted road along N slope of Cadair Idris for 1.5ml (2.5km) from Arthog turning (see no. 49). Opposite track to Cyfannedd Fawr take steep footpath bearing L uphill through forest for c.600m. Pass three groups of stones (the 2nd is possibly a rectangular house). Bedd y Brenin is in clearing at top. Alternatively, reach cairn by continuing W along Ffordd Ddu from standing stone (see no. 49) and turning R into forest before crossing river. Track continues from cairn into Dysynni valley below Allt Lwyd (no. 53)

Bowen and Gresham 1967, p 97; Kelly 1983

This large, round cairn Bedd y Brenin ('Grave of the King') has been badly mutilated, but still remains an impressive monument standing at a most interesting topographical point. Unfortunately, the imposing effect of its siting has been damaged recently by the planting of conifers, but before these trees grew up it was possible to appreciate how the cairn stood on the saddle where all the tracks across the mountain converge – a crossroads where the various valley communities might meet. Those interested in the inter-relationship of landscape and building should make the effort to reach it.

The cairn appears to be a simple structure, 30m in diameter. It was badly damaged by an excavation in 1851, when a large capstone covering a small burial cist was found. It contained four piles of burnt bone, one in each corner. Since then sheepfolds and a high wall have been built over the cairn. The central cist found in 1851 is still exposed at the foot of the wall on the east side.

On the way down, turn left over the stream at the second group of stones. On a level shelf at the head of the gully (SH 631116), in a forest clearing, is a small settlement consisting of a large round hut and enclosure, and a later rectangular building on the edge of a small paddock. The view is magnificent.

51

Bryn Seward Stones, Cadair Idris

Standing stones

2nd millennium BC

OS 124 SH 626117 U1

Site is on N side of Cadair Idris beside asphalted road, passable by car, though very narrow. Continue W from Cyfannedd Fawr (see no. 50); stones are on R, 0.6ml (1km) beyond turning to farm

The fact that these two tall stones are so close together refutes the theory that standing

Bryn Seward standing stones

stones, so often found beside ancient trackways, were simply markers to these routes. They cluster, as here, where the path is straightforward and easy, and are seldom found at points of difficulty, which suggests that they occur where traffic was dense and many people would be reminded of the event or person that they commemorated.

Settlement traces, walls and a possible round hut, occur on the shelf of level ground below the stones, and the mound just west of them, through the gate, may be the remains of a large Bronze Age cairn. There is another about 500m further west on the left of the road, beyond the fields and huts (see no. 88). This has been disturbed, and the central grave has been dug out. The manner in which the covering cairn had been piled around the central feature is clearly visible.

52
Waun Oer Stones, Cadair Idris

Stone alignment

2nd millennium BC

OS 124 SH 617113 U1

Continue 0.6ml (1km) W from no. 51. Stones are just inside field to R of road. Field is private land, but owner allows access to stones. Keep dogs under control

Alignments are relatively rare in Wales, so this one is worth a visit, although none of the five stones is especially impressive. They are all under 2m high, and two have fallen.

Alignments of upright stones, associated with cairns and circles, are a particular feature of Bronze Age Dartmoor, but the lines there are much longer and the stones smaller than in Wales. Short lines of stones, more like the Welsh ones, occur in County Kerry and West Cork. No Welsh alignment or stone row has been excavated, so nothing can be said in detail about this variation on the (assumed) Bronze Age practice of setting up large stones for religious or magical purposes.

Waun Oer stones

There might have been eight stones in this alignment originally, for the spacing is uneven, but only five remain. The first, westernmost, stone is squat; the second one has fallen, and the third is the most impressive but has been obscured by accumulating field clearance. Two stones may be missing between the third and fourth stones, and another may have been lost between the fourth and the fifth, easternmost, stone, which is of rather doubtful antiquity and lies fallen amongst a pile of loose stones cleared from the field.

53
Cairns on Allt Lwyd, Llanegryn

Round cairns, settlement and pillow mounds

2nd millennium BC and ?medieval and later

OS 124 SH 614076 U4

Take turning to Llanegryn, 4ml (6km) N of Tywyn on A493, then immediately fork L; persevere for 1.3ml (2km) up towards Cae'r Mynach. Park just before houses on L; take footpath to RHS. After 2nd gate, fork L and continue uphill; at final field gate bear R towards summit cairn (1ml, 1.6km, walk)

Aerial view of lower slopes of Allt Lwyd, showing pillow mounds

The objective of this walk is the two cairns on the summit of Allt Lwyd, but there are several interesting sites to be seen on the way up or down, and the view from the top is one of the most spectacular in Meirionnydd – a county of spectacular views!

Shortly above the left-hand fork there are several 'pillow mounds' on the right. These are artificial rabbit warrens, low rectangular mounds surrounded with a ditch and low bank. Before gamekeepers existed, birds of prey were very common and rabbits were relatively rare. As a useful food, rabbit farming was encouraged, especially on poor land. Specially designated rabbit warrens are a feature of the medieval landscape, and in the 17th and 18th centuries these special banks were often built to encourage them to burrow.

Just above these mounds can be seen the banks and lynchets of a field system (covered by the modern one) which belongs to a settlement set on a broad shelf in the hillside. At least one round building can be recognised, and other house platforms can be seen in the right light. One has a large white stone inside it.

Above this, on the right of the track, is a small cairn close to a boggy patch, and about 200m higher up is a flat, circular cairn, badly disturbed, on the left of the track. There had been another larger cairn just beyond the final gate, but it has been overlain by a square building, perhaps a house or inn connected with the track, which continues ahead to join the Ffordd Ddu over Cadair Idris. Bear right here and head for the summit, where the northern cairn is just visible.

The northern cairn is a simple mound of stone, 23m in diameter and over 1m high. It has been badly disturbed; a large capstone is exposed in the bottom of a central crater. This is the coverstone of a cist which was rifled a hundred years ago, when bones, charcoal and a flint flake were found. An early Ordnance Survey benchmark has been cut into it.

About 100m north of this cairn, on the flat hilltop, is an arrangement of three vertical stones, presumably the remains of a burial cist robbed of its covering cairn. It is difficult to suggest where the missing stones might have gone, since stone for wall-building is readily available nearby. There are no records of any finds.

The most interesting cairn is the southern one. To reach it, cross the wire fence with care. The cairn is really a group of monuments which partially overlap each other. The earliest is a large (20m diameter) ring cairn – a narrow stone bank without uprights, surrounding a stoneless, dished centre. On the south it is overlaid by a large damaged cairn with a lobe, or perhaps a separate cairn, attached to the north-east. A few metres to the south is a very small, low cairn and a strange rectangular arrangement of stones which are not deeply set. This group of monuments, on the very edge of the summit in an exceptionally commanding position, is unusual. Whereas burial cairns are often placed on such false crests to be visible from below, ring cairns are seldom, if ever, so sited, a position on a lower saddle being preferred. The superimposition of such monuments is also rare, especially since excavation evidence from elsewhere would suggest that the ring cairn should have remained in use for longer than the burial cairn.

54

Croes Faen, Tywyn

Standing stone

2nd millennium BC or ?medieval

OS 135 SH 597015 U1

Site is beside A493 0.7ml (1.1km) NE of Tywyn church, just inside field on R at road junction

This is a straight, narrow stone, 2.5m high, with faceted sides which appear worked, but are simply the product of geology. The top has been broken.

Despite the name Croes Faen ('Stone Cross'), it has no cross on it, and it presents in an extreme form the difficulty of dating such simple monuments. It may be a prehistoric marker – a Christian stone like the one now in the church (no. 113), which was found not far away – or even a simple rubbing stone set up for the convenience of cattle. Without excavation it is impossible to decide.

There is a tradition that it was used in some unexplained way to rid the district of a fiery dragon. It is also said to have been moved in 1840, but later returned to its original position.

55
Eglwys Gwyddelod, Pennal
Stone circle
2nd millennium BC
OS 135 SH 663002 U4

0.6ml (1km) W of Pennal (2.7ml, 4.5km, W of Machynlleth) on A493, fork R (signposted Happy Valley); 1.2ml (2km) along (just before sharp bend) take footpath on R beside small house (park carefully). 20 mins walk up clear but steep path. Site is on rock ledge just after 3rd gate, within triangle of paths

This is a beautiful monument in a very dramatic setting. It stands on a rocky shelf, a point where several tracks converge. Like so many monuments in such settings, it is designed for maximum impact from one direction – in this case, the south. The track continues westwards beyond it and runs along the top of the ridge, passing other cairns and coming down to the valley floor near a fine earthen barrow (visible from the road). These Bronze Age monuments suggest that this trackway, like many others, has its origin in that period.

The circle is relatively small, 8m in diameter, with no stone more than 1m high. It is similar to the lower circle at Moel Goedog (no. 44), but no stone bank or stone in-filling is visible. A single slab of quartz lies in the centre of the circle. It is very probably an original feature, since this perpetually white stone was often used to emphasise significant features of Bronze Age monuments. There has been no excavation, so one cannot tell what it covers.

The circle consists of five upright stones and two stumps just under the grass on the north. A boulder beside the north-eastern stone and perhaps the large leaning stone at the south-east (at first sight part of the circle, but a bit too close to its neighbour) may have fallen from the crag above.

The name Eglwys Gwyddelod ('Irishman's Church') is unusual: the Irish are usually credited with huts rather than churches in Welsh tradition!

Eglwys Gwyddelod stone circle

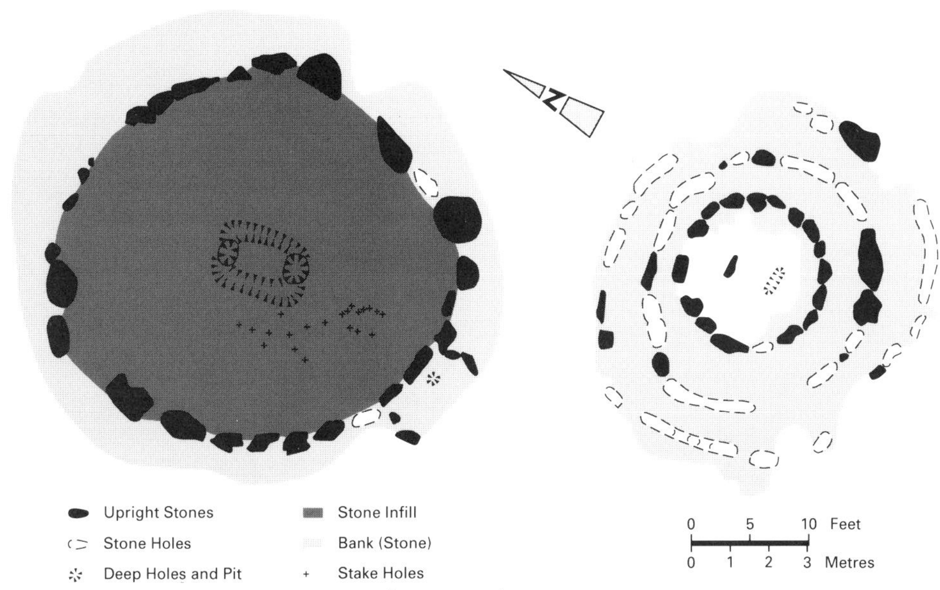

Plan of cairn circle and ring cairn on Cefn Caer Euni

56
Cefn Caer Euni Circles, Bala

Ceremonial/burial monuments

Late 3rd/early 2nd millennium BC

OS 125 SH 993410 U4

From Bala, take A494 NE for 4.4ml (7km) and turn L at Bethel on to narrow road and continue along contour for 2ml (3.6km) to complex junction at Tyn y Bwlch. Turn sharp L (signposted Cwm Main); continue for 0.75ml (1.25km) past No Through Road sign. Park where road bears R and is gated; walk up track ahead to nose of spur (c.0.6ml, 1km). Caer Euni (no. 76) is above on L. Alternatively, reach Tyn y Bwlch from A5 at Maerdy by taking narrow road opposite Goat Hotel

Lynch 1986

These monuments form a pair on either side of the track. Like several such pairs of ceremonial circles, they differ in design: the larger one is a kerb circle, and the smaller a ring cairn. One cannot say which was built first or whether they were strictly contemporary.

Excavation in 1971–2 revealed hearths and wattle fences: evidence of domestic settlement in this very exposed position at the end of the 3rd millennium BC, according to radiocarbon dating – before either monument was built.

The kerb circle consists of a kerb of rounded boulders, 11.5m across, enclosing a level platform of stone. On the south side, four stones project from the kerb to form a 'portal' or porch, within which was a charcoal-filled pit covered with stone. The centre of the monument had originally been stone-free, and two wooden posts had stood there at either end of a ditched rectangular platform. A body may have lain on this platform, but no bones survived in the acid soil. This structure was soon demolished, and the entire central area was filled with stones. One cannot say at what stage the pit in the 'portal' was dug, but charcoal in it provided a radiocarbon date of about 1400 BC.

The ring cairn is unusually small, but its design is complex. It consisted of three concentric rings of boulders surrounding an open centre, 3m across. It is now rather difficult to appreciate this plan because many of the larger boulders from the outer rings were removed in the last century, but the stone-holes remain recognisable. The pointed stone in the centre is an earthfast slab – a natural feature forming the focus of the monument. A slot had been dug parallel to it 1m to the south and filled with black earth and white quartz. Quartz had also been scattered on the top of the stone bank, filling the space between the boulder rings.

The features in both monuments are difficult to explain, but they belong to a well-established range of activities which link burial and symbolic rituals using charcoal (see nos 35 and 44).

A local tradition records that the larger ring was used as a cockpit in the 18th century, when cock-fighting was very popular in this region.

4
The Iron Age

The Iron Age has traditionally been seen as a period of invasion, bringing Celtic-speaking people to these islands and initiating an artistic but warlike society in which innumerable hilltop forts were established to protect the agricultural population against incessant inter-tribal attacks. This view, like so many, must now be questioned. The problem of language is not susceptible to archaeological solution, though there are linguistic reasons for thinking that some form of Celtic was spoken in Britain long before 600 BC. Radiocarbon dating and reassessment of some of the pottery and tools are showing that many hillforts were built in the late Bronze Age, when economic problems within Britain provide an adequate explanation for their construction. If the hillforts are removed from the record of foreign elements, there is little to suggest a serious influx of new people at this time, although it was admittedly a period of unrest in Europe, which could have spilled over into Britain. What does remain is a splendid series of aristocratic and military bronzes designed and decorated in an international style evolved in central Europe and named after a Swiss site, La Tène. The interpretation of these fine pieces – some certainly imported, others undoubtedly made to the new style in this country – is extremely difficult. They could be the equipment of an invading elite, they could be diplomatic gifts exchanged between relatively friendly chieftains, or part of the nexus of international trade which had spanned the Continent since the early Bronze Age.

As in previous centuries, the life of the common people in the Iron Age was centred on agriculture. The farmsteads are exceptionally well preserved in Gwynedd because the vast majority were built of stone, but the equipment of these farms is extremely meagre. Pottery was scarcely used, and both the style of building and most of the stone tools, querns, mortars, pestles, etc., are of types which changed very little over the centuries, so precise dating is difficult. Radiocarbon dating of recently excavated sites has shown a remarkable continuity, with farmsteads being occupied and used in one way or another through from Iron Age to post-Roman times. It would not be surprising to learn that some of the lowland sites were founded in the late Bronze Age, for the house types remain essentially the same and the boundaries of the late Bronze Age trade areas are remarkably similar to pre-Roman tribal areas.

Within this general pattern of settlement, however, some development in the

Artist's impression of the recently excavated stone hut and enclosures at Tŷ Mawr, Holyhead (no. 77)

styles of farms can be recognised. For example, 'concentric circle farmsteads', like Maes y Caerau (no. 46) – a single, large round house placed centrally in a circular yard – belong to the Iron Age but do not seem to continue into the Roman period. Huts within irregular fields, such as those near Trawsfynydd (no. 87), were occupied as iron-making sites in the 1st and 2nd centuries BC, although their surface appearance would suggest a Bronze Age date. Formally enclosed sites – like Din Lligwy or Caer Lêb (nos 79 and 81) – surrounded by either a wall or a ditch and bank, which were thought to belong exclusively to the Romano-British period, may have been founded earlier and continued later. The straggle of round houses along the lower slope of Holyhead mountain (see no. 77) includes farms of Iron Age, Roman and post-Roman date. Excavations on Anglesey and the mainland have shown that, though the fortunes of these farms fluctuated, the 2nd century BC, when the weather improved somewhat, was a period of prosperity when many farms were founded or expanded. Several were abandoned at the time of the Roman invasion, but most were reoccupied later.

The larger establishments – the impressive hillforts with their great stone ramparts and imposing gateways – have been the subject of a similar reassessment, but the lack of recent excavation makes it difficult to be precise about their dates of construction and occupation. For obvious political reasons they are unlikely to have been occupied under Roman rule, but finds of late Roman material suggest that many were reoccupied at a time when Roman power was waning and the native population had to defend itself from Irish raiders.

The exact role of hillforts in society has been a matter of dispute, and several of the Gwynedd examples provide fuel for these controversies. At Pen y Gaer, Llanbedr y Cennin (no. 63), a definitely military, defensive purpose may be argued, since the entrance is unusually well defended; at Tre'r Ceiri (no. 67), on a violently exposed summit of the Rivals, problems of permanent occupation and food resources are raised by the proliferation of stone huts; at Caer y Tŵr on Holyhead mountain (no. 57), in contrast, there appear to be no huts inside the rampart, which may therefore have been designed as a temporary refuge; at Dinas Dinorwic, near Bangor (no. 64) it is possible to see that the defences have been entirely remodelled at some stage.

Very few burials of Iron Age date are known, nor are there any religious monuments of that period in Gwynedd. But Llyn Cerrig Bach, near Valley in Anglesey (no. 58), was one of the sacred lakes of the Celts. Caesar records that it was customary for the European Celts to offer the loot of battle to their gods by casting them into lakes or leaving them in sacred groves. Llyn Cerrig Bach was undoubtedly such a lake, for a great deal of war gear has been found in it – whether the product of local skirmishes or brought from further afield it is difficult to say. If the latter, it raises the question of whether Anglesey might have been a special centre of the Druidic religion, as the presence of Druids at the great battle against the Romans in AD 60 might suggest.

At the time of the Roman invasion, Anglesey was certainly a place of some political importance, if only because of the number of refugees fleeing before the Roman advance through the Belgic kingdoms of south-east England. These refugees, mentioned by the Roman historian Tacitus, can be recognised in the archaeological record by several fine pieces of metalwork – some of them the final offerings to be thrown into Llyn Cerrig Bach.

Aerial view of Caer y Tŵr hillfort from the north-east

57

Caer y Tŵr, Holyhead Mountain

Later prehistoric hillfort and Roman signal station

Later 1st millennium BC and 3rd/4th century AD

OS 114   SH 218830   U4

In Holyhead, follow Ferry Terminal signs, then turn L to Outer Harbour and follow signs to South Stack (3ml, 4.75km). From café car park follow clear but rough track to summit, about 0.9ml (1.4km) but a steep walk. Several tracks circle hill, all come into fort through original entrance and focus on trig. point. Do not leave paths; vegetation conceals very rough surface. Circuit takes c.*1 1/2–2hrs*

Crew 1981

The rocky summit of Holyhead mountain scarcely needs any defence, but on the north and east sides it has a stone rampart of considerable strength. The area enclosed is about 7ha, but no obvious house sites can be recognised within it.

The single drystone rampart survives to a height of 3m in places, with an outer and inner face of massive masonry and a rubble core. It is placed at the top of the steepest slope, taking in several natural crags as bastions to increase visibility. The entrance is at the north-east corner, where a natural gully provides a sloping access overlooked by the incurving ends of the rampart, well preserved at this point. This eastern route may be less steep, but it is not easy: any attacker would have had difficulty rushing the gates over this rocky terrain.

On the north side, a section of rampart seems to have been pushed uphill into the interior, perhaps a deliberate slighting. Such destruction may have occurred during the Roman period, when the authorities, increasingly worried by Irish attacks on the weakened Empire, built a watch-tower on the summit.

The base of this tower (close to the trig. point on the western summit which covers a cairn of assumed Bronze Age date) has recently been excavated and conserved. It was a well-built stone structure, 5.5m square and capable of standing to quite a height. From here look-outs could have seen boats approaching from the west, passed the message down to the naval base in Holyhead itself (no. 89) and – by a series of signal stations which arguably occupied the same spots as the later Mersey Docks and Harbour Board semaphore stations – sent the news on to the legionary base at Chester. Coins found in the building suggest that it was used during the 4th century AD.

58
Llyn Cerrig Bach

Sacred lake

200 BC–AD 60

OS 114   SH 306765   U1

From Caergeiliog, take A5 E for 1ml (1.6km) and turn R (S); cross railway bridge and turn immediately R on to perimeter road around RAF Valley airfield. Site (500m on R) is marked by a large boulder with information plaque. Park and walk a few steps to lakeside

Fox 1946

This is the most important British example of a phenomenon well known on the Continent and described by Caesar – the sacred lake in which the spoils of war were thrown by the Celts as offerings to their gods.

We can never know why this small lake, one among many lakes in this vicinity, should have been chosen. Perhaps some notable event occurred here which gave it an aura of power and fuelled a legend which attracted offerings from many parts of the country.

The remarkable finds – weapons and chariot fittings of iron and bronze – were discovered during the Second World War, when peat was taken from the silted lake to consolidate a new runway. As the material was being spread over the sand, swords, spears, chains and iron tyres from chariot wheels became caught in the teeth of the harrow.

The offerings were largely military, as Caesar describes. Eleven swords and eight spearheads are represented, as well as parts of a beautiful parade shield. Equipment from several chariots is present, both the harness and parts of the structure. Up to 22 chariots can be recognised from the wheels discovered, but this might indicate the offering of wheels alone (which are known to have been sacred to one of the Celtic gods)

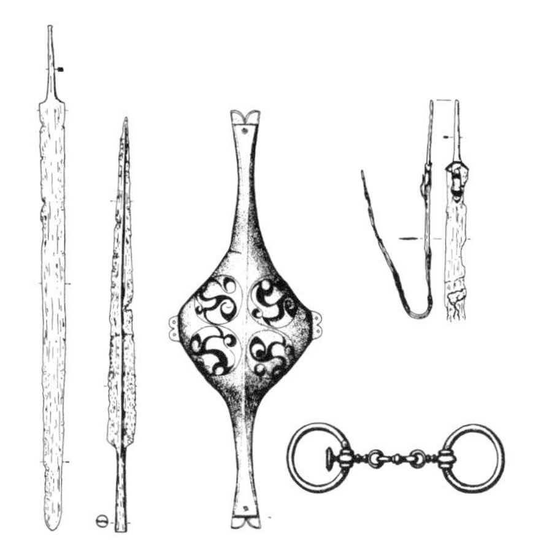

Some of the fine metalwork found in Llyn Cerrig Bach

rather than complete vehicles. The source of all these goods is difficult to pinpoint, but there is reason to think that many pieces may have originated a long way from Anglesey, suggesting a shrine of more than local importance.

The dates of the finds are also of interest. Some of the swords are of types current in the 2nd century BC, others are of later designs, but nothing later than AD 60 can be identified. This suggests that the shrine developed its importance in the latter half of the Iron Age, and that the Roman invasion of Anglesey by Suetonius Paulinus in AD 60 put a stop to the flow of offerings. It is tempting to link this with the defeat of the Druids in the battle at the Menai Straits and the exceptional ferocity of the Romans' attack on the island's sacred sites after their victory.

59
Dinas Gynfor, Cemaes Bay

Coastal promontory fort

1st millennium BC

OS 114 SH 391950 U4 (part NT)

From Amlwch, take A5025 W for 4ml (6.4km) and turn R (N) towards Llanbadrig Church (no. 98) but, ignoring last sign to church, continue ahead for 1ml (1.6km); park carefully on verge just before or after footpath sign. Follow path down to hillfort (c.500m). Alternatively, follow the coastal footpath E from Llanbadrig or W from Porth Wen. All paths meet at causeway; from there take sloping path to R; walk round fort in anti-clockwise direction, returning through original entrance. Bracken is high in

Dinas Gynfor hillfort

summer. Go in winter to see the ramparts, and in summer for the birds, butterflies and scenery

This is a rocky promontory linked to the mainland by a broad, marshy isthmus. The cliffs are steep on all sides, but there is a good harbour at the north-west, used in the 19th century for the export of 'china stone', which was quarried within the hillfort. The ruins on the shore relate to this industry.

The defences are best seen from the approach path – a wide rampart along the crest of the slope and an ancillary bank which protects a path running diagonally from the harbour up to the entrance near the south-east corner of the promontory. The rampart appears to be of earth, but at the south-east end a wall-face is exposed, and minor excavation has shown that it was built of stone dug from an irregular quarry ditch – a rare feature on Welsh hillforts.

Much of the interior is too steep and rocky for building, but there is some flatter ground behind the rampart and on the central saddle. Unfortunately, it is just these areas which have been quarried. The derelict tower on the north end commemorates Edward VII's coronation (1901).

60
Parciau Hillfort, Moelfre

Inland promontory fort

1st millennium BC–1st millennium AD

OS 114 SH 494846 R2

From A5025/A5108 roundabout above Moelfre, take Amlwch road for 0.4ml (0.7km) and turn L at Llanallgo; continue for 200m and enter large iron gate on R to Parciau Home Farm (park carefully). Ask at farm for permission to enter hillfort, which is on private land on promontory to R

This is a flat-topped limestone promontory cut off by three low ramparts. It is chiefly notable for the number of stone hut foundations which can be seen in the interior in high summer, when sun parches the grass over their low walls.

The inner rampart and ditch are substantial; the other two ramparts are much slighter, and are scarcely noticeable under the lines of trees which grow on them. The entrance, on the east, is central, protected by in-turned walls. Only the inner rampart extends around the steep south-east side.

Parciau hillfort

Minor excavations in the 19th century produced Roman pottery dating from the late 3rd–early 4th centuries AD. The defences are likely to be much earlier, but the finds suggest that the fort was reoccupied towards the end of the Roman period, when law and order was beginning to break down. It is a pattern repeated at several sites.

61
Castell Caer Lleion, Conwy
Later prehistoric hillfort
1st millennium BC/AD

OS 115 SH 760778 U4

Several public footpaths run along ridge. Access at E and from Mountain Road off Cadnant Park, Conwy; from 2 paths off Sychnant road (reached from Uppergate Street out of town), and from Sychnant Pass car park at W end. Parking at Sychnant is easy; elsewhere, difficult. From Sychnant follow main path until Conwy Castle is in sight, then turn uphill. Most routes involve a 30-minute walk to reach fort – worth it for the view alone

Hogg 1956, 1975, pp 180–2

On the summit of Conwy mountain is a large stone-walled fort containing about 50 stone huts and levelled house platforms. At the west end is a smaller citadel or keep. Such strongly defended points can be found at other north Welsh hillforts (for example, Garn Boduan, no. 69), and their date relative to the main fortifications has been much debated.

The path along the spine of the mountain comes in at the eastern tip; diverge from it to the lower path on the south side, passing below the fort and turning up to enter by the gate just east of the citadel.

The main enclosure is quite straightforward. On the north side the hill is steep and needs no artificial defence. On the south the huts, quite densely packed, are enclosed within a single thick stone wall. The entrance is a simple gap towards the south-west end; excavation suggested it had been spanned by a wooden bridge continuing the rampart-walk over the gate.

Go to the east end along the spinal path and return via the lower northern shelf, which contains several hut sites.

The complications begin just west of the gate through which you entered, where the citadel was constructed on the rocky summit of the ridge. The general line of the rampart

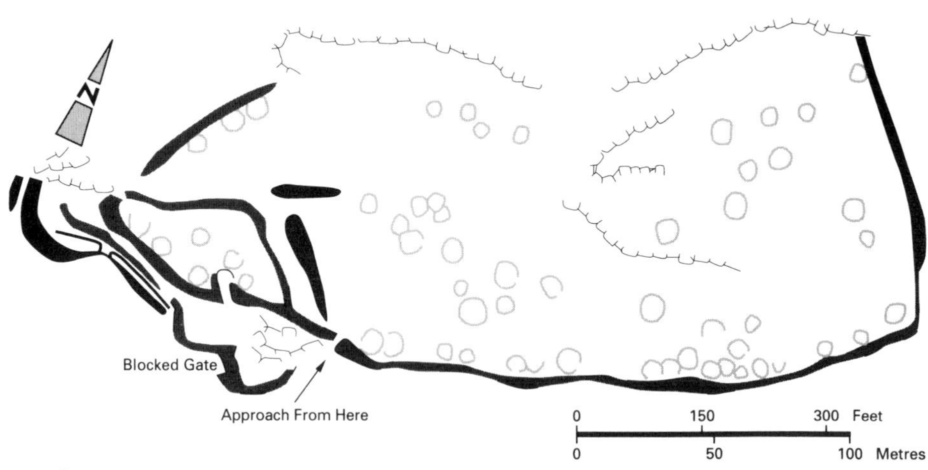

Castell Caer Lleion

would suggest that the original scheme had been a simple line of defence running to the west point of the hill and back to the steep crags on the north. The citadel was then formed by narrowing the area and cutting it off from the main fort by a wall which runs along the north scarp and crosses south to the main gate, taking advantage of a natural line of rock and sweeping over the top of the original rampart (the relationship is easy to see from above). The defence of the citadel was strengthened by an earthen rampart and ditch running across the neck of the hill just outside the east wall. This late bank covered debris from the occupation of the main fort. It is so unlike the stone rampart that it may be a great deal later, perhaps even a medieval fortification.

There is no entrance to the citadel from the main fort; it is entered independently from a small annexe on the south side. This has also been modified and changed, for its wide entrance facing south-west has clearly been blocked, and it is unclear how access was subsequently gained. The entrance from this annexe to the citadel is through a simple gap in what would have been the original rampart. The presence of a demolished hut beneath this gateway confuses the picture: it has been suggested that this whole south-western rampart is a late insertion at a time when the annexe was modified, but problems of access make this an unlikely sequence. The walls of this gateway and the rampart have recently been consolidated, but please take care not to dislodge stones.

Excavations in 1951 were limited: no datable remains were found, only slingstones, querns and stone pestles and mortars. This suggests that, unlike many hillforts in the region, this site was not reoccupied in the late Roman period. There is, however, a traditional association with the 6th-century king, Maelgwyn. Radiocarbon dating, had it been available in 1951, might have resolved the chronological problems, for it is tempting to interpret the citadel, and certainly the earthen rampart, as a post-Roman reorganisation of the site.

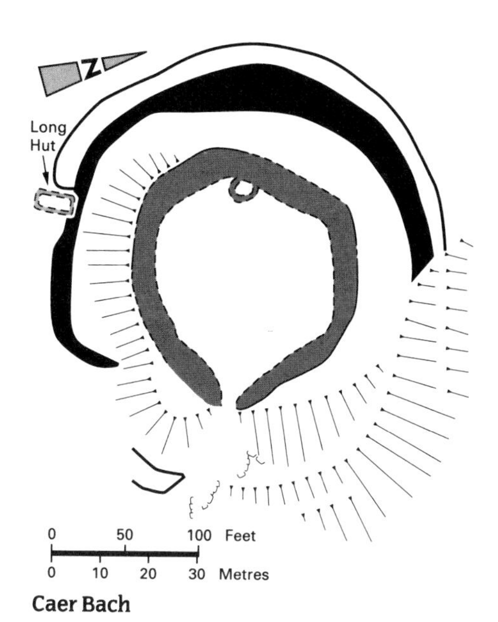

Caer Bach

62
Caer Bach, Rowen

Later prehistoric hillfort

1st millennium BC

OS 115 SH 744730 U4

From Maen Penddu (see no. 36), follow paths over shoulder of hill and down other side for 0.5ml (0.8km); the alternative path up from Llangelynin Old Church (see no. 142) leads 0.6ml (1km) over shoulder lower down to just below fort. Continue c. *1ml (1.6km) SW from fort along path skirting wall to visit settlements above Maen y Bardd and Roman road (nos 82 and 91; see map with no. 37)*

Set on a rocky spur projecting from Tal y Fan, this small hillfort commands a superb view over the valley and has several points of structural interest which make it worth the climb.

The most conspicuous feature is a deep ditch and stone-faced earth bank – unusual in Wales, where forts normally have a single, broad stone wall. It is probable that this was the original defence here too, for the base of such a stone wall survives. Its denudation suggests that it may have become redundant when the ditch and bank were constructed.

The damaged entrance through both enclosures is on the east side. The well preserved outer face of the rampart wall and a round hut attached to the inner face can be seen on the west.

A long hut, perhaps a *hafod*, has been built across the ditch on the south side.

63
Pen y Gaer, Llanbedr y Cennin

Later prehistoric hillfort
1st millennium BC
OS 115 SH 750693 U2

From Llanbedr y Cennin village (off B5106 5ml, 8km, S of Conwy) turn L at the Old Bull Inn, then bear R up steep hill for 0.6ml (1km); 200m after sharp bend take narrow road on L and persevere to top (small car park). Path back to hillfort on projecting spur is through gate opposite and over two large stiles. Fort is divided by a fence – do not cross it. All features of interest lie on accessible west side

This is a particularly interesting hillfort in a dramatic and imposing position, and the walk to it is not steep. The defences are unusual and complex, house sites can be easily recognised in the interior, and there are later foundations built over the ruined rampart on the north-west side.

The last stile brings you out just below the entrance where the defensive feature for which this site is best known, the *chevaux de frise*, can be easily found. A *chevaux de frise* is a sort of raised 'minefield', an area densely

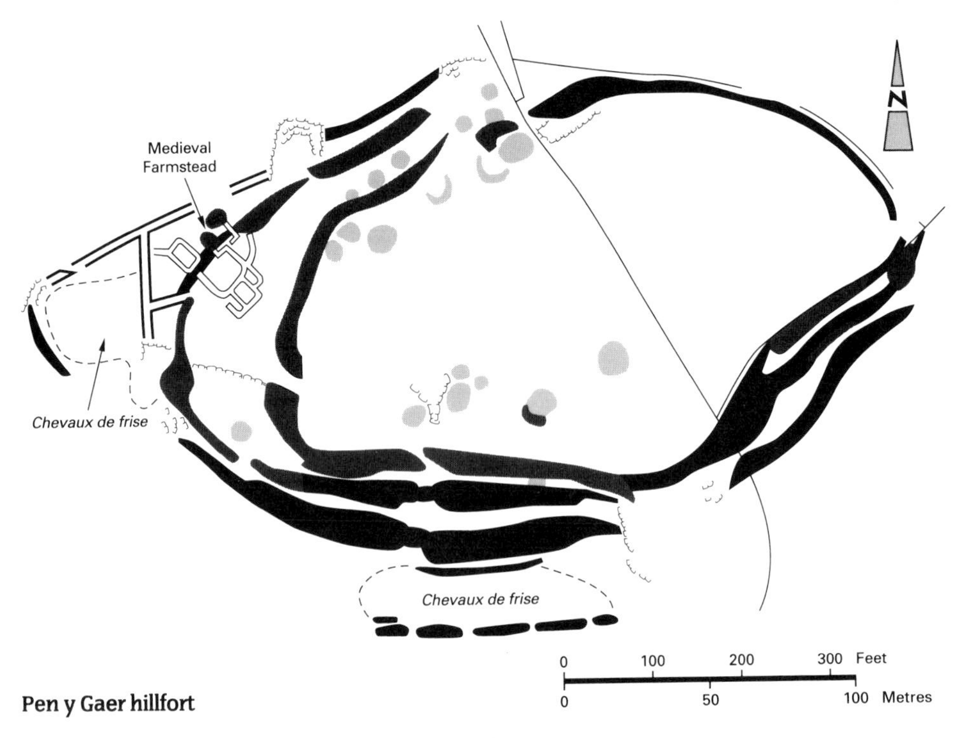

Pen y Gaer hillfort

seeded with small stones designed to break up an attack by tripping unwary runners. A second patch of these stones lies outside the ramparts on the south side, where a modern track has cut through the defences. This system of defence is rare in Britain, but the discovery of pointed sticks used in the same way at Kames in Scotland indicates that excavation at other sites might produce more examples of this defensive stratagem.

The west and south sides of the hill are surrounded by up to three ramparts. The inner one is entirely of stone and goes right round the hill; the middle one is stone on the west, but becomes an earthen bank on the south side, where there is also an outer bank and ditch.

The entrance through the middle rampart on the west is not very clear, but the gateway through the inner one is easy to find, and the massive drystone revetments of the passageway are impressive.

The foundations of 12 huts can be seen in the interior. The group on the south side, tucked in under the rocks, is the easiest to find – circular platforms levelled into the hillside. Wooden houses would have been built on them. Similar platforms occur on the north side.

Minor excavations at the beginning of the 20th century found nothing to indicate the date of these houses or the construction of the fort, but the complexity of the defences would suggest a long history, during which the ramparts and interior arrangements may have been remodelled more than once.

The buildings overlying the middle rampart on the north-west side may be an elaborate sheepfold, or perhaps a later medieval farmstead.

Dinas Dinorwic. The entrance through the earth ramparts is in the trees on the right

64

Dinas Dinorwic, Llandeiniolen

Late prehistoric hillfort

1st millennium BC

OS 115 SH 550653 R3

From A5/A55 intersection S of Bangor, take A5 S towards Betws y Coed, then immediately R (B4366) towards Caernarfon. At next roundabout take B4547 Llanberis road, then 1st R (minor crossroads) for 0.9ml (1.5km) to point on top of rise where road is wide enough to leave a car. Turning to Pen Dinas Farm is 50m on R. Ask at farm for permission to visit site, which is on private land. Gorse can be a problem here

This is a hillfort which was radically remodelled, converting it from a simple stone-walled enclosure to a multivallate fort with massive banks and ditches.

After seeking permission, enter the fort by returning to the front of the farmhouse and climbing up the two steep banks towards the modern wall which overlies the ancient stone rampart (best seen from the inside). The simple entrance through this stone rampart is a few metres beyond the gap in the wall and should be viewed from the inside, where the original thickness (3.3m) of the rampart can be appreciated. Notice how the later, earthen rampart takes no account of this gate.

There was another, smaller, entrance to the stone fort, on the west side. This entrance was maintained when the fort was remodelled, for the entrance through the three earth ramparts runs diagonally from it. These massive banks and deep ditches (12m thick and some 9m in total height) are best seen on the west and south. They represent a rare Welsh example of 'glacis construction', a continuous slope from bottom of ditch to top of rampart, best exemplified at Maiden Castle hillfort in Dorset. Such long, often loose-surfaced slopes were judged particularly difficult to climb.

On the north-west side there was a small annexe to the fort, probably part of the later remodelling. It is now largely occupied by the farmyard and its paddock.

A large flat-topped rock in the second earth rampart about 30m south of the entrance in the wood has been made into a 'stone gun'. Holes for blasting-powder were linked by curving runnels along which the fuse was laid. When this was lit the explosive produced a series of bangs, the timing controlled by the length of fuse between the holes. They were reportedly used in the 19th century to celebrate birthdays or public holidays.

65
Caer Engan, Penygroes

Later prehistoric or post-Roman hillfort

1st millennium BC/AD

OS 115 SH 478527 U2/3

From Penygroes, 5.3ml (8.5km) S of Caernarfon on A487, take B4418 towards Rhyd Ddu for 0.4ml (0.7km); park on L near cottage with elaborate slate roof. Walk E to footpath on R (or cross stile and skirt field-wall), cross river by footbridge; take RH well-built quarrymen's path into monument. Bracken may obscure the monument in summer

This small fort occupies a raised boss of rock right in the centre of the Llyfnwy valley, and commands one of the most famous and dramatic views in the whole of north Wales. Standing in this fort, one looks straight into the grandeur of the Snowdon horseshoe, the archetypal, inviolate mountain view, contrasting with the classic quarrying landscape of the nearer slopes – the terraced houses and scattered farms of Tal y Sarn. It is a view which epitomises much of the historical geography of north Wales.

Against this backdrop the fort itself must be judged a disappointment, but it is typical of a number of small defensive enclosures in this neighbourhood, and consequently worth a visit.

The shape and size of the enclosure are dictated by geology; the rock forms a vertical outcrop, and provides adequate defence on the north and south sides. On the east and west it is possible to recognise an inner earthen rampart topped by the remains of a boulder wall. This defence follows the top of the rock, and the remains of an outer bank can be seen at variable distances outside it. On the east this is in effect a shelf; a modern wall may conceal a third rampart on this gentle slope. The entrance was probably on the south-western side, near the modern farm. There are no signs of buildings in the interior, but there is much loose stone, which may conceal walls.

66
Dinas Dinlle, Llandwrog

Later prehistoric hillfort

1st millennium BC/AD

OS 115, 123 SH 437565 U3

Just S of Glynllifon Park on A499 (Caernarfon–Pwllheli) turn R (signposted Dinlle) and travel 1.4ml (2.2km) NW. Use car park at S end of beach; hillfort is immediately above. Beware of crumbling cliff edges

The classic profile of this hillfort can be seen in the distance from many directions. It has been built on an isolated hill of glacial drift – a remarkable geomorphological feature, of considerable interest in its own right.

Both the hill and the hillfort are being eroded by the sea, which has removed all the

Aerial view of Dinas Dinlle hillfort

western side of the defences and exposed a section through the ramparts which is visible at the southern end. This kind of erosion presents a serious conservation dilemma. A wall would be ugly and futile, but total excavation would be very expensive.

Originally, the fort was surrounded by two earthen ramparts with a deep ditch between. There was only one entrance, a simple, broad gap on the south-east. Erosion has revealed that the ramparts are made from drift material, partly sculpted from the hillside and partly built of material dug from the ditch. The inner rampart was faced by a wall of large boulders from the beach. Where the defences survive they are of impressive size, with an overall height of 6m.

The interior of the fort (not accessible to the public) contained circular buildings and other structures towards the eastern side. There has been no excavation, but casual digging in the past has produced sherds of Roman pottery, suggesting occupation or reoccupation in the 2nd and 3rd centuries AD. The large mound in the north-east corner may be a Bronze Age barrow.

There are steps over the rampart on the north side, giving access to the west side of the fort, but great care should be taken because of the crumbling edge and the wind.

67

Tre'r Ceiri, Llanaelhaearn

Later prehistoric hillfort with Roman-period use

1st millennium BC/AD

OS 123 SH 373446 U4

At Llanaelhaearn, 6ml (9.6km) N of Pwllheli on A499, take B4417 towards Nefyn; 0.9ml (1.5km) from junction take footpath on RHS up hill. Sign is not very prominent and parking may be difficult, but verge can take 1 or 2 cars. Path up hill is clear with two stiles (30 mins walk). Hillside and interior of fort are covered with loose scree; take care not to dislodge stones. Bracken can be a problem in summer

Hogg 1960, pp 10–17

Tre'r Ceiri ('Town of the Giants') is the most spectacular hillfort in north Wales, crowning one of the sharp peaks of the Rivals and commanding breathtaking views in all directions. The inner rampart wall stands over 3m high around almost the entire circuit, and the interior is filled with some 150 round stone huts, many with walls still over 1m high.

The fort is set on the long, narrow summit of the hill and encloses about 2.5ha. The highest point is at the east end, where there is a ruined cairn, probably Bronze Age, pre-dating the defences.

The defences are impressive but simple: a massive stone wall encircles the summit, with the wall-walk and ramps surviving on the north. Additional defensive lines guard the gentle northern slope and the steep western entry. Both can be shown to be late, the northern wall post-dates the path to the freshwater spring, and the western line overlies the unexplained 'enclosures'. These 'enclosures' on the west and north slopes are puzzling since the situation does not seem ideal for fields or garden plots.

The main entrance, dominated by high bastions, is at the lower, west end; another more convenient entry and three posterns can be found on the north. Both main entrances have been conserved; tumbled masonry has been rebuilt under the supervision of Gwynedd Archaeological Trust (1990–4). Replaced stonework is marked with drill-holes. The postern near the summit still retains its (repaired) lintel.

The huts are closely packed together into four or five bands across the width of the fort. They vary in size and shape, and in some cases a sequence of building can be recognised. Some of the round ones are 8m across, others less than 3m. Several of the larger ones have been subdivided, and others seem to have been built as D-shaped structures. A chronological division has been suggested – the earlier phase having fewer, larger houses, the later one a greater number of smaller dwellings, including those created by the subdivision of earlier buildings. Quite large, rectangular structures were built against the rampart, especially along the north side. The houses were built into the scree, so their floors tend to be lower than the level outside. In use, the floors must have been packed or boarded.

Aerial view of Tre'r Ceiri from the east

Excavations at the beginning of the 20th century and in 1956 revealed that the site had certainly been occupied during the Roman period, but this was very probably the reoccupation of an older site.

The modern path leads to the ridge beneath the south-west entrance, and from there climbs up through the walled enclosures and between the ends of the additional rampart to the imposing gate.

Inside the fort, take the left-hand path towards the north gate. Go out to view the lower gate where it blocks the original track. Return and continue along the north side. About 50m from the gate, one of the ramps to the wall-walk is reasonably well preserved, but the walk is clearer at the east end, just beyond the postern.

Go up to the cairn, which is a good vantage point for looking down on the huts. Take the path which winds down through them. The most interesting group is at the west end, where a sequence of building can be demonstrated. A very large, round hut was divided into three, and D-shaped and rectangular houses were built against its outer walls. The exterior enclosures can be seen well from the top of the rampart on the south side. Return to the main gate.

68
Porth Dinllaen, Nefyn

Coastal promontory fort

1st millennium BC

OS 123 SH 275416 U3/4

In Morfa Nefyn, 1.2ml (2km) W of Nefyn, follow signpost to Porth Dinllaen; park in official car park (charge). Walk through golf course (15 mins) to defences (cut by road to Tŷ Coch Inn and beach). Walk to tip of promontory takes c.15 mins from here

There are surprisingly few coastal promontory forts in Gwynedd, but this, though damaged, is a good example, and one that is very strategically placed, for it

Porth Dinllaen. The rampart is above the houses in the middle distance

overlooks the only good natural harbour between Bardsey Island and Caernarfon. As such it was a candidate for development as the main port for Ireland. The less energetic can appreciate its strategic position from the main road at SH 320418. Rectangular foundations at the tip of the headland (below 15th tee) belong to an early 19th-century barracks for workmen building the projected harbour installations.

The prehistoric remains consist of two lines of defence cutting across the isthmus just north and west of the Tŷ Coch Inn where the road goes down to the harbour. There is no sign of huts within the 7ha enclosure.

The road has badly damaged the southern defensive line, which originally consisted of a high rampart with a ditch and counterscarp bank outside it. The road now occupies the ditch; a section of the counterscarp bank can be seen on the right where the road turns around it and the badly eroded rampart (built from sand and gravel above a darker, cultivated soil) is exposed above the retaining wall of the road.

The inner rampart – a large bank 12m wide and 4.5m high, without a ditch – survives rather better, but has been cut by the concrete RNLI access road as it curves to the right about 60m further north.

A bank at the southern end of the promontory looks like an outer line of defence, but it is modern.

69
Garn Boduan, Nefyn

Later prehistoric hillfort

1st millennium BC/AD

OS 123 SH 310393 U4

Access from B4354, 0.2ml (300m) E of junction with A497, Forestry Commission gateway on L (room to park, but do not block access), stile and good track. At 2nd hairpin bend take upper path into wood and follow round to top of plantation. Scramble up steep track to east end of summit (c.30 mins altogether). Beware of treacherous terrain

Hogg 1960, pp 1–10; Hogg 1975, pp 214–16

Garn Boduan is one of the line of volcanic hills forming the backbone of the Lleyn peninsula, and its rocky summit is crowned by a stone-walled fort filled, like its more famous neighbour, Tre'r Ceiri (no. 67), with well preserved stone houses. In addition, Garn Boduan has, at the east end, a small fort or citadel which may belong to a later period of occupation, perhaps even that suggested by the name Boduan ('Residence of Buan' – a quasi-legendary figure of the 7th century AD).

The best strategy for a visit is to go up to the citadel, then to the north-east corner to see the best-preserved stretch of the main rampart and wander through the huts towards the south-east end of the spur (where some of the individual huts contain features of interest), then leave by the southern entrance whence a narrow track leads back to the Forestry Commission path.

Excavations in the strongly defended citadel provided evidence of occupation in the Iron Age and the later Roman period, but the style of rampart suggests that the defences were not of the same date as the main fort, and were probably later. There was a fine gateway on the west side but it was eventually blocked by a carefully inserted wall. This sequence and the well-preserved wall-faces can still be easily recognised,

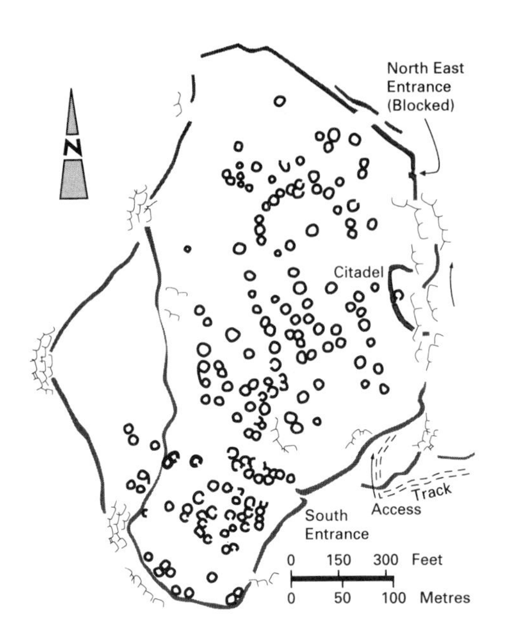

Garn Boduan

especially from the outside, though, sadly, much other evidence here has been wrecked by the recent construction of two round shelters. These have removed the original steps in the rampart wall and other details of the interior, including the southern gate.

In the north-eastern corner of the main fort there was an entrance (blocked in antiquity). The duplication of the main rampart is clearest here. This duplication of defences is the basis for the belief that the main fort was remodelled at some stage. The original stone rampart is the lower one, less massive and well-built than the upper, whose inner face is well preserved in this stretch. The remodelling made little difference to the plan of the fort, except on the west side where the later rampart drops down the slope to enclose a prominent boss of rock and provide a wider field of view. Only a few huts were built in this steeply sloping annexe.

The hillfort covers about 10ha and contained at least 170 houses, though it is unlikely that they were all occupied at one time. The interior is divided into a series of natural shelves descending from east to south-west; all were occupied. The huts are visible as collapsed rings of stone about 5–6m in diameter, except on the upper shelf where they are grass-grown. Walk towards the prominent boss of rock on the south side. Just west of it are two rebuilt huts with higher walls; 90m west of the smaller one are two superimposed huts. The lower one was built at the same time as the earlier rampart against which it stands. Some 20m to the east is a hut with an unusual spiral wall which may well have been a blacksmith's workshop, like the one revealed by excavation at Bryn y Castell (no. 72). Nearby are two freshwater springs. Unlike so many hillforts, notably Tre'r Ceiri (no. 67), Garn Boduan was well supplied with water throughout the year.

The southern entrance to the fort lies in a natural gully almost directly east of these huts. It is not a complex structure, but passes diagonally through the rampart in such a way that defenders could trap an attacking force. A fort on a steep, isolated hill like Garn Boduan is so well protected by nature that the man-made defences do not need to be very sophisticated.

70

Castell Odo, Aberdaron

Later prehistoric hillfort

?Late 2nd millennium BC–1st millennium AD

OS 123 SH 187284 R4

On B4413 1.6ml (2.5km) N from Aberdaron, park car on R and go through gate on L beside isolated stone byre; walk to top of hill (10 mins). Fort is on private land. Seek permission to visit from farmer by phoning 0175 886212 or going down to Bodwrdda (through wide white gates on R, 250m S of access point). No dogs allowed

Alcock 1960

Even though the defences on this low hill are badly eroded, the site is worth a visit. The hill itself, though not high, has a commanding position; the two ramparts encircling it have a particularly long and well-documented history, and huts in the interior can be easily recognised.

The outer rampart, set below the summit of the hill, has the longer history. Excavation in 1958–9 revealed that the first defence of the hill was a wooden palisade with a very small ditch outside it. This was burnt down before the circuit was completed. It was later replaced with a broader earthen bank. When this decayed it was covered by a stone revetted bank, the remains of which are still visible today. The inner rampart is simpler, a stony bank revetted with boulders, perhaps contemporary with the final stage of the outer rampart.

The first settlement on the hilltop, however, may have been totally undefended, for postholes of round houses were found beneath the banks. Pottery from this occupation layer (in Bangor Museum) is now recognised as late Bronze Age, and palisades like the one subsequently built on Castell Odo are also of this date. This hilltop, therefore, was one of the earliest defended sites in Lleyn, but after an attack – or perhaps an accident – which burnt the incomplete palisade, it was abandoned.

The second settlement may have been of stone houses. It was enclosed within a low earthen bank, but the precise date is not known. At a later stage the hill was more strongly defended. The inner rampart was built and the outer bank was revetted in stone, but no deep ditches were dug. The entrance on the north-east side was a simple gap through both ramparts.

It is not clear how many stone houses stood within the double ramparts. At least eight can be seen in the interior today, but the one just inside the gate on the left was built over the remains of the rampart, which seems to have been deliberately dismantled. It has been suggested that this destruction of the defences was ordered by the Romans in AD 78, but that the inhabitants were later allowed to return. It is very seldom possible to prove this type of historical hypothesis by

Aerial view of Castell Odo from the north-west

excavation, but the scenario is by no means impossible.

The rectangular mound surrounded by a shallow ditch which lies to the south of the trig. point is a post-medieval 'pillow mound' – an artificial rabbit warren (see no. 53).

71

Creigiau Gwineu, Rhiw

Later prehistoric or post-Roman hillfort

1st millennium BC/AD

OS 123 SH 228274 U4/NT

At crossroads in Rhiw village (3.5ml, 5.6km, E of Aberdaron) turn R (S); park with discretion on LHS just beyond footpath sign. Walk up path, turn R over stone stile; turn L uphill; cross stile to LHS of wall; continue to ladder stile which is just outside SW end of fort (10 mins). Turn L over crags and down behind blocked entrance. Bracken fills interior in summer but main walls remain visible

This fort is in a dramatic position overlooking the sea and making optimum use of the natural defences of the rocks and crags on which it stands.

The fort occupies a craggy ridge which, on the west, forms a high cliff, except where a wide gully gives access to the interior. The original entrance was probably here, but all trace of it has been lost in rock falls or masked by modern walling. The east side has a gentler slope, and is protected by a single, broad stone wall linking the crags which form natural bastions at intervals along it. Two narrow gaps in this wall are not necessarily original. The interior is divided into two unequal parts by a wall incorporating the central spine of rock. There have been no excavations or casual finds to indicate the period of occupation. Such simple fortifications might be early, even Neolithic, for defended sites of that date have been identified in Cornwall. However, a post-Roman alternative is more likely.

72

Bryn y Castell, Ffestiniog

Later prehistoric hillfort

c.*300 BC–AD 250*

OS 124 SH 728429 U4

From Ffestiniog, take B4391 towards Bala (L immediately after railway bridge); after 1.2ml (1.9km) turn L at minor crossroads into gated lane; leave car beyond waterworks at junction of tracks. Take track bearing R for 0.3ml (0.5km); Bryn y Castell is small, steep hill on L; access from N side

Crew 1986

This small defended hilltop was completely excavated from 1979–85 and the rampart and stone buildings in the interior have been partially reconstructed. The site produced remarkable evidence of iron-working carried

Aerial view of Bryn y Castell

on both within the fort and in the round hut later built outside on the northern slope.

The defences are relatively simple, consisting of a stone rampart encircling the very top of the hill, but the entrance must always have been rather awkward for bringing in heavy or bulky industrial materials. The original 2m-wide gate was near the north-east corner, but that was blocked early in the history of occupation and a new one made 9m further west. The position of the gate-posts is now indicated by stones standing vertically in their postholes.

The interior was crowded with buildings of varied construction. The most unexpected discoveries were two stake-wall round houses in the central area (indicated now by cobbling and the porch postholes). Wooden houses of this type had not previously been found in Welsh hillforts, where stone huts were considered the norm. However, more careful excavation (for the stakeholes are extremely difficult to recognise) is likely to produce evidence of others.

The stone building in the north corner was originally a conventional round hut with a doorway facing south-east. Later the south wall was moved to create the unusual snail-like plan. This provided a draught for ventilation, and shade for smithing hearths along the east wall. The interior was full of smithing debris. A hut of this shape may be seen at Garn Boduan (no. 69) and is also probably a smithy.

Concentrations of iron-working debris and the remains of smelting furnaces were found at the south end of the fort and just outside the entrance, in the lee of the rampart.

Iron-working, both smelting and smithing, seems to have been the chief activity of the inhabitants of Bryn y Castell. They used bog-ores from the nearby peat bogs and cut trees for charcoal to fuel their furnaces on a very large scale.

Radiocarbon and archaeo-magnetic dating show that the settlement was occupied from the late Iron Age until the coming of the Romans. The industry was re-established, probably after a withdrawal of the local garrison in the 2nd century AD, but the hillfort was no longer occupied. Activity was centred instead at a building just outside. This was filled with slag and surrounded by dumps (including, on the west, a large stone anvil with smithing slag on its surface), suggesting intensive production, but perhaps over a short period.

Moel Goedog hillfort from the east. Entrance is in top left-hand sector

73
Moel Goedog, Llanfair

Later prehistoric hillfort

1st millennium BC

OS 124 SH 614325 U4

Continue up hill from Moel Goedog Circles (no. 44). Fort is on private land but owner permits access to SW section. Do not attempt to climb walls which divide site into three. Essential features can be appreciated from SW section

This small hillfort has relatively slight defences but stands in an exceptionally commanding position. It is reminiscent in many ways of Castell Odo, near Aberdaron (no. 70).

The almost circular summit of the hill is surrounded by two close-set concentric ramparts with shallow external ditches. The banks are nowhere more than 1m high, and it has been suggested that they must have been surmounted by a wooden palisade if they were to provide effective defence. The entrance – a simple gap through both ramparts – is in the south-west, where there is a natural line of approach between two rock ridges.

There has been no excavation to provide evidence of date or occupation, but Castell Odo, which it resembles, is one of the earlier hillforts in north Wales, established in the late Bronze Age. By the Iron Age the preferred settlement unit in this part of Meirionnydd seems to have been the concentric circle farmstead (see Maes y Caerau, no. 46).

74
Castell y Gaer, Llwyngwril

Later prehistoric hillfort

1st millennium BC

OS 124 SH 592090 U3

On hill immediately S of Llwyngwril (on A493 10.5ml, 16.8km, SW of Dolgellau). From N, take 2nd turning L after bridge (steep road between church and war memorial); site is on R shortly beyond end of walls. Fort is on private land but owner allows access to monument

This is a small fort on a spur overlooking the sea. It is very similar in size, design and situation to Caer Bach in the Conwy valley (no. 62). They both use a combination of stone and earth defences, but it is difficult to tell whether or not the two systems are contemporary.

The stone rampart originally surrounded the flat top of the hill completely, but almost all of it has been removed from the west and north sides. On the south and east enough survives to show that it was about 4m thick with a simple entrance at the south-east corner.

The outer defences exist only on the south, where two ditches with a high bank between them cut off the promontory from the rising ground behind. The distance from the top of the bank to the bottom of the ditch is about 3.5m. The bank ends with a slightly out-turned bastion on the east side, where a path curves in to enter the fort by the gate through the stone rampart. The northern side may have been slightly steepened by an artificial scarp, but the bank and ditches do not continue around it.

No excavation has been carried out to date the sequence which is implied by the different types of defence, but which is not proven because both circuits use the same entrance (contrast no. 64).

Castell y Gaer hillfort from the air

75
Tal y Gareg, Tywyn

Later prehistoric or early medieval hillfort

1st millennium BC/AD

OS 135 SH 574036 U4

From Pont Dysynni on A493 3.1ml (5km) N of Tywyn, take minor road W towards seaward tip of ridge N of Broadwater (1.6ml, 2.6km, from junction). Park car carefully at footpath sign; steep path up S side of hill, double back at top towards summit. Go either side of wall; easy to cross. Alternatively take footpath from Castell Mawr (SH 581049) – a bracken-infested fort – a gentler, longer walk. Visit on Sunday when quarry is not working

This is a fortification in an exhilarating position, fronting the sea and all the winds that blow! Its date is very uncertain, and it may have been occupied at more than one period.

The defences are built on the very top of the narrow ridge. They consist of two relatively low earth and stone banks enclosing a rectangular space about 45m long and 22m wide. At the seaward end there is a much stronger point – the base of a tower or small circular enclosure (10m in diameter) fronted by a rock-cut ditch now virtually filled with stone. If this stone comes from the collapse of the tower, it must have been quite high. Beyond the ditch is a curving bank with another deep rock-cut ditch beyond. This ditch is now right at the edge of the quarry – take care! The ring of concrete pegs on the collapsed tower once anchored a shipping signal.

The small stronghold is likely to be early medieval or possibly medieval; the outer defences may belong with it, or may be prehistoric.

On the lower slope, closer to the sea, is another defended enclosure (inaccessible).

76

Caer Euni, Bala

Later prehistoric hillfort

1st millennium BC

OS 125 SJ 000412 U4

See Cefn Caer Euni Circles (no. 56). From gate where car is parked, either walk directly up fence to L or follow path ahead and walk back along ridge to enter fort at SW end. Fort is on private land but owner allows access. Bracken can be a problem in high summer

Aerial view of Caer Euni hillfort

This long, narrow fort is of interest because of the surface evidence for enlargement, the existence of vitrified stone in its south-west rampart, and for its superb views.

It is built in a naturally defensible position, with a steep, unbroken slope to the valley floor on the south-east. The original fort ran from the north-east tip to the highest point of the ridge – a narrow, triangular enclosure with a curving south-west bank and an awkward entrance in the apex, with perhaps three gateways in direct line one behind the other. The south-east side needed little extra defence; on the other there were two banks, essentially scarps, with a small ditch between.

The curvature of the south-west end is the clue to the enlargement of the fort, for the smooth line of the extension is broken where the original incurve began. This can be seen on the ground quite easily on the south-east side, and on aerial photographs it is very obvious; even the line of the demolished rampart across the hill can be made out.

The added defences on the south-west are much more substantial than the original ones, largely because the hill becomes less steep here. The most notable feature is a deep rock-cut ditch fronting a higher and stonier rampart with its own counterscarp bank. No new entrance was provided, which must have made life difficult for the inhabitants, for access to the north entrance is awkward, even for friendly visitors! The present gap in the western defences is modern, though a little further south is an original uncut section of ditch, perhaps an informal crossing point.

Vitrified stones, presumably fallen from the rampart above, have been found in the ditch on the north-west corner. Vitrification of stone normally arises from the burning of a timber-laced rampart (a stone wall braced by a timber framework) but only excavation could confirm the presence of this feature. It is an aspect of military design which was thought to be restricted to a certain period and to certain groups, possibly with Scottish connections, but this has not been convincingly demonstrated.

Patches of dark vegetation can be seen in the fort on aerial photographs, and sometimes on the ground. These may mark sub-surface features, either house sites or perhaps filled-in storage or rubbish pits. No finds have been reported from the site, although the interior has been cultivated at some period, for cultivation ridges can be seen on the summit in suitable lighting conditions.

77

Tŷ Mawr Huts, South Stack, Holyhead

Iron Age and later settlement: hut group

1st millennium BC/AD

OS 114 SH 212820 U1 Cadw

In Holyhead, take South Stack road (see no. 57). Car park on L 0.4ml (0.64km) after RH turn, signposted huts opposite. Bracken obscures field system in summer but huts are kept clear

Smith 1987

This is one of the best known of the early settlements in Anglesey. It was first excavated in 1862–8 by the Hon. W O Stanley, the local landowner and MP, who did a great deal to preserve and elucidate the prehistory of Anglesey (see exhibition in Ellen's Tower nearby).

The remains consist of 10 large, round stone huts or houses scattered along the hillside and interspersed with smaller rectangular buildings which are partly subterranean, entered by one or two steps. Stone walls cross the area, and terraced fields can be identified among the modern fields on the slopes below. Through a gate at the east end is a further group of huts, re-excavated in 1978–82.

The round stone huts are about 7m in diameter with thick, low walls. They would have had a high, conical roof supported on a ring of posts and thatched with straw or reeds. It is unlikely that the walls would have been much higher than at present. The low, outer part of the room could be used for storage and sleeping. The houses contained hearths, usually in the centre. The only source of light would have been the wide doorway. The mortar for grinding roots and vegetables in Hut D must have been in a rather dark part of the room. Notice that all the doors here face away from the prevailing winds! One house had been subdivided late in its history.

The small, rectangular buildings are sufficiently narrow to have been spanned by flat beams. Stanley's excavations suggested that these had been used as workshops. He found hearths, slag, crushed quartz and other evidence of metal-working. Industrial activity was not confined to the workshops: he found similar hearths in some of the round houses, but perhaps those had been abandoned as dwellings. The excavations in 1978–82 found little industrial evidence, but provided more information about the agricultural side of the community's activities.

These later excavations, with the benefit of radiocarbon dating, demonstrated the very long history of settlement on this site. It is not a single village, established and abandoned within the Roman period, as Stanley thought (basing his view on 12 Roman coins found in Hut C), but rather a series of farmsteads of various dates, occupation being concentrated at different points along the hillside at different periods. The economic base of the community may also have varied and their prosperity fluctuated.

There is evidence for intermittent human occupation from the Middle Stone Age, Neolithic and Bronze Age, but the visible buildings in the eastern group belong to the Iron Age, and were used in one way or another up to the 6th century AD.

These eastern huts, unlike the western ones, had an enclosed yard in front of them. The earliest structure, the now-demolished hut in the centre, cannot be dated precisely. A larger house was built beside it in about 200 BC, originally with its doorway facing south-east. When the yard was altered this became inconvenient, and that door was moved to the east. At that time the original central house was partly demolished and a large granary was built in front of it, raised on seven stone blocks.

These developments belong to the Iron Age. No Roman material was found here, but the neighbouring land was worked during the Roman period, and dumping of stones and straw on the ruins in the 6th century AD demonstrates continuing occupation of the area at the time of St Cybi.

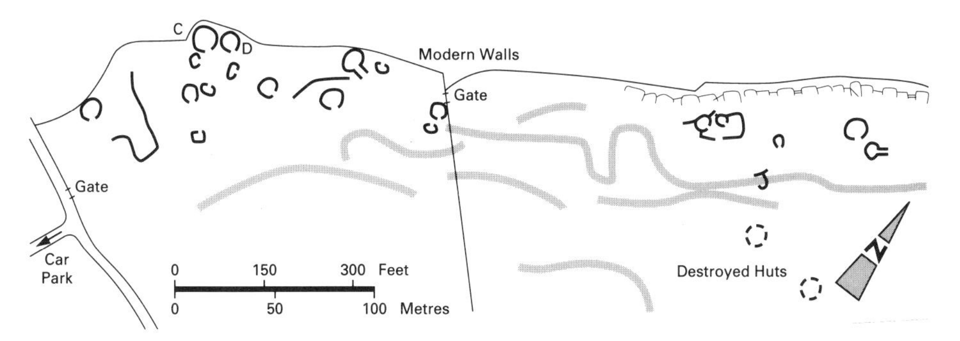

Tŷ Mawr huts

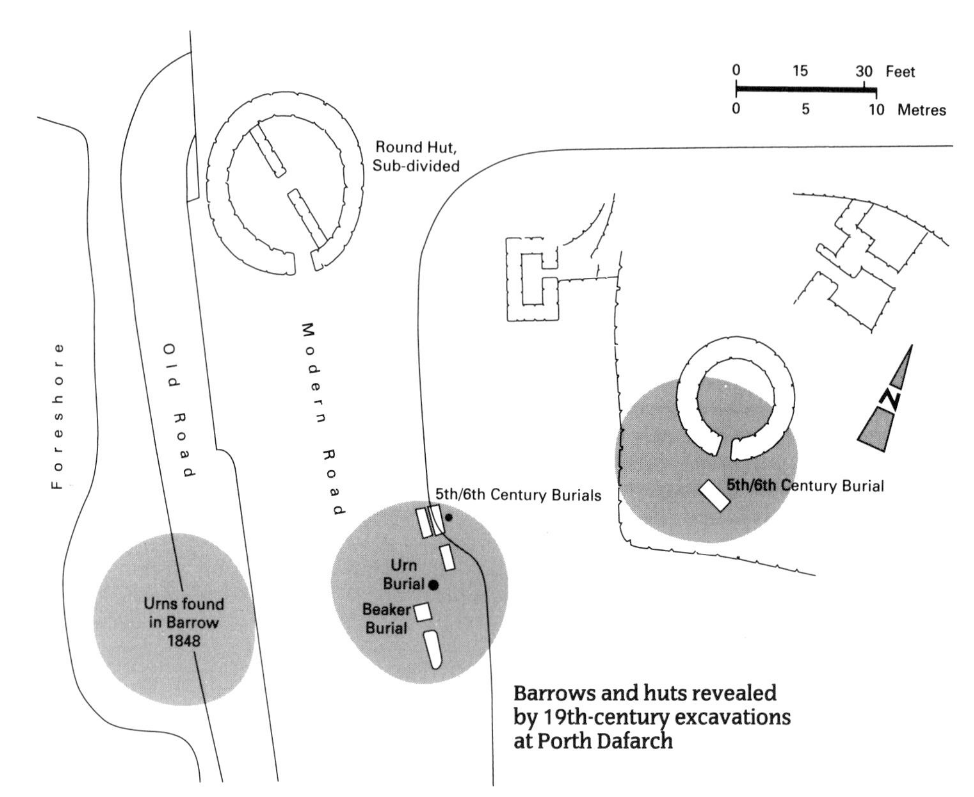

Barrows and huts revealed by 19th-century excavations at Porth Dafarch

78
Porth Dafarch, Trearddur Bay

Burial monuments and settlement

3rd, 2nd and 1st millennium BC/AD

OS 114 SH 234801 R3

At Holyhead railway bridge, follow sign to Trearddur Bay; after 0.2ml (300m) bear R (signposted Porth Dafarch). Site is in E corner of T-junction at bay (1.3ml, 2.2km). Land is private: do not enter, but huts visible over wall

Stanley 1876

This site is worth visiting even though the present remains are not easily intelligible and are inaccessible to close examination. Its importance lies in the evidence of a long period of activity, from late Neolithic onwards, and for continuity of use from the Roman period through to the early years of Christianity. Radiocarbon dating is now revealing this continuity at other sites, but this is one of the few places where there is a clear structural sequence, demonstrated by W O Stanley's excavations at the end of the 19th century.

The earliest activity here belongs to the Beaker period (about 2200 BC) when a young woman was buried with two Beaker pots in a stone cist marked by a tall stone and covered by a mound of sand. Both this mound and another Bronze Age barrow closer to the sea were destroyed by the road. The second barrow was disturbed in 1848, when cremation burials from about 1600 BC were found. A third Bronze Age barrow was built in this little valley, and that survives, but badly disturbed by the stone huts built over it.

The hut group consisted of round huts and at least one rectangular 'workshop' like those at Tŷ Mawr (no. 77). This is the structure which is easiest to recognise from the road. Stanley's excavations produced some rather fine pieces: a carved agate from a ring, a bronze tankard handle, and imported Samian pottery, which suggest a wealthier community than those on the mountain. These finds indicate occupation during the 2nd–4th centuries AD but, as at Tŷ Mawr, one may suspect that the settlement was established earlier.

Details of continuity into the 5th–6th centuries AD are not clear, but by then some houses must have been ruined, for the site was used for burials. Several long cist graves, normally assumed to be Christian, were dug into the earlier barrows and in amongst the ruined walls of the huts.

79
Din Lligwy, Moelfre

Enclosed hut group

Early 1st millennium AD

OS 114 SH 497861 U2 Cadw

From roundabout on A5025 SW of Moelfre, take road signposted Din Lligwy, pass Neolithic tomb (no. 13) and park where road widens (0.6ml, 1km, from A5025). Follow footpath past no. 138 (350m – kissing gate and rock steps)

Baynes 1908

A very well-known monument, Din Lligwy, with its neat white buildings and well composed vista, has an immediate appeal – rather like a not-too-grand country house. And this is what it seems to be – a well-regulated 'estate centre' with houses and working buildings arranged within an

Din Lligwy from the air

imposing wall. Though described as a 'hut group', it is really comparable to the contemporary Romanised 'villas' of the south of England.

The site is well chosen, standing on a low cliff with a superb view over Lligwy Bay. Excavation revealed evidence for earlier occupation – a less coherently planned set of buildings. The date of the reorganisation which resulted in the present arrangement is uncertain. The angularity of the enclosure and the presence of several rectangular buildings would suggest that they belong to the Roman period, built by a native chieftain, perhaps impressed by the commandant's house at Segontium (no. 92). Finds suggest occupation in the 4th century AD, but these may reflect only a small segment of the site's history.

Entry to the pentagonal enclosure is through a rectangular building on the east side – an imposing barn which doubled as a gatehouse.

Once inside, the eye is drawn to a large house in the right-hand corner, a superbly built circle of large limestone slabs with steps up to the entrance flanked by tall door jambs. This is the principal domestic building, and its traditional 'native' plan reveals the ancestry and conservatism of the owner. The finds here include a silver ingot, imported pottery (much of it carefully mended), and even glassware. Generally, the standard of living and sophistication is high. Even in this house there was evidence for some industrial activity (slag around the hearth), but perhaps this may belong to a period of later dilapidation.

It is assumed that the other round building in the south-east corner was also domestic, whereas the two largest rectangular buildings, in the north-east corner and against the south wall, were clearly workshops with rows of iron-working hearths and dumps of slag. The square building on the west side contained a hearth, and may have been lived in; the enclosure beside it, probably unroofed, may have been an animal pen. The buildings against the south-east wall are also somewhat informal; there has been a good deal of patching, changing and propping of walls in this area.

The small buildings outside the enclosure on the south side are rather puzzling. They seem to be later than the wall, and the authenticity of the little gate beside them is uncertain. What *is* certain is that the gap between the two walls was used, not surprisingly, as a rubbish dump.

The present plan is undoubtedly the result of a long period of development during which several buildings may have been modified and converted to different uses. Even the imposing enclosure wall may have been built in two stages, for there are some suggestive changes in building style.

Unfortunately, no excavation or analysis could confidently identify the amount of land belonging to this estate and the range of influence of its owners. This part of the island contains many hut groups which are probably contemporary with Din Lligwy, but we cannot recreate their social hierarchy.

80
Castell Bryn Gwyn, Brynsiencyn

Defended enclosure (multi-period site)

Late 3rd millennium BC; late 1st millennium BC/early 1st millennium AD/?11th century AD

OS 114 SH 465670 U3 Cadw

Site is signposted off A4080, 0.9ml (1.5km) W of Brynsiencyn (W corner). It is possible to drive to site but lane is tortuous and narrow. Those who can walk 500m should do so, leaving cars in lay-by

Wainwright 1962; Lynch 1991, pp 101–3

This is a well preserved circular earthwork; a clay and gravel bank 10m wide and 2m high surrounds a level area 17m in diameter, now revetted by stone walls and damaged by the

Aerial view of Castell Bryn Gwyn

insertion of a farmhouse. It was originally surrounded by a deep ditch, now completely silted up and quite invisible. Its presence was revealed by excavations in 1959–60, which also showed that the site had a very long and complex history, still the subject of some discussion and dispute.

Late Neolithic flints and pottery from under the bank suggested that the site was first constructed at that time – a bank and ditch enclosure with perhaps two entrances. This has been interpreted as a henge monument like the one at Bryn Celli Ddu (no. 8), but with the bank inside the ditch. This arrangement, unusual in a henge, made the site suitable for reuse as a defended farmstead at a later date.

The original ditch had silted rapidly in the unstable gravels and had then been filled in. The later bank, enlarged on more than one occasion, was built over the first ditch, and new V-profiled ditches were dug outside. The date of these rearrangements is uncertain. No later prehistoric material was found, but it is likely that there was some occupation at that period. Pottery from the interior indicated occupation at the end of the 1st century AD, but no coherent house plans were discovered. Some rebuilding of the defences occurred slightly later, making it an establishment to rival Caer Lêb (no. 81).

There is a documentary reference to a castle built by King Olaf, grandfather of Gruffudd ap Cynan, somewhere near the Menai Straits. It is tempting to identify this 11th-century base with Castell Bryn Gwyn, but nothing has been found to confirm such a suggestion.

81
Caer Lêb, Brynsiencyn

Settlement with defended enclosure

1st millennium BC/AD

OS 114 SH 473674 U1 Cadw

From Brynsiencyn, take 1st turning R after sharp corner (W end); site is 0.3ml (0.5km) on L (signposted). Park carefully on verge. Ground may be boggy in autumn and winter

This settlement, surrounded by impressive banks and deep water-filled ditches, is not well placed in military terms because it is overlooked by higher ground to the east. The defences, therefore, may have more to do with status than protection.

These defences consist of two banks and ditches. The inner bank is complete, and its sharp profile indicates that it was topped by a stone wall. The entrance was on the east. The outer bank follows the same pentangular line but it has been levelled on the north and east sides, where it can be traced only as a line of drier ground between the two silted ditches. Gaps in the banks on the west side have been caused by animals.

The site was partially excavated in 1866, when the footings of rectangular buildings were found against the inner rampart on the east and a circular hut was discovered in the southern half of the enclosure. The northern half contains a raised platform. Finds included

Caer Lêb from the air

pottery dating from the 2nd, 3rd and 4th centuries, suggesting occupation throughout the Roman period, but – as at other sites of this type – earlier and later phases, lacking distinctive finds, may have escaped recognition.

Other huts may be seen in the field on the right beside the bridge, Pont Sarn Las, 500m north-west along the road. Three round houses are clearly visible in the corner which has escaped ploughing. These are all that remain of a large settlement recorded in the 19th century and destroyed by agricultural improvement in the 1870s.

82
Huts near Maen y Bardd, Rowen

Late prehistoric–medieval settlement

Late 1st millennium BC–16th century AD

OS 115   SH 737717–SH 741720   U4

See no. 15 and map with no. 37. Settlement evidence occurs along Roman road (no. 91) and up slope NW of tomb (no. 15). Remains are described from road junction at W end (SH 732715). Bracken obscures many field boundaries in summer

The first enclosure is near the first standing stone on the left. It is typical of many on this slope: an oval platform levelled into the hillside, with an enclosing bank or wall and huts within it (in this case round), set against the slope.

Return to the track. Just after crossing the stream, notice a large stone in the left bank. This is inscribed with a cross within a circle (rather faint) – a prayer-station dating from the 7th–9th centuries AD, demonstrating the continued importance of the Roman road network in later centuries.

Just through the next gate, above the road on the left, is another oval enclosure with three round huts. Field-walls running downhill from here are cut by the road, suggesting that the settlements are earlier than the formalisation of the route by the Romans.

Just before Maen y Bardd (no. 15), below the road, there is a large, circular enclosure. The later track curves around it. Such kinks in modern walls are often an indicator of earlier structures.

From Maen y Bardd, go diagonally up the hill in a north-easterly direction, crossing several early field boundaries (lynchets) and passing levelled enclosures. Huts, either round or rectangular, can be seen in most but not all of these. A particularly interesting one

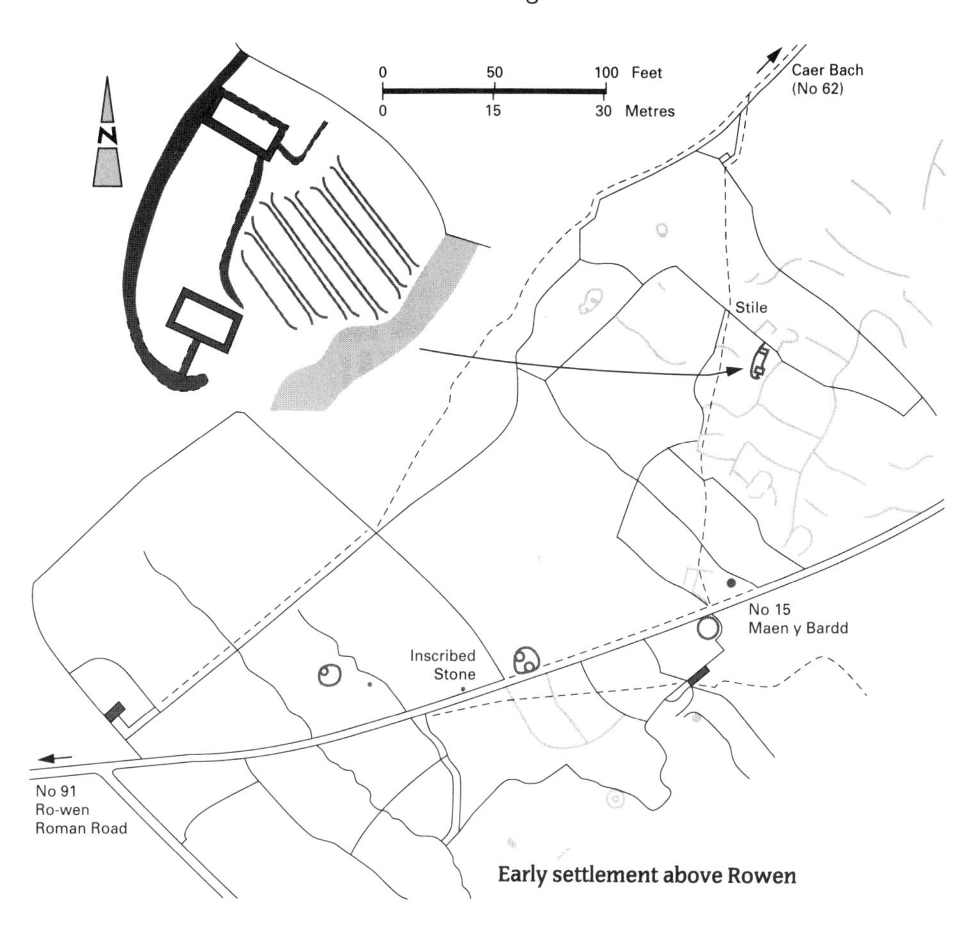

Early settlement above Rowen

is just west of a long, modern field-wall running down the slope. Set on the levelled platform are two long houses (8m by 3m) fronted by an area of lazybeds (spade-dug raised beds), probably a vegetable garden. Houses of this type are thought to belong to the 12th–16th centuries, but could be later.

A short way above, there is a stile over the wall and the path leads on to a modern ruin, a small farm on a levelled terrace where, in the last century, many aspects of life might still have been familiar to those who had occupied the medieval and even prehistoric sites around it. A gate in the wall leads to the track to Caer Bach (no. 62).

83
Hafod y Gelyn, Abergwyngregyn

Prehistoric and later settlement

1st millennium BC–?16th century AD

OS 115 SH 677717 U2

See no. 38. Park at end of road. Huts are on slope below Carnedd y Saeson. Bracken may obscure lower site in high summer

From just above the car park a good view can be gained of the enclosed farmstead (A) west

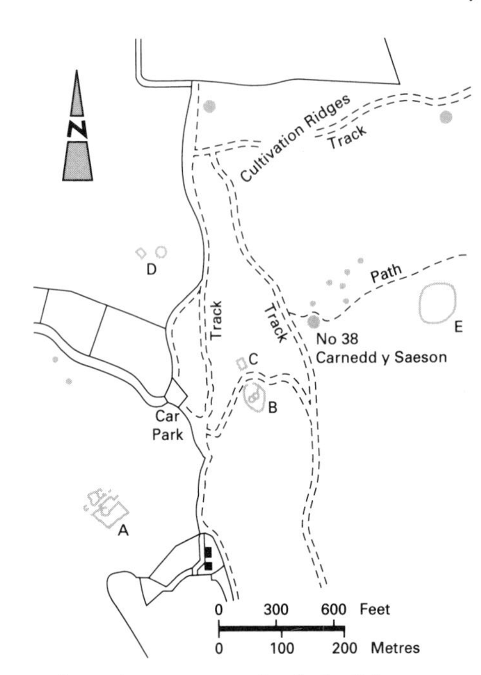

Early settlement around Hafod y Gelyn

of Hafod y Gelyn. The site itself is on private land, but the square yard with a large, round house foundation near the centre can be clearly seen. Just outside is another free-standing house, and perhaps another two, overlain by a later rectangular building.

The slope is crossed by a number of hollow ways – early tracks cut by men and pack-horses following the old route across the hills towards Bwlch y Ddeufaen (no. 37). The slope is a sunny one, occupied by several prehistoric and later farms. At the top, where the track takes a wide curve to the right, quite extensive cultivation ridges can be seen when the sun is low.

The two clearest farmsteads are B and C, midway between the two tracks. B is cut into the hillside; a thick stone wall with a clear entrance on the north-west surrounds two round houses. It is likely to be Iron Age or Roman in date. Levelled fields can be seen around it, and in the corner of one of these to the north-west is a single rectangular building of medieval type (C). The inner and other wall-faces and the square corners are clear. Other houses and terraced fields (D) can be seen by looking over the wall to the west (also visible from the path up to Carn Meuryn, no. 39), and a large, oval enclosure (E) on the upper slopes can be recognised as earlier than the modern sheepfold built inside it.

The Bronze Age burial cairns above the upper track are described under Carnedd y Saeson (no. 38).

84

Moel Faban, Bethesda

Prehistoric and later burial monuments and settlement

2nd millennium BC–?16th century AD

OS 115 SH 636678 U2/4

From A5 in centre of Bethesda, opposite Bethesda Chapel, turn up hill; fork L; take upper L turn at complex T-junction at top, then double back, acute R at Carneddi PO. Turn first L up steep narrow road (Cilfoden), persevere to row of cottages on open hillside (0.75ml, 1.25km). Park in lay-by to L and continue up footpath. At mountain gate bear R along clear track at foot of hill. Bracken can obscure some details in high summer

The smooth eastern slope of Moel Faban is divided into a series of large, rectangular fields associated with at least two groups of round stone houses. They are likely to be late prehistoric in date, with occupation continuing through the Roman period into the first few centuries AD. At both of the larger sites, rectangular houses (probably medieval) have been built over the ruins of the round ones.

Follow the 19th-century leat to the corner of the modern wall, where the early fields become clear. The two huts just below the track here are not easy to find, but the first group – about 150m to the north, higher up the slope – is easier. One round house and a

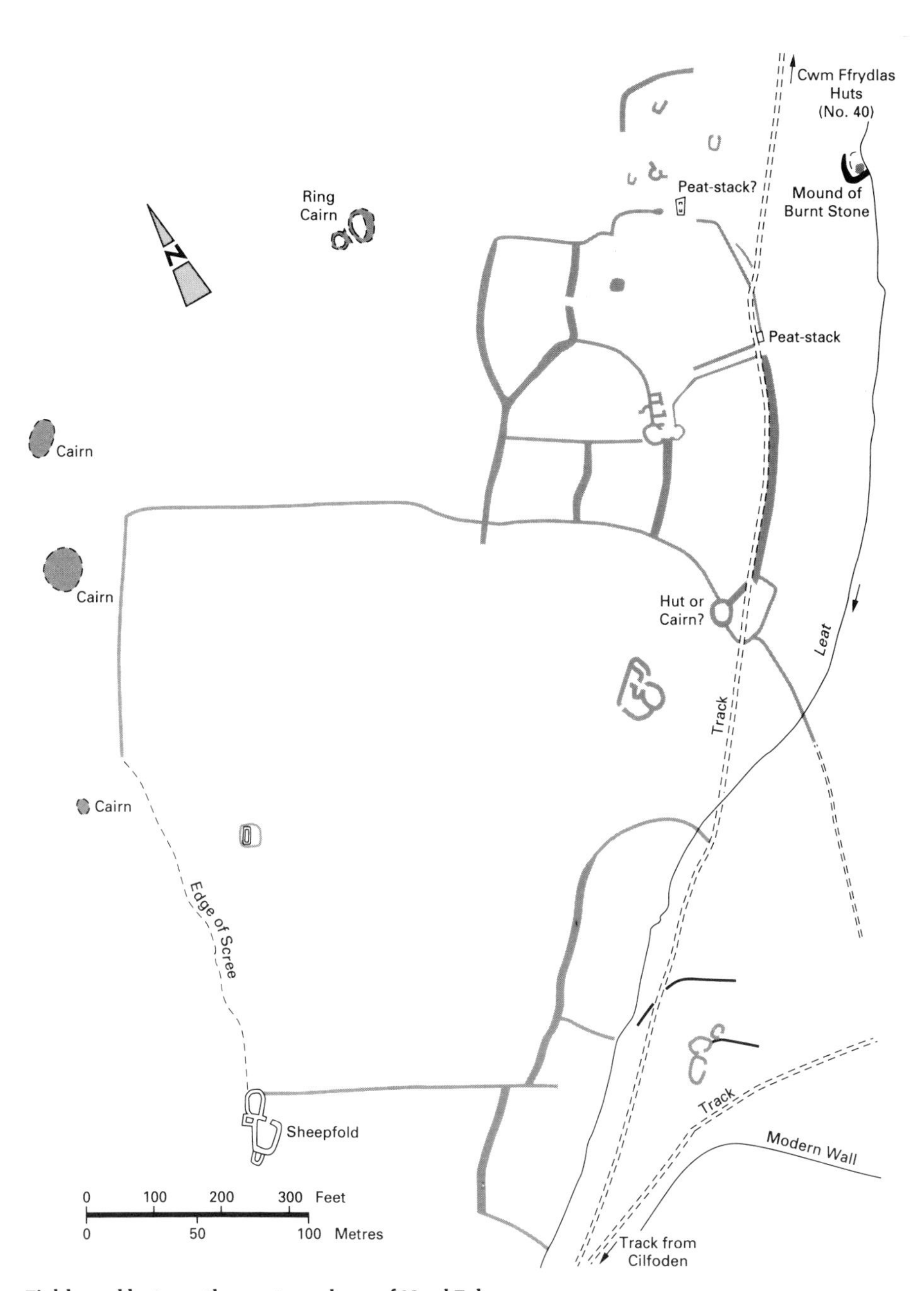

Fields and huts on the eastern slope of Moel Faban

curving wall of its 'farmyard' are clear; the later buildings are a jumble of stones. Return to the path, which cuts the edge of the fields, until a double-walled lane on the left is reached. This leads up to the 'farm'. On the left, two round house foundations within the yard can be recognised easily. The upper side of the yard is overlaid by a rectangular building with three rooms. The integration of the 'farm' with the fields around it is shown by the way the field-walls run into those of the yard and houses. Their coherent layout and the contrast between their relatively stone-free surface and the boulder scatter beyond can be appreciated from the flat land to the north.

From the lower end of the 'lane', a typical small burnt stone mound can be seen beside the stream to the north-east. The mound is horseshoe-shaped, surrounding a rectangular patch of rushes indicating the position of the boiling trough, the whole enclosed by a low bank. This could have been a cooking place for the occupants of the round houses, but may be an earlier, Bronze Age, establishment. Meat was cooked in water brought to the boil by throwing heated stones into the trough (see no. 46).

From here it is possible to continue along the main track to the Cwm Ffrydlas settlement (no. 40) and Drosgl cairns (no. 41).

There are three round cairns – Bronze Age burial monuments – on the summit of Moel Faban, and on a spur at the north-east end is a damaged ring cairn, recognisable by its hollow centre with slabs on the inner edge of the low stone ring.

On returning over the summit, other enclosures and huts can be seen on the south-west slope. The most impressive is on a promontory between two small slate quarries. It is a small area with at least six round huts built against its substantial enclosing wall. The entrance is at the west end, giving on to an awkwardly steep slope, and at the other end it is defended by a length of bank and ditch.

85
Cwm Dyli, Nantgwynant

Later prehistoric hut group

1st millennium BC/AD

OS 115 SH 655541 U2

From Beddgelert, take A498 NE for 3.8ml (6km) to Bryn Gwynant Youth Hostel, then 0.9ml (1.4km) further N bear L to Cwm Dyli Power Station. This turn is awkward from N. Drive 1.5ml (2.4km) to junction with track to power station; leave car here and walk 300m to site on R of track just before river. South enclosure obscured by bracken in summer; can be wet underfoot

The huts and fields here take advantage of a small area of flat land beside the river. There are two clusters of round huts. The southern (nearer) one consists of four huts within an oval enclosure. The northern group – which is easier to see – has four, more widely spaced, huts which are unenclosed. Two of these four huts have exceptionally well preserved walls, but the floor areas have been damaged by recent drainage ditches.

A lot of small stones have been thrown on to the walls during field clearance. This may have been done when the settlement was occupied, and indicates intensive cultivation nearby. Small enclosures or fields can be seen radiating from the huts and extending up the slope to be lost in the bracken. Another group of huts exists under the bracken just across the river, indicating the population pressure on these small parcels of fertile ground in this rocky landscape.

86
Cors y Gedol Huts and Fields, Tal y Bont

Prehistoric and later settlement

1st millennium BC–?16th century AD

OS 124 SH 604230 U2

See Cors y Gedol tomb (no. 25). Fields cover area on LH (E) side of road from gate almost as far as café above Pont Fadog. Land is private but owner allows access. Please follow the Country Code and respect livestock. Bracken obscures field boundaries in high summer

Griffiths 1958

This is an exceptionally extensive and well preserved ancient landscape, containing settlement sites and their fields dating from late prehistoric and Roman times to medieval and perhaps later periods. In some places one boundary was built over another, at others, later farmers no doubt accommodated themselves to the earlier layout.

One of the settlements has been excavated. It can be found by turning left at the gate and walking up the wall to a water tank. The enclosed hut group is just below this, tucked in below a high lynchet. There are two round huts on the west side, with a rectangular one between them at the back. The enclosure wall is best seen on the south side. Excavation in 1956 produced part of a burnt wooden bowl and pottery of 2nd-century AD date.

From here walk south-east, crossing an open area containing a number of field clearance cairns. Then cross some stone banks and walls, amongst which is an obvious lane. Continue down the north–south lynchet (much more developed than the south-west–north-east ones because of the lie of the land) until you reach an oval enclosure. This is a

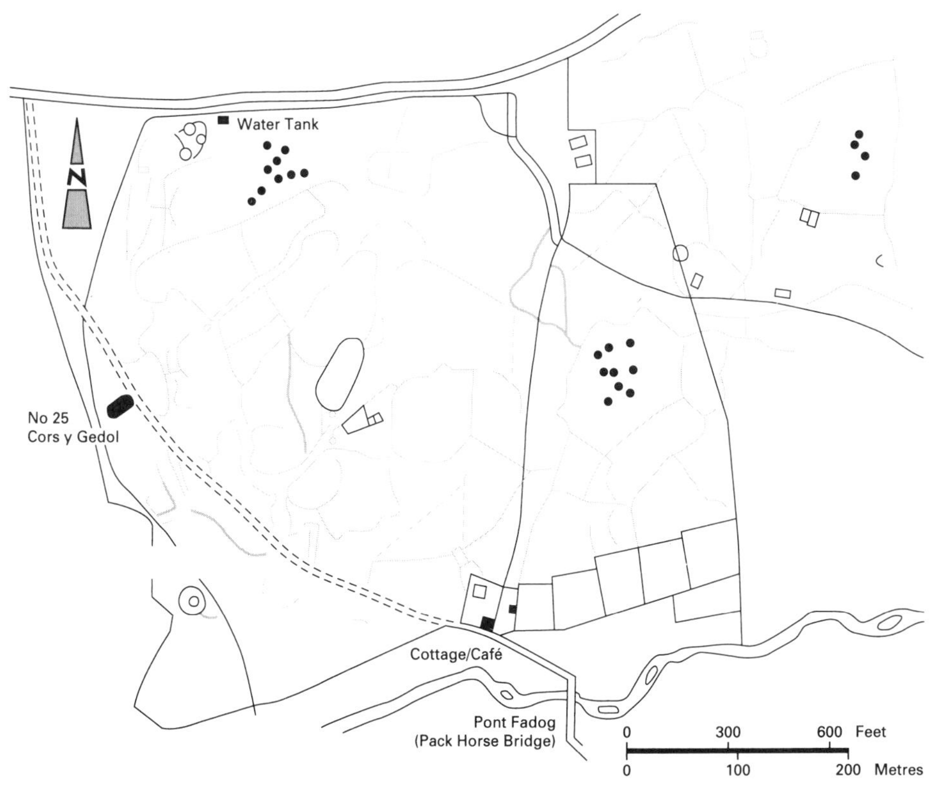

Early fields and farms above Cors y Gedol

better-preserved wall than the others, and is probably medieval or later. At the south end it can be seen to overlie a circular hut at the corner of an earlier field. Just east of this point is an enclosure with two rectangular houses at the east end – a farm and paddock dating perhaps from the medieval period, or even the 16th century.

Walking down to the modern road at this point, you emerge above a circular enclosure of Iron Age type, not very easy to find amongst scrub trees. Walk back to the gate via the Neolithic tomb (no. 25).

The field system extends much further east, but the western area provides a good sample of the types of fields and huts present.

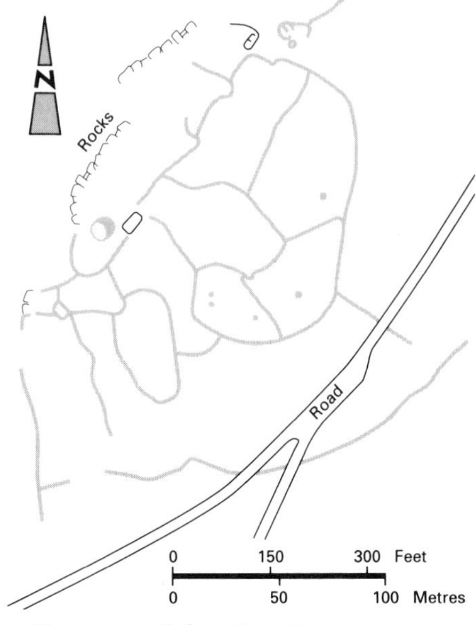

Settlement on Cefn y Clawdd

87

Cefn y Clawdd, Trawsfynydd

Prehistoric and medieval settlement

1st millennium BC and ?12th century AD

OS 124 SH 688337 U2

From Trawsfynydd, go S on A470, 0.6ml (1km) and turn R; continue for 0.9ml (1.5km) and take L fork; continue for another 0.9ml (1.5km). Site is in rough ground to R of road, opposite a track leading down on L. Vegetation can be a problem in high summer

This site is not dramatic, and it is quite difficult to appreciate on the ground, but it is typical of a number of imprecisely dated settlements on these hills and, unlike most, is easily accessible.

The settlement (5.6ha) is placed just below low crags, and consists of an outer ring of discontinuous walls which define three fairly large enclosures encircling a core of small, lobe-like fields with clearance cairns. The round huts are not obvious, but there is a small one at the west end, and a significant bend in a wall at the north-east end may indicate the site of a wooden house. Stake-wall round houses of Iron Age date have been revealed by excavation at a similar site at Crawcwellt, 1.5ml (2.5km) to the south. The community there was heavily engaged in iron-working, but the fields suggest that the industry was underpinned by an agricultural economy.

Close under the crag are two long house foundations which are likely to be of medieval date, or possibly later *hafodau* (summer grazing bases).

88

Cyfannedd and Bryn Seward, Cadair Idris

Prehistoric and medieval settlement

1st millennium BC–15th century AD

OS 124 SH 634122 and SH 623117 U1

Both areas of settlement can be reached from asphalted road running along N slope of Cadair Idris (see nos 49–52). The 1st is 120m S of road, taking footpath turning sharply back on L 0.5ml (800m) SSW of Cyfannedd Farm. Other is bisected by road, N of which huts are clearly visible

Kelly 1983

The most conspicuous feature of the Cyfannedd group is a large, circular enclosure lying between two tracks. It is a broad stone wall with three rectangular buildings abutting it. It may have been a group of *hafodau* (summer grazing bases) sharing a stockade. Other rectangular buildings, some circular ones and a number of clearance cairns may also be recognised in this unplanted area.

The Bryn Seward settlement is more extensive, and probably earlier, since most of the buildings are round. It extends from north of the standing stones (no. 51) to the cairn at SH 622116; the clearest features are to the north of the road. No plan of the site has ever been drawn, and much of it is quite difficult to interpret, but at least one large round hut within a circular enclosure can be very clearly seen below the road. Other features include field-walls and clearance cairns, suggesting that this fairly level shelf was once intensively farmed. At the western end, on a lower shelf, there are two very large, rectangular buildings of unknown date and purpose. They seem much longer than the normal platform house, and might possibly be of 10th-century Viking origin – a period with very few field monuments in Wales.

These walls and huts are indicative of the wealth of archaeological evidence which awaits proper study in these upland regions, still vulnerable to the spread of commercial forestry.

Aerial view of settlement remains on Bryn Seward

5
The Roman Occupation

The Roman invasion of Britain in AD 43 saw the beginning of a north-westward advance of the Roman legions. The attitude of Rome towards the conquest of its new province was sometimes faltering or equivocal, but by AD 57 there was a serious commitment to campaigning in Wales, which by AD 60 had brought Suetonius Paulinus to the shores of the Menai Straits. The Romans exerted control, sometimes by diplomacy and the establishment of client kingdoms, and sometimes by conquest. In the case of the Ordovices of north Wales it was conquest, and the struggle seems to have been a hard one. However, only one marching camp has survived from that early campaign (no. 93).

The main Roman base for control of north Wales when victory was achieved by Agricola in AD 77 was the legionary fortress at Chester; from there emanated a series of military roads linking the various auxiliary forts placed at strategic intervals. Snowdonia was hemmed in by several forts: Canovium at Caerhun (no. 90), to cover the Conwy crossing; Caer Llugwy, near Betws y Coed; at Tomen y Mur, near Ffestiniog (no. 94), and at Pen Llystyn, to cover the route across the neck of the Lleyn peninsula. Finally, there was the most important of the north Welsh forts, Segontium at Caernarfon (no. 92), where a garrison was maintained throughout the period of Roman rule in Britain, despite the demand for troops elsewhere which led to the reduction of garrisons at other forts in the 2nd century.

Another series of roads and forts ran from Chester down the Bala gap to the coast but, despite its economic importance, there seems to have been no Roman base in Anglesey until the small coastal fort was built at Holyhead (no. 89), probably in the 4th century.

Vici (civil settlements and, in some instances perhaps, shanty towns) grew up outside the gates of the military establishments, and many of the elements of Roman urban life may have come to north Wales in this informal way. Caernarfon, where a Mithraic temple has been found, provides the best evidence for the growth of such a settlement of camp followers, hangers-on, merchants and veterans, but there is no true Roman town, of the type found at Wroxeter, Caerwent or even Carmarthen; north Wales remained an essentially rural area.

In the countryside, the period of Roman rule seems to have been an era of prosperity. It is no longer believed that all the various stone hut settlements were established at this date, but most of them seem to have prospered in the 2nd, 3rd

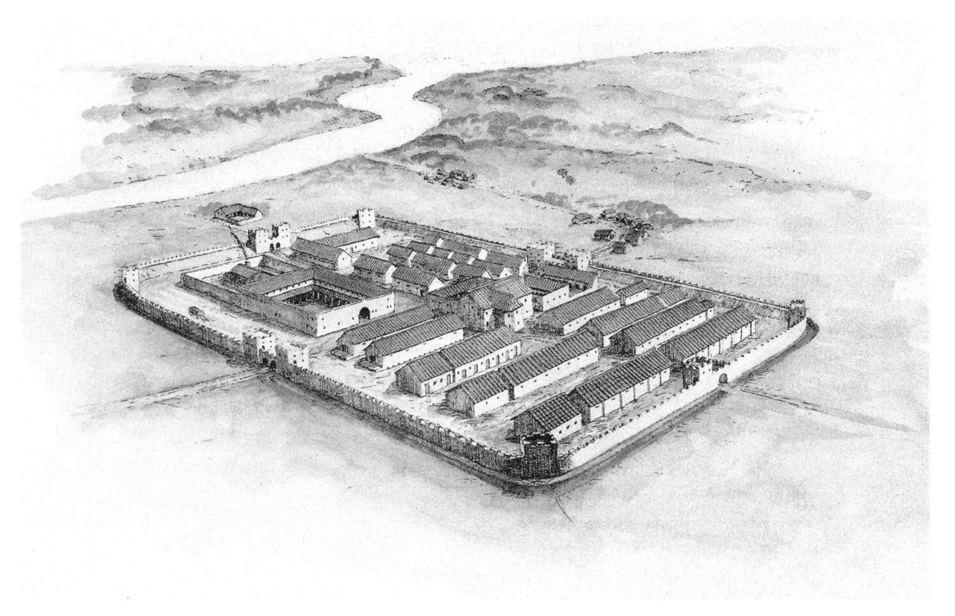

Segontium Roman fort as it might have appeared in the 2nd century AD

and early 4th centuries, and the formation of terraced fields around many of them provides a picture of intensified agriculture which is typical of most parts of Roman Britain. In the heavily Romanised south, these prosperous estates, whether owned by natives or by Roman officials, were *villas* in the true Mediterranean style. Such establishments may be found in Glamorgan, but in north Wales the rural settlements cling to the old native tradition of round houses and less formal grouping. A good example of such a Romanised farm which may have pretensions to *villa* status can be seen at Din Lligwy (no. 79), near Moelfre in Anglesey. Some of the pottery there had come from as far away as the New Forest, and silver was in use for some metal-working process in one of the hearths.

The Romans encouraged – and taxed – not only agriculture, but also industry. The fate of iron-making from bog-ores in Meirionnydd is not clear, but the earlier copper mines at Parys mountain in Anglesey and probably those on the Orme (no. 34) were exploited and possibly expanded. Evidence at this date lies, not in the mine galleries, but in the numerous copper ingots in north Wales, several of them with official Roman stamps. At Caer Llugwy, Betws y Coed (see Appendix), the military may have been mining the nearby lead ores, and in the workshops at Brithdir fort they were using slate from deep quarries. Although much domestic pottery was factory-made in other parts of Britain, there was a local tile industry in Gwynedd, with kilns probably operated by the army (see no. 96).

The Roman administration in Wales fell victim to pressures on the centre of the empire in the 4th century. Troops were removed to fight for their provincial generals on the Continent, and outlying areas such as north Wales became prey to sharp-eyed raiders from across the Irish Sea. It is in this context that we may see the establishment of the fort at Caer Gybi, Holyhead (no. 89), and perhaps the reoccupation of hillforts by the native population. Once the legions had gone and even Segontium was deserted, the historical record becomes extremely obscure. Agricultural settlements continued, but with the collapse of Roman marketing systems, coinage and distinctive pottery are no longer found, and a detailed chronology is impossible to construct.

89
Caer Gybi, Holyhead

Roman naval base

Late 3rd–late 4th century AD

OS 114 SH 247826 U1 Cadw

In centre of Holyhead; from railway bridge, either walk up Market Street (pedestrianised) and through S gateway or drive towards ferry, turning L up Boston Street (signposted Library); car park on L

Before the modern dock was built, this fort stood on a rocky slope overlooking a sheltered beach. In the late 3rd century AD the declining Roman empire was threatened by pirates in the North Sea and on its western frontiers, and several coastal forts were built in Britain and on the Continent. Although no Roman material has been found in Holyhead, the style of masonry, the three-sided plan which can be matched in the Rhineland, the recognition of a Roman signal station on Holyhead mountain (no. 57) and references in the *Life* of St Cybi all combine to reinforce the identification of this structure as a late Roman naval base for ships which patrolled the Irish Sea.

The fort is a three-sided enclosure (75m by 45m) with solid masonry towers on each corner and indications of a wall projecting towards the sea on the north-east side. This wall might have protected a quay. The 1.5m-thick walls stand 4m high on all three sides, topped by the remains of a wall-walk and parapet. The walls are built with a rubble core and, in places, a facing of obliquely pitched stones with regular lacing courses. This style of building is indicative of a late Roman date.

The corner towers are 5m in diameter, and the well preserved western ones are solid masonry up to the height of the wall-walk. The base of the north-eastern one is Roman, and on the east side the stub of a thick (Roman) wall can be seen where the narrow modern wall abuts the tower. The upper part of this and the whole of the south-eastern tower have been rebuilt. The eastern wall of the graveyard and the quarried cliff beneath it are modern features.

The narrow northern gate is entirely modern; the original gate was in the south

The walls of Caer Gybi

wall, but the existing double arch is not Roman.

There is no historical record for the building or use of this fort but the *Life* of St Cybi says that Maelgwyn, the 6th-century AD king of Gwynedd, gave him the land here for a monastery, of which the fine parish church standing within the fort is the successor. Abandoned Roman forts were often given to the church, so the legend has considerable credibility.

90
Caerhun/Canovium, Ty'n y Groes

Roman auxiliary fort

1st–mid-2nd century AD

OS 115   SH 776703   U1

0.75ml (1.3km) S of Ty'n y Groes (4.5ml, 7.2km, S of Conwy on B5106) turn L (E) up private road to Caerhun church (signposted). Land is private but road crosses fort since church stands in NE corner of it, and surviving ramparts are clearly visible. Please do not stray from path

Reynolds 1938

The position of this fort on a river crossing at the upper tidal reach of the river Conwy is one of great strategic importance in the communication network of Roman Wales. Although the military garrison may not have been maintained at full strength for very long, there was certainly spasmodic occupation in the fort, or the nearby civilian settlement, into the early 4th century.

The site was extensively excavated in 1926–9 and two main periods of building were revealed in the interior, which contained the standard range of Roman military buildings: headquarters (*principia*), commandant's house (*praetorium*), barracks and granaries. An annexe on the south side was shown to be defended with a stout wall and ditch, but no buildings were found inside it. Between the fort and the river there was a bath-house and, on the flat land on either side of the Roman road as it approached the southern gate, there was a very extensive civil settlement or *vicus*, which may have continued to flourish after the military importance of the fort had declined. Cremation burials were found to the north and south of the fort, but no large cemetery was located. The remains of a possibly contemporary dock were found near the river bank.

Canovium Roman fort from the air

The fort was probably built during Agricola's north Welsh campaign in AD 77. Its defences were a clay and rubble rampart, 7m wide, fronted by a single ditch which may have been dug only on the south-west side. The internal buildings at this stage would have been of timber. Almost 2ha in extent, it was probably designed for a mixed cavalry and infantry garrison of about five hundred men.

In the mid-2nd century AD the defences were rebuilt in stone, and detached corner towers and stone guardchambers were built at the gates. But the roadways through them were only of single carriageway width, and it seems that the military role of the fort may have been rapidly reduced.

The road to the church crosses the south-west corner of the fort, overlying the corner tower. The ditch can be seen to the left, and the highest section of rampart to the right. The road continues over the *praetorium* and a corner of the *principia*; the church overlies four barrack blocks, and the granaries lay in the field to the left of the car park. The main northern gate is under the north end of the parking area. The remains of the bath-house can be seen over the churchyard wall. The ditch of the southern annexe is visible from the road, as are the 'humps and bumps' which indicate the position of the *vicus*.

91
Roman road from Canovium to Segontium, above Rowen

Roman road

2nd–4th centuries AD

OS 115 SH 750722–SH 665735 U2/4

See no. 15 (or no. 37, with map, for those who do not want such a long walk). Road is less clear and accessible W of Bwlch y Ddeufaen

Jones 1985

This road from Caerhun to the Menai shore must have been one of the best-signposted roads in the province of Britannia! No less than four Roman milestones have survived from this section. Three of these stones may be seen in Bangor Museum.

The two earliest – set up in the reigns of Hadrian and Septimius Severus, in AD 121 and 208 respectively – were tall, cylindrical, well-cut stones of a type standard throughout the empire. They symbolise the powerful international organisation of Rome. Both stood at the same spot (Rhiwiau Uchaf, SH 679727).

Those set up in the 3rd and 4th centuries were much less impressive: misshapen and roughly cut. They reflect the increasing troubles of an empire overstretched and threatened with political disintegration. The latest one, set up during the reign of

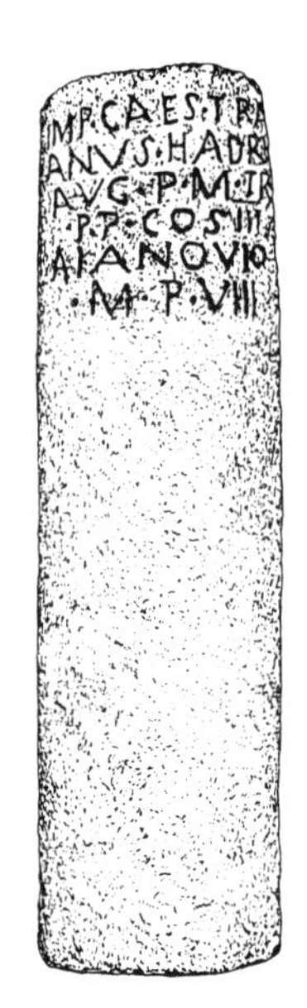

The Hadrianic milestone found at Rhiwiau Uchaf

Constantine the Great in the early 4th century, was found just to the east of the pass at SH 719716. The most westerly one was found near the coast, near Madryn Farm (SH 669734). It was set up in AD 262 under the Emperor Postumus, but about two hundred years later it was turned upside down and used as a gravestone for a local saint or chief. The cross-inscribed stone from the middle of the route (see no. 82) belongs to roughly the same period, when the Roman road network remained vitally important.

The road marked by these stones had been a regular route through the mountains for many centuries before the Roman armies formalised it. Neolithic and Bronze Age monuments can be seen to either side (see nos 15 and 37) and the hillside is covered with farms and fields of later prehistoric date (see no. 82). The paved road cuts across some of these fields in an arbitrary fashion, showing that the Roman engineers laid out a new track.

The road is about 4.5m wide, and appears as either a shelf cut into the hillside (visible from Bwlch y Ddeufaen car park, eastward, where the Roman line is above the modern road) or as a slightly raised bank (over the summit section). The present stone paving is not Roman, but it had been paved originally with flat stones. In fact, limited excavation in the pass when the electricity pylons were erected revealed two layers of these stones separated by gravel, suggesting careful repairs.

92
Segontium, Caernarfon

Roman auxiliary fort

1st–4th century AD

OS 115 SH 485624 R1 NT/Cadw

Segontium is signposted from centre of Caernarfon. A4085 to Beddgelert passes through fort. Admission charge and standard opening hours. Site museum

Official Guide leaflet, Casey and Davies 1993

This fort was the main Roman base in north Wales from the conquest till the end of the 4th century. It was garrisoned for longer than any other fort in the region, which suggests that it may have had additional economic and administrative roles in the collection of taxes (paid in grain and other goods which needed protection) and the organisation of mining operations.

The fort was founded by Agricola in AD 77 or 78, when he finally conquered the Ordovices. At that time the defences were of earth and wood, and all the internal buildings would also have been timber. It was a typical auxiliary infantry fort, designed originally to hold about a thousand men – non-citizen soldiers, serving in the Roman armies for 25 years and given citizenship on retirement, when they might settle down locally.

The original timber defences were rebuilt in stone in the first half of the 2nd century, and the internal buildings were changed to stone in a piecemeal way over the same period. The history of rebuilding, with major activity at AD 140, 200, 300 and 350, may reflect native revolts and attacks, or it may simply result from changes in imperial policy.

Segontium (named after the river Seiont) is clearly identified in late Roman military route descriptions, in the *Antonine Itinerary* and the *Ravenna Cosmography*. A unit of men called Segontienses is recorded in the Balkans in the 4th century AD, but the fort does not feature in historical documents. However, it does play a major role in Welsh legend, where it appears as Caer aber Seint, 'the many-towered fort at the mouth of the Seiont' in the 'Dream of Macsen Wledig', one of the stories of the *Mabinogion*. Macsen Wledig may be identified with Magnus Maximus, the late Roman general of Spanish origin who made his reputation defending the north-western frontiers against Picts and Irish, and who made a bid to become emperor in AD 383. There is no record of Magnus Maximus – nor his wife, Helen, nor Constantius, nor Constantine – ever having been at Segontium, yet they all feature fleetingly in its legends. Poets have obviously made an amalgam of all the famous 4th- and 5th-century figures who had the slightest connection with Britain – and the Welsh bards have set their stories in the most notable Roman fort they knew: Segontium.

The site has been extensively excavated, and the foundations are exposed so that visitors can appreciate the layout of a typical Roman fort, with its four gateways, central headquarters buildings and serried ranks of barracks and stores. The modern road lies approximately on the more important Roman axis, and most of the site lies to the north, behind the museum, which should be visited first.

The defences consist of a rampart fronted by a double ditch (now filled in). The core of the Roman wall still stands to an impressive height on the south-east corner (access by a lane opposite the museum). There were originally four gates, all of which were narrowed in the course of their history. The most interesting is the north-western one.

Aerial view of Segontium Roman fort from the north-east

The barracks and store buildings (distinguished by their buttresses) changed little in design from the 2nd to the 4th century. Each building would have housed 80 infantrymen, or alternatively, 64 cavalrymen.

The headquarters buildings in the centre of the fort consisted of the *praetorium* (commanding officer's house) and *principia* (regimental offices). In the early 3rd century a cellar, probably a bank vault containing pay and other valuables, was put in below the floor of the regimental shrine at the back of the *principia*, and the next-door room was enlarged and heated to act as an accountant's office. This is perhaps an indication of the growing importance of economic rather than military activities at the base. The identification of the room comes from an altar to Minerva dedicated by an *actarius* who worked there (see museum).

The barracks in the south-eastern quarter of the site were demolished in the 2nd century, when a large courtyard house with a private bath building was constructed there (visible across the road, but not officially open). It may have been for an imperial procurator – a high-ranking official in charge of mining in the region.

The fort was the centre of Roman administration, but evidence for Roman activity covers a much larger area. The informal town (*vicus*) which housed families, hangers-on and traders, spread down the hill to the south and west. To the east there was a temple to Mithras and a cemetery (under the new cemetery opposite Llanbeblig church).

Only one of the ancillary buildings is visible today – Hen Waliau, about 150m away on the road to Pwllheli. It forms the garden wall of a large stone house near the petrol station, and can be seen where it abuts the pavement. The site was a substantial walled enclosure (three sides remain, in places up to 4.5m high) probably built in the 3rd century as a warehouse for stores landed from ships in the river below.

93
Pen y Gwryd Camp, Llanberis Pass

Roman marching camp

1st century AD

OS 115 SH 660557 U1

Site is at junction of A498 and A4086, 6ml (9.7km) SE of Llanberis. Junction signs on all three roads stand alongside bank where Roman defensive circuit is cut by modern roads. Leave car in car park on A498 and walk back 100m (to signpost) where bank is best seen in field to E of road near footpath sign

Marching camps are a relict of the early campaigns of the Roman army in Britain. Each night the soldiers would have to dig themselves in behind a defence of ditch and turf wall topped by a wooden palisade. Each soldier carried stakes and a pick as part of his standard equipment and, at the end of a day's march, they would construct the camp and pitch their tents inside. As one late Roman writer put it, 'the army carried with them a walled town, as it were, wherever they went.'

These temporary camps are relatively insubstantial, and this is the only one which survives as a field monument in Gwynedd. It must belong to the period of active campaigning between AD 48 and 77, and seems to be designed to hold an army of some two thousand men. At just under 4ha it is about half the size of the standard legionary campaigning camps.

It is strategically placed at the junction of three routes through the mountains (notice the Second World War defences at the same spot). The south side of the camp is the best preserved; on the west of the road, a modern wall tops the Roman bank, on the east it is unencumbered. From the top of the eastern ridge it is possible to see the 3m-wide (unprotected) south entrance and the south-eastern and north-western corners of the camp. The west side is visible from the A4086 above.

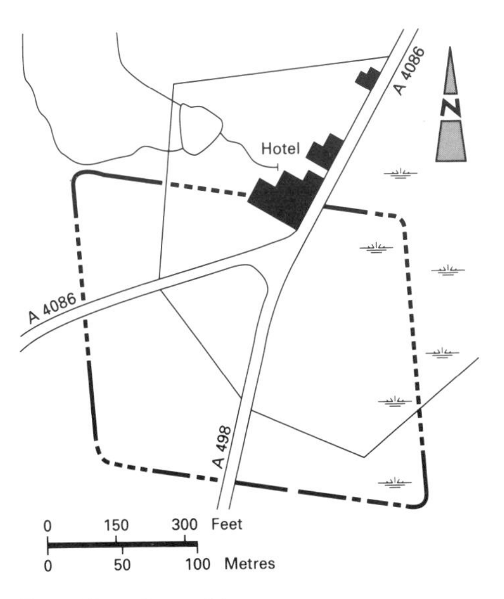

Pen y Gwryd marching camp

94
Tomen y Mur

Roman military complex; medieval motte

1st–2nd and 11th centuries AD

OS 124 SH 707388 U2/R2

From Maentwrog, go SE on A487 for 2ml (3.2km), pass junction with A470 and take 1st turn on L. Go under low railway bridge and continue for 1ml (1.6km), leaving car beyond cattle grid and amphitheatre. Amphitheatre and other earthworks are on open Crown land, but fort itself and features to N and S of it are on private land. Visitors should seek permission to enter these fields at Tyddyn Du on A470, 1st farm on L

Gresham 1938; Jarrett and Nash-Williams 1969, pp 111–13

The name derives from a late 11th-century earthwork castle built over the rampart of the Roman fort, which thus provided a ready-made bailey, or outer enclosure. This motte is a most conspicuous feature, but little is known of its history except that William Rufus campaigned here in 1095. Mur y Castell ('Castle Wall'), the earlier name of the site mentioned in the *Mabinogion*, suggests that

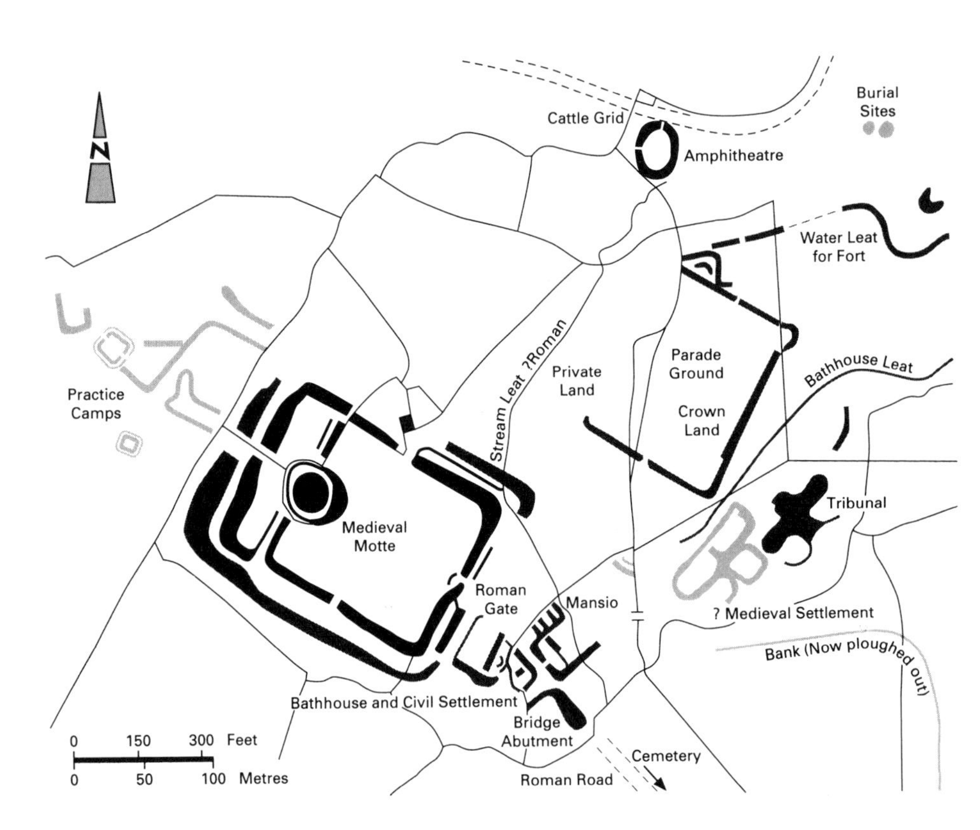

Roman military earthworks at Tomen y Mur

the walls of the fort were still standing in the early medieval period. A 5th-century gravestone found nearby indicates continued settlement, though the military role of the fort itself ended at an early date.

The fort was probably built in AD 77 or 78 as a result of Agricola's campaign; it then had earthen defences enclosing 1.7ha. In about AD 120, under Hadrian, it was reduced in size and the defences were rebuilt in stone. The progress of this rebuilding is exceptionally well recorded in a series of ten centurial stones (recording completion of a section of wall by a gang, or 'century' of soldiers). These were found in the 19th century. One is now set into the outer doorway of the bar at The Grapes Hotel, Maentwrog. However, the fort was not garrisoned for long after this rebuilding, and may have been abandoned by the middle of the 2nd century AD.

The earthworks as they stand today constitute one of the most interesting Roman sites in Britain, not only because of this sequence of construction, reduction and medieval reuse, but because the fort is surrounded by an exceptionally complete and well preserved series of ancillary buildings: bath-house, *mansio* (guesthouse), practice earthworks, leats, roads and burial monuments. A circular tour may take from one to two hours. Experienced fieldworkers will find the site particularly rewarding.

The clearest of the ancillary earthworks is a small amphitheatre close to the cattle grid: an oval area surrounded by quite high banks; it would have been used as an arena for weapons training. As it stands, the structure is confused by the road, a modern wall and a raised tramway from the Braich Ddu slate quarry which bisects the central arena.

If you have obtained permission, go through the right-hand gate and walk towards the ruined farm which stands close to the north-east gate of the fort. The rampart is well preserved here, fronted by a modern wall built from well-cut, undoubtedly Roman, stone. Walk towards the motte, crossing the levelled platform on which the stone-built headquarters building (*principia*) stood. The motte, surrounded by a sharply cut ditch, covers the narrow stone bank which was the western rampart of the reduced fort. The rounded earthen banks of the original, larger fort can be seen to the west and south-west. Return along the south-western side, where the junction of early and late ramparts is clear. Leave the fort by the south-east gate, where the double guardchambers, central pier and stone blocking (probably original) have been exposed by 19th-century excavations.

On leaving the fort, head towards the bridge abutment. On your right is a large, rectangular platform; beyond is the bath-house excavated in the 19th century. Remains of plastered walls and the stoke-hole (outside the modern field-wall) can still be seen. On the left-hand side of the road was a large courtyard building, probably a *mansio* or guesthouse. The northern wing, in stone, can be easily recognised.

From this group of domestic buildings turn north towards the parade ground and a series of more problematic structures. A narrow opening in the wall leads to the Crown land. Detouring right, follow the turnpike road (now a footpath) and cross the stream to join the Roman road heading south-east past an enclosed cemetery (300m away, just north of the road). The most notable monument is a fine, square, ditched barrow (on private land but visible from the path).

Returning over the river, climb the rocky ridge to the high mound on its summit from which there is a fine view of the fort and parade ground. On the way up you pass low banks, thought to be medieval field boundaries. The roughly square mound with two narrow extensions on either side has been the subject of much debate. It has been variously identified as a saluting base or tribune, the foundation for a catapult, or the base of a temple and colonnade. However, it is surrounded by quarry scoops, and its unusual shape may be fortuitous.

The parade ground – a levelled space about 120m square – is a rare survival. The short military history of the fort may explain its unfinished state: the northern half, in contrast to the crisp southern section, is insufficiently levelled.

The leat which supplied water to the bath-house runs between the 'tribune' and the parade ground. It can be followed for some way up the river. Two other leats carried water through this valley. The upper one, which can be traced for 200–300m to Llyn yr Oerfel, runs at the level of the *principia* and may have reached the fort on a raised launder.

North of the quarry tramway are a number of natural hillocks. On one is what has been claimed to be a catapult emplacement. Seven small square burial mounds, very low, can just be recognised on the nose of the westernmost rise, close to the later field bank. Like the cemetery on the east side, these graves were placed in accordance with Roman tradition, close to the road.

95
Dolddinas Practice Camps, Trawsfynydd

Roman practice camps

1st–2nd century AD

OS 124 SH 735378 U4 (map essential)

From A470 at Trawsfynydd turn E on to Bala road (A4212); continue for 1.2ml (1.9km) and take 1st L, farm road to Bwlch Gwyn Uchaf. Ask permission to leave car near farmyard and walk c.*1ml (1.6km) up rough but clear track to deserted farm, Dolddinas. (Road passable to 4-wheel drive vehicles.) To reach Camp E, walk N on a line from corner of field wall towards nearest pylon. On edge of boggy land its raised bank is visible on L. Others can then be recognised despite confusion of drainage ditches. Those E of river are in rough vegetation and very difficult to find. (Alternative walkers' approaches can be identified from OS map)*

Davies 1968

Military manoeuvres and training exercises were a great part of the life of a Roman soldier, and several manuals written by retired generals emphasise the value of hard work in rough, exposed terrain to keep the men from becoming soft, and to ensure that they were not only fit but skilled in the techniques of camp construction and defensive and offensive warfare.

Throughout the empire there is evidence of this training programme, but Britain has more surviving small 'practice camps' than any other province, and this group at Dolddinas are judged the best preserved in Britain. Practice camps are much smaller than real camps. Corners and entrances are the most difficult parts of the circuit to build properly, and the small size gave troops plenty of experience in them. The training manuals give an insight into the high standard of work expected of the troops, and the rigour of measurement and inspection by officers.

Practice camps normally occur a short distance from the main fort, close to military roads and in a variety of soil conditions to give troops varied experience. The group at Dolddinas, so near the fort at Tomen y Mur (no. 94), is therefore typical. There are five camps in all: two on the east of the river (A and B), and three just north of the farm (C–E). Three are almost exactly the same size, 44m square; the other two are 33m and 22m square. Rather unusually, most of the entrances are unelaborate and do not have the normal extra protection. There is, however, a *titulus* or external bank covering the northern entrance in Camp C, and there is another on the north side of Camp E, the smallest camp, whose low bank and external ditch are quite easy to see. Camps C and D have been badly damaged by modern drains. The visibility of the group varies according to season and light.

A small, round turf mound just south of the road near the field-wall may cover a Roman cremation burial. The modern track, as it runs east–west beside the farm, is part of the Roman road from Tomen y Mur (no. 94) to Caer Gai (see Appendix). It can be easily traced

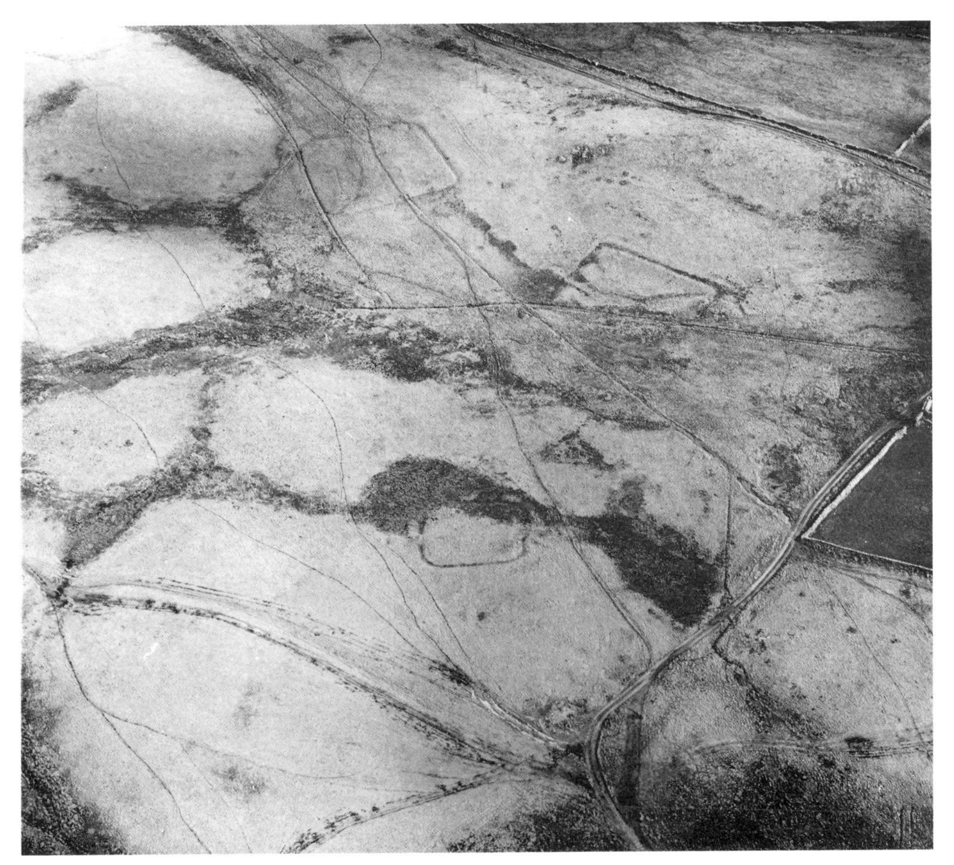

Aerial view of the three western practice camps at Dolddinas, camp E at the bottom, C at the top

for much of this route, and on the return journey it is possible to see (from SH 726372), in an improved field on the north of the river, not only the road but also the regularly placed scoops from which its material was quarried.

96

Pen y Stryd Kilns and Sarn Helen, Trawsfynydd

Roman tile kilns and road

1st–4th centuries AD

OS 124 SH 726319 U1/2

From Trawsfynydd, go S on A470 for 2.5ml (4km) to Bronaber; turn L to Rhiw Goch holiday village, skirting N of it. Follow road till it merges with another coming in from L (1ml, 1.6km, from A470). Leave car by gate at stream. Kilns are 100m from road above first rise on S side of stream. Roman road runs N–S between them and modern road, just E of gas pipeline (easily mistaken for Roman ditches). Bracken can obscure parts of the Roman road in summer

The two kilns are situated conveniently close to the Roman road and a source of water. Suitable clay could be obtained from about

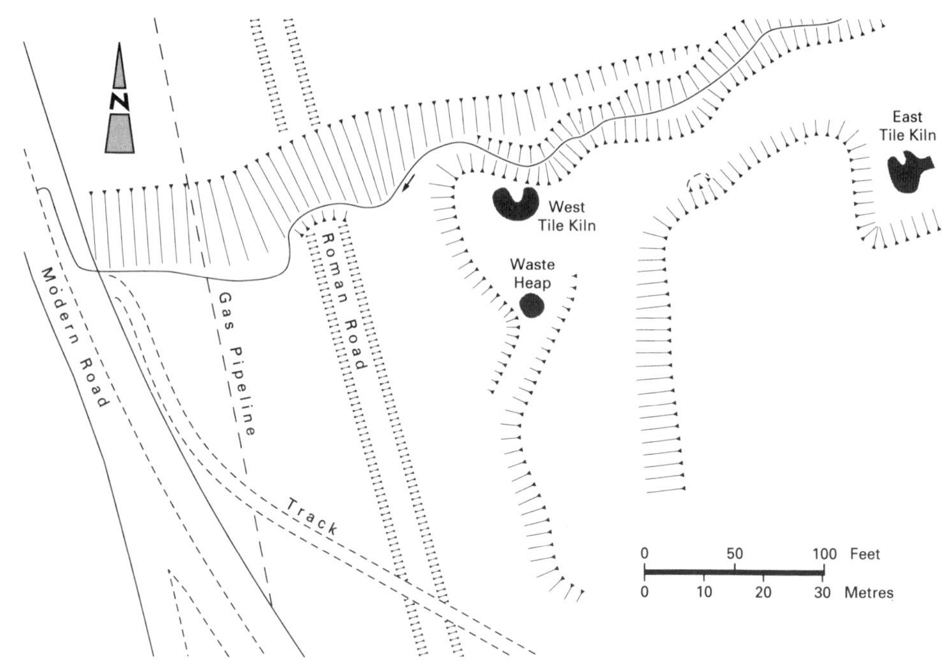

Roman road and tile kilns at Pen y Stryd

1ml (1.6km) away. They lie between the Roman forts at Tomen y Mur (no. 94) and Brithdir (near Dolgellau) and may have supplied both bases with bricks and floor and roof tiles for the fort buildings.

The Roman road from Tomen y Mur to Brithdir is visible as two parallel ditches with a slightly raised roadway or *agger* between them as it runs down the northern slope and approaches the stream, where there must have been a wooden bridge. Unusually for north Wales, it approximates to the classical Roman road construction: ditches about 1m wide, 0.3m deep and 5.5m apart. It can be followed for a short distance on the south side of the stream until it becomes lost where the modern road crosses.

The first kiln is a large semicircular mound with a hollow (the stoke-hole and access point) facing the stream. To the south is a smaller mound which seems to be composed of 'wasters' (broken and fused tiles and bricks). The second kiln is higher up the stream, tucked into a recess in the hillside. Its stokehole also faces the stream.

The hills here contain a lot of evidence for military training manoeuvres, not only by the Roman army but the British one, which had a base at Rhiw Goch from the 1890s to the 1960s (see no. 48).

6
Early Medieval Gwynedd

The 5th century saw the birth, from the ruins of the great Roman empire, of new British kingdoms, their national identities forged in battle against the Saxon invaders and burnished by their bards.

The history of the kingdom of Gwynedd from the 5th to 11th centuries reflects its struggles against its neighbours within Wales, notably with Deheubarth to the south and Powys to the south-east, and against the increasingly powerful Saxon kingdoms of Mercia and Northumbria, which threatened the area east of the river Clwyd. Gwynedd, with its capital at Aberffraw, was naturally strong, its rich Anglesey farmlands protected by the barrier of Snowdonia. At several periods it was Wales's major power, its princes dominating the whole country; but such hegemonies were short-lived, for Celtic society did not recognise primogeniture, and the reluctance of princes to accept any hierarchy among themselves prevented effective consolidation of previous gains. To the swaying struggles of cousins and neighbours were added external forces – the Viking raids of the 9th and early 10th centuries and, in the late 11th century, the advent of the Normans.

The details of this history are few and uncertain; the events and personalities of the 5th century, the nature of the crucial Roman withdrawal and the establishment of Christianity as the dominant religion, are all veiled in legend. One historical figure was assimilated into legend: the Roman general Magnus Maximus, who seized the western empire in AD 383 – traditionally from his base at Segontium – became Macsen Wledig, husband of Helen, a British princess and founding ancestor of many Welsh 'tribes'. The story of Cunedda – reputed to be a 5th-century chieftain from near Hadrian's Wall, invited south to defend north Wales against Irish raiders – is more controversial. In contrast to west Wales, there is little evidence for Irish settlement in north Wales. This may indicate that Cunedda was, indeed, successful, but archaeological investigation has failed to confirm his arrival or that of other settlers from the north.

The association of Vortigern and Emrys with Dinas Emrys, near Beddgelert (no. 110), is also legendary, although excavation there has revealed 5th–6th-century imported pottery. Other legends are associated with older hillforts and with Roman forts, and most leaders would probably have been based within some long-established centre of power. It is tempting to identify the 'citadels' within forts such as Garn Boduan (no. 69) and Carn Pentyrch (see Appendix) as work of this period, but archaeological proof is lacking, since distinctive artefacts are frustratingly rare. There is now no trace of the palace at Aberffraw – the principal court of the princes of Gwynedd from the 6th–13th centuries. Secure within Anglesey, this palace does not seem to have had formidable defences.

Excavation shows a similar continuity of settlement at the lower end of the social scale. There have been no finds of pottery (perhaps replaced by wood once Roman mass-produced bowls were no longer imported) and characteristic tools from this period, but radiocarbon dating has shown that occupation continued at many sites. At Tŷ Mawr, near Holyhead (no. 77), some farms were ruined but fields were still worked, and at Graeanog, near Llanllyfni (see no. 42), the round stone houses were still inhabited during the 6th century.

The first historical (rather than legendary) figure ruling in Gwynedd is Maelgwyn, who is associated with Degannwy (no. 117) and who died in AD 549. He is mentioned by the contemporary writer Gildas, and also features in many of the *Lives* of the north Welsh saints. A reasonably complete list of kings and princes can be compiled though some are little more than names mentioned in the 9th-century *Annales Cambriae* or on gravestones (see no. 101).

In AD 825 the dynasty of Maelgwyn ended and was replaced by that of Merfyn Frych – his son, Rhodri Fawr (844–78), being the first acknowledged leader over both north and south Wales. The court of Gwynedd was then a noted centre of learning and culture where all travelling scholars would be royally entertained. Rhodri was successful against both the old Saxon enemy to the east and the new Viking one from the sea. As in England and Ireland, the Vikings did great damage, especially to wealthy ecclesiastical foundations; their passing is recorded in the names of islands and headlands, but there is little evidence of settlement – in contrast to northern England and Ireland, where they established successful kingdoms.

The raids eased in the early 10th century, during the reign of Rhodri's grandson, Hywel ap Cadell, better known as Hywel Dda ('the Good'). His main base was in the south, and his was a time of peaceful consolidation, with the introduction and widespread use of coinage leading to an expansion of trade. But he is best known for his codification of the customary law of Wales, from which a picture emerges of a broad social pyramid with ruler and noblemen at the top, freemen in the middle, and, at the bottom, bondmen or even slaves, tied to the land, living in 'bondvills' close to the *llys* or court, where they worked the lord's land.

When Hywel died in AD 950, disunity returned; 35 Welsh princes were killed within 120 years either by Saxons, Vikings or fellow Welshmen. In 1012 Olaf, a Norseman from Dublin, was describing himself as 'King of Anglesey and Gwynedd' and in 1018 the line of Merfyn Frych was ousted by a new dynasty, whose most notable member, Gruffudd ap Llywelyn (1039–63), reunited Wales under his sole control. But by the end he had overreached himself, attracting retaliation from Edward the Confessor's lieutenant, Harold Godwinson.

Very little of this history – from the *Annales Cambriae*, which supported the legitimacy of Merfyn Frych's dynasty, and the less reliable *Historia Brittonum* of Nennius – is complemented by archaeological or architectural evidence. There are no traces of Gwynedd's palace at Aberffraw, nor of Deheubarth's at Dynefwr, and lesser centres are equally elusive. Some hillforts indicate that reoccupation and farming continued on some old sites during the 5th–11th centuries, but there are no distinctive structures or settlements attributable to this period.

Today the only visible remains from the 5th and 6th centuries AD are those of Christianity. This religion had been well-established in Roman Britain, but whether it survived here after the empire's collapse is debatable. Certainly, whether coming to known communities or launched into the unknown, a great wave of missionaries and preachers from western Gaul and from Ireland were sailing the Irish Sea during these centuries. The evidence of their success lies in church dedications, in the legends they generated and, most tangibly, in their gravestones and those of their flock. Few of these stones are overtly Christian in their markings, but the practice of identifying a grave by name, of east–west alignment, and the absence of personal belongings for the purely spiritual journey, are traditions still followed in Christian countries today. Most have been found close to churches, emphasising the antiquity and continuity of these sites, even though all trace of the original building is lost.

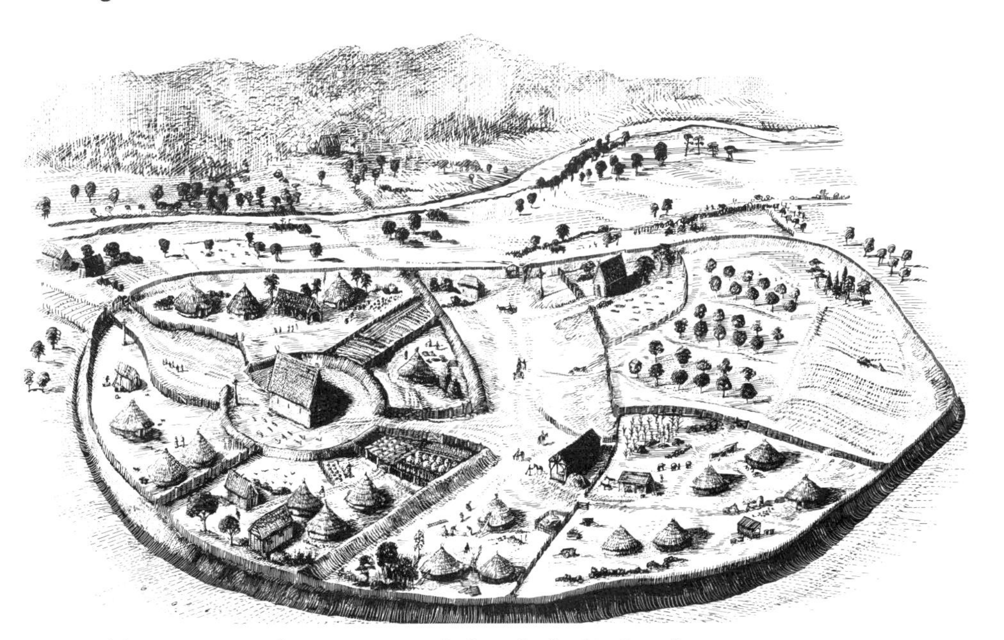

A view of the monastery of Bangor as it might have looked in the 8th century AD

These memorials are normally quite small stones, smooth but not carefully dressed, standing at the head of the grave. The inscriptions usually read vertically from the top, although there are also horizontal ones; the message is normally very simple: 'X lies here' (a Gaulish formula), or 'The stone of X, son of Y' (the preferred Irish form), or, later, 'X, son of Y, lies here.' Sometimes a profession is given, or a place of origin. The language is Latin, but the names are usually Celtic, adapted to Latin grammatical form. The inscription on the stone at Tywyn (no. 113) is in Welsh, the earliest 'public' use of the language.

Dating depends upon the lettering style and formulae used. In the late 5th–early 6th centuries the letters are simple capitals; during the 6th century a cursive hand becomes more common, and in the 7th century a rather complicated half-uncial script is preferred. One or two stones refer to historical characters or events, which enables them to be dated more closely (see nos 101 and 109). From the 9th century names become rarer; graves were marked with simpler cross-inscribed stones, like those at Llangaffo (see no. 102).

Despite the Viking threat, the 10th century was a period of growth and development for the monasteries. In Ireland and Northumbria, art in many forms flourished – as it did in south Wales, where there are still many large stone crosses. Fewer have survived in north Wales, but the two from Penmon (see no. 103) and the fragments from Bangor (see no. 144) and other sites indicate the wealth now lost to us. No buildings of this period survive at any of the *clasau*, the early monasteries at Bangor, Penmon, Llangaffo, Beddgelert, Bardsey, Anelog, Penmachno and Clynnog. Like their contemporaries in Ireland, they would have consisted of several small churches, probably built of wood, with the huts of the individual monks scattered amongst them, the whole surrounded by a wall. The enclosure was usually circular, and its line may still be recognised in the circular churchyards of many old foundations (see no. 99) or in the street layouts, as at Bangor.

Key to Transcriptions

This chapter uses the following conventions in the transcription of early Christian gravestone inscriptions:

The inscriptions are written in capital letters. Editorial insertions within inscriptions (also in capitals), and the translations of the inscriptions themselves appear in italics.

Square brackets indicate letters which are assumed, but indecipherable on the stone.

Round brackets indicate letters or words which are inserted for comprehension or translation, but which are not present on the stone.

An oblique line indicates the beginning of a new line in the inscription (quite often in the middle of a word).

Drawing of the eroding edge of Towyn y Capel at the time of Stanley's excavations

97
Tywyn y Capel, Trearddur Bay
Early Christian graveyard and church site
5th–17th century AD

OS 114 SH 256790 U1

Site is on B4545 in Trearddur Bay, 1.5ml (2.4km) S of Holyhead. Park in main car park and leave by path in RH corner; site is immediately on R abutting promenade

Stanley 1846

This now rather featureless sand dune is all that remains of a large early Christian cemetery which surrounded a chapel dedicated to St Bride (Bridget). A noticeboard fronting the site tells the legend of her arrival from Ireland on a square of turf which took root here and grew into the mound on top of which she built a church.

The chapel was still standing in 1780 but by 1846, when excavated by W O Stanley, it had collapsed and was buried in sand. He recorded a simple building, 10m by 6.5m, with deep foundations protected by a mass of stone. Many human bones came from beneath the chapel, and slab-lined graves were found all around it, up to five layers deep. Many of these 'long cist graves' may have dated from the 5th century, but records suggest that the graveyard continued in use up to the 17th century AD. Until the promenade was built, autumn storms used to expose graves in this mound every year, and bones were frequently found on the beach.

98
Llanbadrig Church and Stone, Cemaes Bay
Early Christian stone
9th–11th century AD

OS 114 SH 375946 R1

From Cemaes Bay, take A5025 E towards Amlwch; church is signposted at 1st L and all subsequent junctions. NT car park; many

Early gravestone in Llanbadrig church

footpaths begin from here – Dinas Gynfor (no. 59) is 1ml (1.6km) E along coastal footpath. Church is normally open on Monday and Wednesday afternoons in summer

Nash-Williams 1950, no. 7

The early gravestone stands against the west wall of the church. It is a narrow, rectangular stone, decorated with a crudely carved wheel-cross above a simple linear cross. This is perhaps the most inept of the early gravestones from Anglesey, but the church itself is worth visiting. It is a simple, pleasing building in a beautiful position, and notable both for the blue tiles of Islamic design placed in the sanctuary by Lord Stanley (W O Stanley's twin brother), who was a convert to Islam at the end of the 19th century, and for its recent double restoration. It was restored at great expense in 1987, only to be burnt by vandals in 1989. This tiny parish managed to raise the money for new repairs. They deserve support!

99
Llanbabo Churchyard, Llanddeusant

Early medieval graveyard

5th century AD onwards

OS 114 SH 378867 U1

From Llanddeusant church (2.2ml, 3.5km, SE of Llanfaethlu), drive N for 0.6ml (1km); take 2nd R (signposted Rhoscoch); after 1.8ml (2.8km) turn L overlooking lake; Llanbabo church is 300m. Key to church is kept at Bryn Drofa, 1st farm on L, 0.25ml (400m) beyond Llanddeusant turn. Parking for 2 cars

This is one of the best and most attractive examples of a circular churchyard in Anglesey – a quiet and meditative spot. The presence of a circular churchyard is a good indication of an early foundation, even when the church itself has been rebuilt.

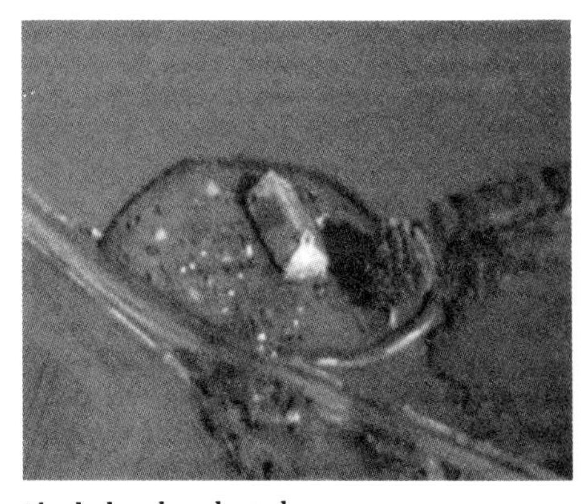

Llanbabo churchyard

The church here is a small and simple building, typical of many on the island. The walls are probably 12th century (characteristic chevron carving has been reset above the south door) but the east window was remodelled in the late 14th century. A carved stone head of uncertain date is set above the south door.

The church contains a very fine early 14th-century carving of the legendary King Pabo, one of a group carved by the same hand which includes the Eva Stone in Bangor Cathedral (no. 144). The interior is simple and moving.

100
Bodfeddan Stone, Llanfaelog

Early Christian stone

6th century AD

OS 114 SH 356746 U1

Stone stands beside A4080 (A5–Rhosneigr), 1.5ml (2.5km) S of A5/A4080 junction; on L behind wall opposite isolated cottage

Nash-Williams 1950, no. 9

This stone, over 2m high by 1m wide, is unusually large for a Christian gravestone, and it might be a prehistoric standing stone reused in the 6th century AD. The ground has been disturbed by quarrying, and there is no record of what graves or other features were found there. A notable grave would usually be found close to a church and surrounded by other burials.

The two-line inscription, CUNOGUSI (the I is turned horizontally) / HIC IACIT, or: (*The stone*) *of Cunogussus. He lies here*, is set vertically in the centre of the north-eastern face. The U and N are the easiest letters to see. The Celtic name Cunogussus is more common in Ireland than Wales, and is thought to survive in the name of the nearby village, Pencarnisiog, 'Headland of Cunogussus'. The 6th-century date is based on the use of simple Roman letters and the formula '*hic iacit*' which was popular in Gaul at this time.

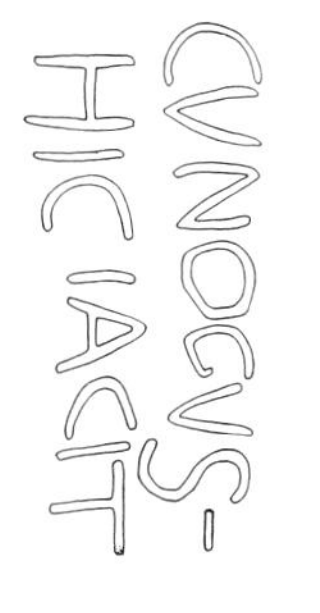

Inscription on the Bodfeddan stone

101
Cadfan Stone, Llangadwaladr

Early Christian stone

7th century AD

OS 114 SH 384693 R1

On A4080 in Llangadwaladr just E of junction. Church is behind old vicarage on L. Key is kept by Mrs Rockey, Wayside, Hermon, 0.5ml (0.8km) to SE on same road, tel: 01407 840418

Nash-Williams 1950, no. 13

The stone now set in the north wall of the church, opposite the door, is the most important gravestone in Anglesey – a historic document of multiple significance.

It was undoubtedly found close to the church, since before the 19th-century restoration it was used as a lintel to the south door, and thus it demonstrates that this site was the royal burial ground associated with the court at Aberffraw on the other side of the river. This slight separation of secular and religious centres is typical of early royal capitals.

The inscription refers to one of the early kings of Gwynedd – Cadfan, who died about AD 625 – so it provides a key to dating other stones where a similar lettering style is used. The lettering is a mixture of Roman capitals (C I N O X) and half-uncials, a manuscript

The gravestone of King Cadfan

hand. The A and three variant forms of M are reminiscent of lettering in the famous *Book of Kells* in Trinity College, Dublin.

The grandiloquent phraseology has echoes of the Imperial Byzantine court and reflects the far-flung European contacts, the ambitions, and indeed the standards of elegance and learning, at the court of Gwynedd in the 7th century.

The stone was designed to stand upright at the head of the grave, the cross vertical above the inscription, which would have been read downwards from the top right-hand corner. It has been reset horizontally, which makes it easier for us to read it. CATAMANUS / REX SAPIENTISI/MUS OPINATISIM/US OMNIUM REG/UM, or: *King Catamanus* (Cadfan in Welsh) *wisest* (*and*) *most renowned of all kings* (*lies here*).

Nothing survives of the church of Cadfan's day, or of his grandson, Cadwaladr, to whom the present church is dedicated. It is likely to have been a wooden building. The present church, however, though mostly post-dating the period covered in this guide, contains some of the best ecclesiastical architecture in Anglesey. The south transept, built in 1661 by Anne, widow of Col. Hugh Owen of Bodowen, is a splendid example of very late Gothic; their Renaissance memorial is very fine, and the east window in the chancel contains the only medieval glass to survive in quantity on Anglesey. Even the 19th-century gargoyles are worth looking at!

102
Llangaffo Cross and Gravestones

Early Christian cross, inscribed stone and gravestones

7th–12th century AD

OS 114 SH 446685 U1 (cross and inscribed stone R1)

Site is at N end of Llangaffo (2.2ml, 3.5km, NW of Newborough on B4419). Key to church is kept at cottage at entrance to graveyard

Nash-Williams 1950, nos 14–24, 35

The bleak 19th-century church in this small ridge-top village gives no hint of the historical importance of the site in the early Middle Ages, or of the wealth of sculpture which still survives here today.

St Gaffo is mentioned as a friend of St Cybi, a member of the circle of 6th-century saints who were the chief evangelisers of north Wales. It is likely that a monastery was established here from an early date.

The earliest stone in the collection dates from the 7th century; it was not found at the church, but at Fron Deg about 800m to the south. This stone is in the sacristy. The inscription, written horizontally on a rather awkward piece of schist, is in a mixture of capitals and half-uncials like those on the Cadfan stone (no. 101). It reads [G]VI/[R]NIN / FILIU[S] / CUURI[S] / CINI / ERE/XIT / HUNC / LAPI/DEM. The name is very uncertain, but has been read as *Gvernin* (perhaps an early form of Gwern), *son of Cuuris Cini, set up this stone*. The wording suggests that this is not a gravestone but some other memorial. The formula is often used later by those who set up crosses.

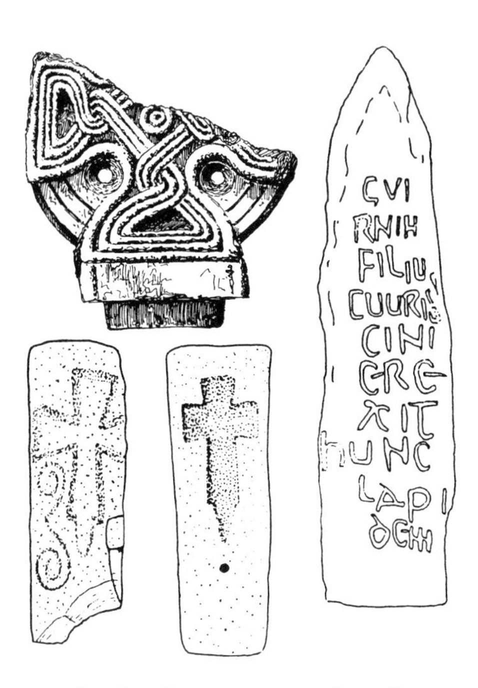

Crosshead and gravestones at Llangaffo

The broken head of one such cross is lying beside the sacristy door. It was a wheel-cross cut from a single piece of stone, with a projecting tenon by which it would have been fixed to a tall shaft. The head is of 10th–11th-century type with the same triple-beaded strap decoration on both faces. When complete it would have looked like those at Penmon (see no. 103), and would probably have stood at the entrance to the monastic enclosure. The presence of this cross-head and the very badly eroded shaft which stands near the foundations of the old church in the graveyard shows that this was a major site, perhaps equal in importance to Penmon in the 10th century. The tall wheel-crosses show a combination of Scandinavian and Irish styles, but the cross-shaft with its wheel-head carved onto the face is a type more common in south Wales.

The exceptional feature of Llangaffo is the number of cross-inscribed gravestones which have survived at the site. Five stand against a low wall opposite the church door, and two pieces of another may be found built into the graveyard wall facing the road. The largest stone among the group by the church door is 12th–13th-century in date, the others belong to the 9th–11th centuries. They all have outline crosses with barred or expanded arms and spiked shafts, a design imitating wooden crosses driven into the ground above a grave. The one in the graveyard wall (in the second course below the coping in the section between the telegraph pole and the gate to the war memorial) is also inscribed with spirals, very like the fragments built into Llangeinwen church wall (see Appendix), and indicative of a local school of sculptors.

The old church whose foundations can be recognised by the modern war memorial contained features dating from the 12th and 15th centuries. It was demolished in 1846 when the village population outgrew it.

103
Penmon Crosses, Church, Priory and Holy Well

Early medieval monastery and later priory

10th–13th century AD

OS 114 SH 630807 U1 Cadw

From Beaumaris, take B5109 N for 1.7ml (2.7km) and turn R at crossroads; continue for 1.1ml (1.7km), turn R at T-junction and continue into priory car park. The church is open throughout the day, all year

Nash-Williams 1950, nos 1, 37, 38

This group of monuments – sculpted crosses, the 12th-century church and 13th-century conventual buildings – encapsulates the development of Christian history on Anglesey.

The original monastery is reputed to have been founded by St Seiriol, one of the 6th-century preachers, and a friend of St Cybi. The monastery prospered, and in the 10th century fine crosses were set up at its gates, but the Viking raids have destroyed all other evidence of this date. During the 12th-century revival under Gruffudd ap Cynan and Owain Gwynedd the abbey church was rebuilt, and it remains the finest and most complete example of a church of this period in Gwynedd. In the 13th century the Celtic monasteries were persuaded by Llywelyn ap Iorwerth to adopt a more regular rule, and Penmon eventually became an Augustinian priory with quite substantial conventual buildings. The priory survived the Edwardian conquest and expanded slightly, but was dissolved in 1538. The buildings passed into the hands of the Bulkeleys of Beaumaris, who enclosed much of the land as a deer park and built a fine dovecote. They also converted the prior's lodging into a rather attractive house. Throughout this time the priory church remained in use, as it does today.

The two high crosses are the only tangible evidence for the early medieval monastery. Both are now inside the church (entered through the chancel). One had been used as a window lintel in the later refectory; the other used to stand in the deer park but was moved to the church to prevent further weathering. Both would probably have stood close to the gates into the monastic enclosure.

The smaller cross is in the south transept; the one from the deer park is in the nave. Light switches to illuminate them and the nave are in the north transept.

The small cross is carved from a single piece of stone: the head is a cross within a cross, a plain wheel-cross carved on a disc with very short projecting arms (one was cut off when used as a lintel). Apart from the cross and two animal heads within the fret pattern on the sides, the decoration is entirely non-figural. The patterns vary, but the scheme is the same on both sides.

The deer park cross is larger, and retains its original base. The head is a separate piece (compare no. 102). The decorative scheme is more complex and includes one figural panel in the manner of the Irish pictorial crosses which fulfilled a teaching role. Unfortunately weathering makes this very difficult to see, but earlier photographs show a figure between two standing beasts, who whisper in his ears – the 'Temptation of St Antony in the Desert', a favourite theme in these monasteries where the hermit was so much admired. There are other figures, perhaps a hunting scene, on the bottom on the left-hand side. The very striking ring-chain motif on the back of the shaft was a particularly popular pattern in the Isle of Man during the 10th century.

The square font at the end of the nave is decorated with three panels of very similar fret decoration, and it is possible that it was originally the base of another cross. Its origin is uncertain. It came to light in the last century in a stonemason's yard in Beaumaris.

All three of these pieces belong to a school of sculpture which absorbed stylistic traits from northern English, Viking and Irish art. They date from the late 10th or early 11th centuries, perhaps from the relatively

The cross formerly in the deer park at Penmon

peaceful reign of Gruffudd ap Llywelyn, and the sculptors who created them may have had close connections with Cheshire.

The cruciform church is the most complete 12th-century structure on Anglesey, built during the reign of Owain Gwynedd, the Golden Age of Welsh independence. The nave is believed to be a little older (AD 1140) than the tower and the transepts (AD 1160–70). The large chancel was added by Llywelyn ap Iorwerth in AD 1220–40, perhaps because the newly reorganised canons needed this space, since the rest of the church remained in parochial use. It was entirely rebuilt on the old foundations in 1855.

The nave is quite plain, with small, high windows. The south door has a carved tympanum, now rather weathered, showing a crouching beast with head turned back to bite its own tail. (Open door from inside and rebar it on return.)

The squat, conical tower is a well-known landmark. At ground level the crossing has richly carved pillars and arches. The decoration – chevrons and chequer patterns – belongs to an international romanesque style, but details suggest that inspiration, and perhaps skills, were derived from Ireland, where the princes of Gwynedd had close contacts. The south transept is embellished with a blind arcade of chevron-decorated arches. A series of carved stones found during restoration have been reset in the south transept, where the small window contains fragments of medieval glass.

The conventual buildings date from the 13th century, when the positions of Penmon and its sister foundation on Ynys Seiriol (Puffin Island) were regularised. The cloister, now a garden, stood on the south side of the chancel – an unusual, easterly position which reinforces the idea that the nave was a public church. The eastern range of buildings has gone, but the southern one, containing the refectory with dormitory above, still stands. Enter by a door in the south side which gives access to a cellar. A 12th-century gravestone which had been used as a lintel to this door stands nearby. The beam-holes for the refectory floor and the large windows which lit this dining room can be seen above. Meals were accompanied by spiritual readings, and the reader's seat can be seen beside the window in the south-east corner. In the 16th century a califactory or warm common room was built against the end of the refectory (notice the straight joint and ground-floor fireplace). The western range was occupied by the prior's lodging, modified as a private house in the 18th century.

The Holy Well is a spring emerging from a cliff behind the church. It is reached by a path on the left, just beyond the car park, which skirts the monastic fish-pond. Although it is the source of water for the monastery, the structures here are all relatively modern. The roofed inner chamber around the pool is of brick, and dates from 1710. The lower courses and the open antechamber with seats to either side may be somewhat earlier, but no medieval finds were made during recent excavations. The so-called 'cell', beneath the cliff on the left, is of uncertain date and purpose. Its angularity does not suggest a 6th-century hermitage, nor does it support any association with St Seiriol.

104
Memorials at Llanfaglan Church, Caernarfon

Early Christian and medieval gravestones

5th/6th century and 13th century AD

OS 115 SH 455607 U2

From Caernarfon, take A487 S, cross Seiont bridge and take 1st R, then turn immediately R again to Coed Helen. Llanfaglan church is 3ml (4.75km) along coast road; path to church is signposted. 13th-century stones can be seen in 'porch' but earlier stone is inside locked church; key is kept at 4 Uwchmenai, Saron (1ml, 1.5km, S of Llanfaglan village), tel: 01286 831335

Nash-Williams 1950, no. 89

Llanfaglan church

This is a beautiful little church with an unchanged 18th-century interior; it is in an exceptionally peaceful setting with wonderful views all around. The approach road provides a superb view of Caernarfon Castle (no. 128).

The porch has an air of great antiquity but was built in the 19th century, incorporating medieval roof beams. A long window opening has been formed on the east side using two 13th-century gravestones as lintel and sill. Both have long-stemmed crosses (cross pattée) but bear no name. The lower one may commemorate a sailor since it has a masted ship carved beside the cross stem.

The 5th/6th-century inscribed stone has been used as a lintel to the north door. It is a large stone, 2m long, which would originally have been upright with the inscription reading vertically, FILI LOVERNII / ANATEMORI, or: (*The stone of*) *Anatemorus, son of Lovernius*.

105
Llystyn Gwyn Inscribed/ Ogam Stone, Bryncir

Early Christian stone

6th century AD

OS 123 SH 482455 U2

From Porthmadog, take A487 NW for 7.2ml (11.5km); stone is up 1st farm road on R after sharp bend at Bryncir gravel pit; leave car in lay-by on L on A487 just beyond farm turning. Take care crossing road. Farm road is a public footpath, and owner allows access to yard

Nash-Williams 1950, no. 84

The stone, which was found in about 1901 on the flat-topped hill just south of the farm, is now set into the garden wall to the right of the farmyard. Because of the frame it is easy to recognise, but, if the light is flat, it is often difficult to see the alphabetic inscription in the top right-hand corner, and even more difficult to make out the Ogam letters on the right-hand edge.

The inscription records: ICORI(*X*) FILIUS / POTENT/INI, or: *Icorix, son of Potentinus* in Roman capitals of 6th-century style on three lines. This is a normal form found on many Welsh memorials, but this stone is unusual because the information is repeated in Irish Ogam script up the right-hand edge. This simple 'tally-mark' script of 20 letters is formed by groups of straight or angled cuts to right, left or across the sharp edge of the stone. Such bilingual inscriptions are quite common in south-west Wales, where Irish settlement was dense in the post-Roman period, but this is the only Ogam inscription from north-west Wales. It reads upwards: ICORIGAS, or: (*the stone*) *of Icorix*.

Returning down the hill you can see the rampart of Pen Llystyn Roman fort. The 1st-century AD fort was quite large, but as control was established the size of the garrison was reduced. All the interior has now been removed by gravel digging, but the plan of the buildings was salvaged as quarrying advanced.

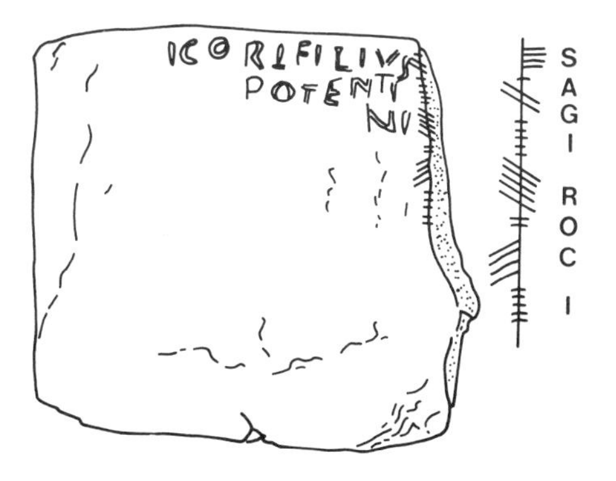

Stone with Latin and Ogam inscriptions, Llystyn Gwyn

106

Inscribed Stones, Llanaelhaearn

Early Christian stones

5th–6th century AD

OS 123 SH 387448 R1

From Pwllheli, go N on A499 for 6.3ml (10km) and turn L on to B4417; turn 1st L to parish church; parking for 1 or 2 cars. Key is kept at Bryn Llan, on corner where you turned in

Nash-Williams 1950, nos 86, 87

The earlier and more interesting of these two stones is in the north transept of the church. It was found in 1865 in a field next to the church. It is a pillar-stone, 1.3m high, with a two-line vertical inscription in Roman capitals reading downwards (now set horizontally). It reads ALIORTUS ELMETIACO(*S*) / HIC IACET, or: *Aliortus a man of Elmet lies here*. Elmet is the district around modern Leeds, an independent British kingdom in the 5th century, but soon swallowed by the Saxon advance. The stone shows the persistence of local loyalties even when people had lived and died far away from home. It is also interesting that the correct classical form IACET is used, not IACIT, which is more common in Wales. The reference to birthplace and a consciousness of local loyalties is seen again at Penmachno (no. 109), where a citizen of Gwynedd is commemorated.

The second stone, in the graveyard just to the right of the path to the church door, has a less interesting inscription: ME.LI.TV[*S*], or: *Melitus* (*lies here*), but it is an important survival because there is every chance that it

The two stones at Llanaelhaearn

is in its original position. Another stone of a similar size has been carefully built into the wall by the door, but there is no sign of any mark or inscription on it. A stone marked with an M is built into the outer face of the churchyard wall just above and to the left of a very large stone opposite the last house in the terrace.

Gravestone of the doctor from Llangian

107
Melus Stone, Llangian

Early Christian stone

5th–6th century AD

OS 123 SH 295289 U1

From Pwllheli, go SW on A499 for 6.2ml (10km) and at Abersoch turn R to Llangian. Stone is in graveyard on S of parish church in centre of village. Inscription is easiest to see in late morning light

Nash-Williams 1950, no. 92

This is a simple granite pillar with a vertical inscription in three lines written in simple and rather inelegant Roman capitals. The inscription reads MELI MEDICI / FILI MARTINI / IACIT, or: (*The stone of*) *Melus the doctor, son of Martinus. He lies* (*here*). The names here are both Latin rather than Celtic, and the stone is notable for the reference to the man's profession. This is rare in itself, and the profession of 'doctor' even rarer. It is also an important stone because it might be in its original position over the grave; though having supported a sundial in the last century (note the flattened top), it may well have been moved.

108
Anelog Stones, Aberdaron

Early Christian stones

Early 6th century AD

OS 123 SH 173263 U1

Stones are in parish church just above beach at E end of village. Church is open for most of day in summer. Inscriptions can be seen best in morning light

Nash-Williams 1950, nos 77, 78

These two stones were found at Capel Anelog, a site on the eastern slope of Mynydd Anelog, a few miles north of Aberdaron. It may have been the original monastery of the community which was later established on Bardsey and at Aberdaron. Both stones date from the early 6th century and look as if they were carved by the same sculptor.

Both record the graves of priests (*presbyter*). One is inscribed VERACIUS / PBR / HIC / IACIT, or: *Veracius the priest lies here*. The letters PBR with a line above are an abbreviation for PRESBYTER, shortened 'by

Gravestones of two monks from Anelog near Aberdaron

contraction': by omitting letters from the centre of the word. This system originated in Hellenistic Greek but became popular in Latin writing in the 4th century. The distinctive form of the capitals, with forked serifs, is also thought to show Greek influence.

The other stone reads SENACUS / PRSB / HIC IACIT / CVM MULTITV/D(*I*)NEM / FRATRVM //PRESB(*IT*)E[R], or: *Senacus the priest lies here with the multitude of the brethren. Priest.* The last word, very faintly written in a different style near the bottom of the stone, seems to be a later addition – a gloss on the abbreviation PRSB which, though unique, would not seem to need explanation. The phrase CUM MULTITVDINEM FRATRVM is grammatically incorrect, an indication that people were by then beginning to find difficulty with Latin.

Aberdaron had a monastic community linked to that on Bardsey, the centre of great pilgrimages. The fine 12th-century west door and the extension of the church in the early 16th century are evidence of the wealth these pilgrims brought.

109
Inscribed Stones, Penmachno

Early Christian stones

Late 5th–mid-6th century AD

OS 115   SH 790506   U1

Stones are in Penmachno parish church in centre of village, on B4406 3.8ml (6km) S of Betws y Coed. Church is open in summer

Nash-Williams 1950, nos 101–104a

Three of these five stones were found in the immediate vicinity of the church. The others were found close to the Roman road which runs south to Tomen y Mur (no. 94) – one from Rhiw Bach (SH 740460) and the other possibly from Beddau Gwŷr Ardudwy (the graves of the men of Ardudwy), a legendary site near Bryn y Castell, Ffestiniog (no. 72).

The content of the inscriptions gives a moving picture of a community of the 6th century anxious to retain some link with the firm political structures of Rome and the secure society that their ancestors had known before the withdrawal of the legions.

The four earliest stones are set against the chancel wall, the Carausius stone above, the Cantiorix stone below on the left.

The Cantiorix stone, which may have come from Ffestiniog, is a pillar-stone with a vertical inscription in Roman capitals on the front and continuing on the left-hand side. CANTIORI(*X*) HIC IACIT / [V]ENEDOTIS CIVE(*S*) FVIT / [C]ONSOBRINO(*S*) / MA[G]LI / MAGISTRATI, or: *Cantorix lies here. He was a citizen of Venedos* (*and*) *cousin of Maglos the magistrate* (the final I is laid horizontally as on the Bodfeddan stone, no. 100). There are many points of interest in the inscription. The terms 'citizen' and 'magistrate' appear in no other British inscription of this date, though on the Continent there are Christians who mention their offices within the secular hierarchy. What is amazing is that such a hierarchy should have still existed, or be claimed to exist, here in Venedotia so long after the legions had left. The name Venedos is the Celtic/British form of the Welsh Gwynedd and, like the reference to Elmet on the stone at Llanaelhaearn (no. 106), it reveals the existence of formally recognised administrative units or kingdoms. It also shows that boasting about your powerful relations is not new!

The next stone, found near The Eagles Hotel, is another with interesting political implications. The stone has been split; a line of vertical lettering and half the horizontal words have been lost. The damaged inscription now reads [ ] FILI AVITORI / IN TE(*M*)PO[RE] / IVSTI[NI] / CON[SULI(*S*)], or: (*The stone of. . .,*) *son of Avitorius* (*Set up*) *in the time of Justinus the consul.* Justinus was consul (or chief magistrate) in Constantinople in the eastern Roman empire in AD 540, almost the last one whose consular year was used as a record of date. Inscriptions naming him occur particularly often in Burgundy, a

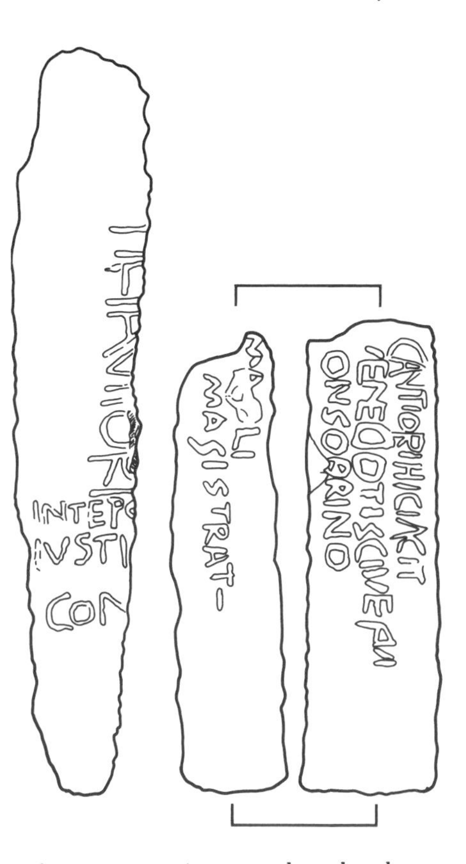

Early gravestones in Penmachno church (above and right)

region of Gaul much visited by British and Irish pilgrims and scholars. Someone from this community in Penmachno must have been among them.

The Carausius stone was found in 1820 near the Rhiw Bach quarry at the end of the valley. Its interest lies in the *chi-rho* symbol which precedes the inscription. Such unambiguous Christian symbols are surprisingly rare. It reads: CARAVSIVS / HIC IACIT / IN HOC CON/ GERIES LA/PIDVM, or: *Carausius lies here in this heap of stones*. The Latin syntax here has several mistakes, but the lettering is very clear and careful. The reference to a heap of stones suggests that the burial was beneath a cairn like the Bronze Age ones. No such monuments survive over graves of this date, but Christian burials have occasionally been inserted into prehistoric barrows.

The broken stone in this group was found while dismantling the old church. The inscription is in the standard form [ ]ORIA (*H*)IC IACIT, or: . . . *oria lies here*, written vertically.

The fifth stone, standing at the other end

near the font, is a later (7th–9th-century) gravestone marked only with a cross. It demonstrates both the survival of the religious community and the way in which fashions in monuments change uniformly (compare Llangaffo, no. 102). The church continued to be important, for Iorwerth 'Snubnose', the father of Llywelyn the Great, is reputedly buried here, but the sixth stone, a 13th-century gravestone, cannot be proven to be his.

110
Dinas Emrys, Beddgelert

Early medieval defended settlement

5th–12th century AD

OS 115 SH 606492 R4 NT

Site is on A498 1.2ml (2km) NE of Beddgelert. Owing to vulnerability of remains and difficulty of access, all visitors must first contact NT warden at Beddgelert (tel: 01766 890293, or via shop during summer). A way-marked route (45 mins attractive walk) brings you to summit up NE ridge. Western ramparts are fragile and dangerous; exploration is not advised. Bracken can obscure inner rampart and pond in summer

Morris 1980, pp 29–31; Savory 1960; Edwards and Lane 1988, pp 55–7

This is a legendary fortress, believed to be the setting of one of the most enigmatic tales in early British history – a tale which encompasses both the fantastic world of wizards and magic and the reality of the political struggle, in the ruins of the Roman empire, between native British and invading Saxon.

The story, left to us by Nennius, the 9th-century writer, concerns Vortigern, a genuine historical figure of the 5th century AD. He was the British king who invited the Saxons into his kingdom to help defend it. They then ousted him from his land and he had to flee westward, searching for a strong site on

The rock of Dinas Emrys viewed from Sygyn, across the valley. The tower on the summit is obscured by trees

which to establish a fortress. His wizards identified a site in Gwynedd and he ordered building to commence, but each time work began the materials disappeared overnight. His wizards declared that the spell could only be broken by finding a child without a father, killing him and sprinkling his blood upon the rocks.

A search throughout Britain eventually found such a child, who was brought to the fortress, but the boy questioned his fate. Under interrogation by the boy, whose name was Ambrosius (Emrys the Overlord), the wizards had to admit their ignorance of the true situation and the boy revealed that the king had been trying to build his tower on a lake. He also prophesied that in the lake they would find two vessels, one inside the other, and between them a white cloth.

When these things had been found he ordered the cloth to be opened, and inside were two sleeping dragons, one red and one white. When these awoke they fought for possession of the white cloth, first the white and then the red dragon gaining ground, until finally the red dragon chased the white one across the lake and the cloth vanished. The boy interpreted the sign for Vortigern and his wizards, identifying the red dragon with the native British people and the white with the new invaders, the Saxons. He predicted the final victory of the British, but declared that Vortigern would never succeed in building the fortress here. He, Ambrosius, as son of one of the consuls of the Roman people (an interesting indication, like the Penmachno inscriptions, see no. 109, that legitimacy of power still sprang from the Roman tradition) would remain on the hill – hence its name, Dinas Emrys ('City of Emrys').

Excavations in 1954–5 showed that there had been some occupation of the hilltop in the late Roman period (3rd–4th century AD), but that the rough stone banks at the west end were later, and might be contemporary with the period of Vortigern. They consist of a series of two, or possibly three, poorly built stone ramparts down the western end of the rock (inaccessible to visitors) and lengths of thinner walling on the north and south sides. The poor construction of the ramparts and the strategy of linking crags rather than providing a full circuit is thought to be characteristic of post-Roman defences. The discovery of sherds of broken amphorae from the eastern Mediterranean, and a pottery roundel with a Christian *chi-rho* symbol, indicate that the hilltop was indeed occupied in the 5th century AD – and by those who could afford to import wine! The buildings of this period are difficult to interpret: both timber and stone structures were found in the deep hollow around the spring and on the level shelf behind the inner rampart at the west end.

The archaeological features of the hilltop appear, in an astonishing way, to correspond to the situation described in the ancient story. It is certainly a most precipitous rock, which might well be judged the strongest natural fortress in Gwynedd, but the most notable coincidence is the discovery of evidence for 5th–6th-century AD occupation around the spring or pool in the centre of the site. Its present regular shape, however, is due to the construction of a medieval cistern within it. The footings of a rectangular stone tower now stand on the rock above the pool, but this, of course, is a great deal later than Vortigern and Ambrosius, and later than Nennius, who wrote down the story in the 9th century AD. There is no documentary evidence for its construction but it is likely to belong to the reign of Llywelyn ap Iorwerth (d.AD 1240), the most active castle builder among the Welsh princes.

111

Llanaber Stones, Barmouth

Early Christian stones

Late 5th–early 6th century AD

OS 124 SH 599180 U1

Stones are in Llanaber church on seaward side of A496, 1.9ml (3km) n of Barmouth harbour. Neighbouring garage more visible than church. Park in lay-by; church usually open. Stones stand against N wall at W end where light is good

Nash-Williams 1950, nos 271, 272

Neither of these stones was found in the churchyard; the first comes from the beach below; the other from Ceilwart Isa, a farm about 0.5ml (0.8km) to the south.

Inscribed stones in Llanaber church

Both stones have simple inscriptions in Roman capitals reading horizontally. The first reads: AETERN[I] / ET / AETERN[(*A*)E], or: (*The stone*) *of Aeternus and Aeterna*. Both names are a bit uncertain, but possibly these are a brother and sister buried together. The second reads CAELEXTI(*S*) / MONEDO/RIGI(*S*), or: (*The stone*) *of Caelestis Monedorix*.

The church in which they are housed is the finest 13th-century church in Gwynedd. It was built by Hywel ap Gruffudd ap Cynan, a great-grandson of Owain Gwynedd, who became overlord of this part of Meirionnydd in 1202 but was dead by 1216. It is an aisled church with a narrow chancel, a design which was traditional for secular, as distinct from monastic, churches. It is built across the contour of the hill, and the long chancel stands well above the aisled and clerestoried nave with its five-bay arcade and decorated capitals. One can best appreciate the strength and beauty of the building by standing beneath the chancel arch and looking down into the nave on a sunny afternoon.

112
Bedd Porius, Trawsfynydd

Early Christian stone

Late 5th–early 6th century AD

OS 124 SH 733315 U1

From Trawsfynydd, travel S down A470 and take 2nd road on L (signposted Abergeirw); after 2.2ml (3.5km) take LH fork; continue for 0.3ml (0.5km) then take RH fork. Site is 300m on L

Nash-Williams 1950, no. 289; Gresham 1985

The stone within the little caged enclosure is a cast. The original is in the National Museum in Cardiff, but it is interesting to visit the approximate site of its discovery because, unlike most Christian graves, this one is remote from any church site and must have been placed beside the road. This spot has been a significant point in the communication

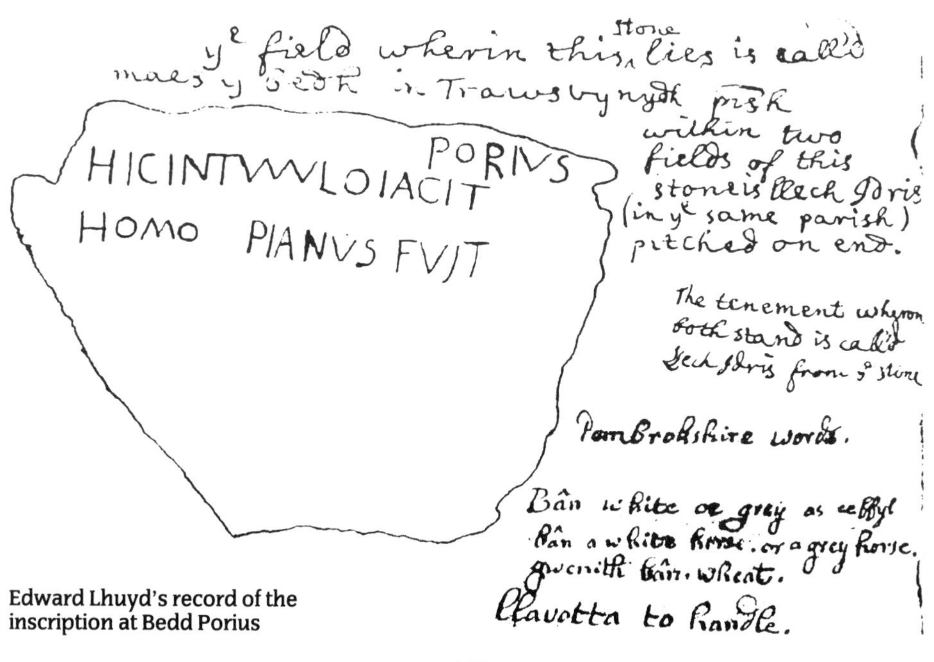

Edward Lhuyd's record of the inscription at Bedd Porius

network for millennia (see nos 48 and 96).

The exact nature of the grave found in the 17th century is unrecorded; it is assumed that the square kerb belongs with the railings set up in about 1830, but some of it may be original. The inscription speaks of the burial being beneath a mound. The inscription is in thinly incised Roman capitals and reads: PORIUS / HICINTUMULOIACIT / HOMO PLANUSFUIT, or: *Porius lies here in the mound. He was a plain man.* There has been a good deal of dispute about the meaning and validity of PLANUS. Some have suggested that he was a leper who had lost his nose, hence 'flat', and others that it was originally XRIANUS, or: *Christian*. Those who adopt the latter theory point to the fact that all the other words are run together, and believe that the stone has been damaged at this point, removing the X. Edward Lhuyd and other early recorders of the inscription gave PIANUS, not PLANUS; the foot of the L seems to have appeared between 1846 and 1884. The latest discussion of the stone (Gresham 1985) favours this view, but unfortunately readers can only decide for themselves by visiting the original in Cardiff. The numbers were added later by the army, who used this area as a training ground.

113
Inscribed Stone, Tywyn

Early Christian stone

7th–9th century AD

OS 135   SH 588009   U1

Stone is in parish church in centre of Tywyn, on A493. Church is normally open throughout year. Stone is set up opposite door, light switches on W wall

Morris-Jones 1918, 1921; Williams 1949

A vitally important stone, it is the only inscription in Welsh among the early stone monuments of Gwynedd. However, it has to be admitted that it is hideously difficult to read, let alone understand! At least two significantly different readings have been suggested.

The stone was found in the 17th century, about 800m from the church, and the first record of the inscription was by the noted antiquary Edward Lhuyd, who saw it before it was damaged. It had been used as a gate-post and broken before it was brought into the church in 1761. It is now set up with the broken section standing beside the main piece.

Tall, thin and narrow, the stone originally stood over 2.3m high, with a carefully tapered foot designed to fit the socket of a stone base. The inscription is written vertically on all four sides. It reads both downwards and upwards, and includes two interpolations, two initial crosses and two sets of reversed brackets (a unique symbol whose grammatical role is obscure). The lettering, moreover, is very coarsely pecked and clumsily designed. It appears to be intended as half-uncial script (compare the lettering on the Cadfan stone, no. 101).

The reading established by Sir John Morris-Jones in 1921 identifies the beginning of the inscription on the narrow right-hand side, starting with an initial cross and reading downwards: CINGEN CELEN, or: *the body of Cingen*, with a reversed bracket beneath. This is continued on the back reading upwards: TRICET / NITANAM, or: *lies beneath*. The top of the stone is damaged, but there is no early record of any lettering higher up. The three lines of very awkward script at the bottom of this side (mostly on the separated piece) are a different sentence, reading upwards: MOLT / C reversed bracket PE/TUAR *The tomb . . . four*. A second main inscription starts on the front, reading downwards, with another initial cross: TENGRUIN MALTE[C] GU/ADGAN, or: *Egryn, Mallteg, Gwaddian*, a series of personal names. Two lines near the bottom, awkwardly cut by the break in the stone, are another interpolation: M[C]/ARTR, which defied translation. The second inscription continues on the left-hand side reading downwards: ANTERUNC DUBUT MARCIAU, or:

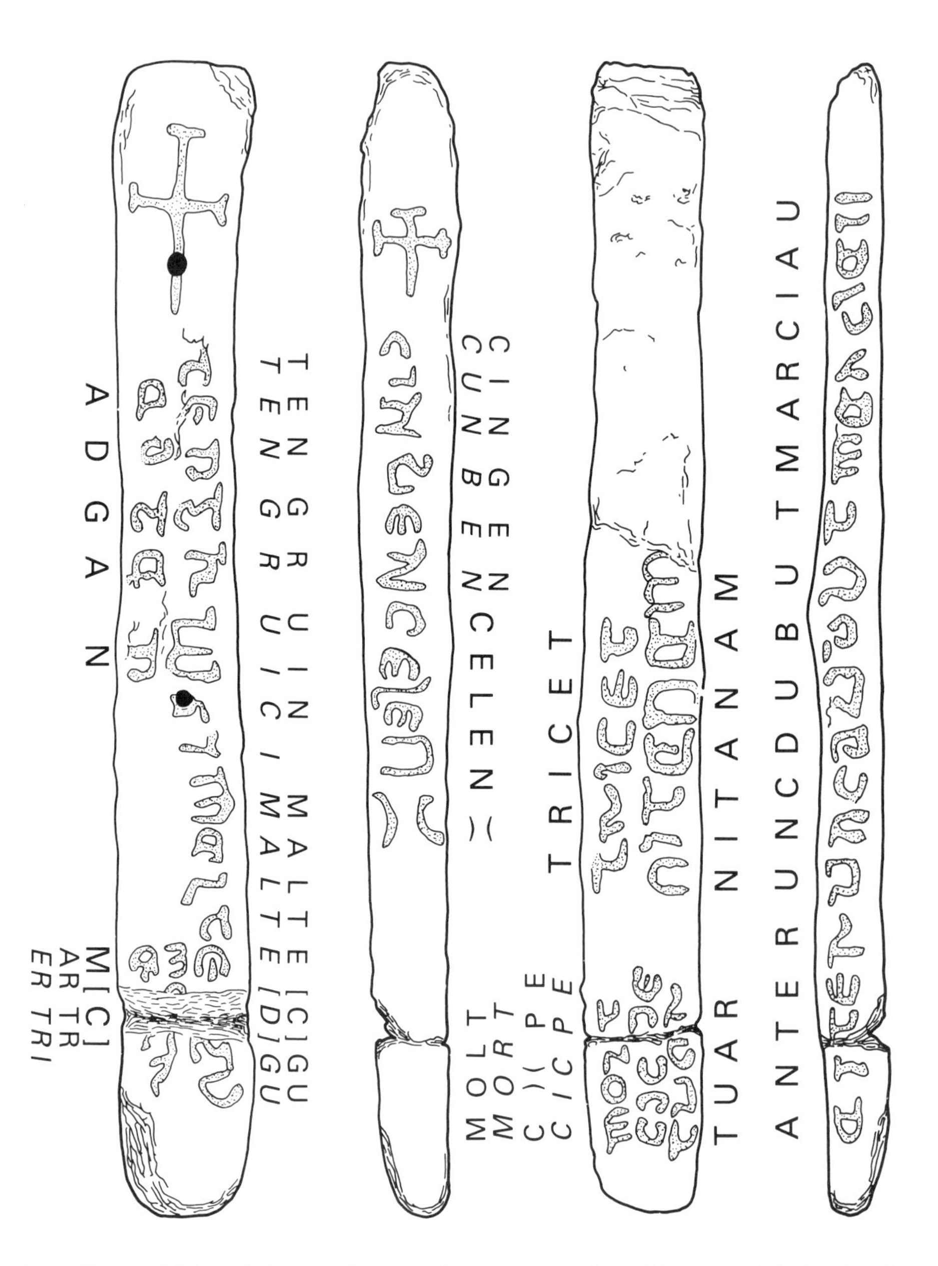

The earliest Welsh inscription, on the stone from Tywyn. Left to right: front, right, back and left sides

together with Dyfod and Marchiau.

In this reading, therefore, the stone marks the grave of Cingen and invokes the protection of a number of other persons, presumably local saints. Sir John claimed to identify only one – Egryn, who is the patron of the neighbouring parish, Llanegryn.

The next attempt to read the stone was by Sir Ifor Williams in 1948. He saw two hands at work, distinguished by the quality of carving. He believed that the earlier inscription began with an initial cross on the front (the more normal place for a beginning), and read downwards: TENGRUI CIMALTE[D] GU/ ADGAN, which he translated as: *Ceinrwy, wife of Gwaddian* (*lies here*), and continued on the left side, which he read as Sir John had done, but divided the words differently: ANT ERUNC DU BUT MARCIAU, and translated them as: *close to Bud* (*and*) *Marchiaw*, perhaps her children. The disputed word CIMALTED, which he translated as *linked/associated* and thence *wife*, occurs at a point where the stone is very rough and has been damaged by its use as a gate-post. This reading refers to three graves, and Sir Ifor interprets the letters MC ER TRI at the bottom of his first side as a 'footnote' emphasing this: *the memorial of three*, perhaps necessitated by the confusion caused by forgetting to put 'and' between BUT and MARCIAU.

In Sir Ifor's reading, the inscription starting on the right-hand side is a later one. He reads it as: CUN BEN CELEN, or: *Cun, wife of Celyn*, continuing on the back with the same reading as Sir John, but providing a completely different translation of the word NITANAM which gives the memorial a touchingly personal tone: *the grief and loss remain*. Since a new name had been added, the stone was now a memorial to four persons, and Sir Ifor interprets the 'footnote' on this side: MORTCIC (a variant reading following Lhuyd) PETUAR, or: *the memorial of four*.

Whatever the reading preferred – and that of Sir Ifor Williams has more adherents today – the stone must be acknowledged as having enormous linguistic importance. This is because it is the earliest record of the Welsh language as it emerged as a distinctive form of British Celtic. One characteristic of Welsh is that it has lost the case endings which are a feature of Latin and are retained to this day in German. These had existed in the earliest written form of Celtic used in Europe, but by the 7th century, while they survived in Latin, they were beginning to be dropped in the vernacular languages. In Sir John Morris-Jones's reading, this development was well illustrated: CINGEN CELEN, or: *Cingen's body* has no genitive ending, whereas if it had been British it would have been CUNOGENI. In Sir Ifor's reading, only PETUAR, also a genitive, is relevant to this point of crucial linguistic development.

Another early stone, a long gravestone with a simple cross, probably 9th-century AD in date, has been built into the outside of the south side of the modern church tower and can be seen beneath the main window.

The church of St Cadfan is an impressive structure in its own right. It is a cruciform monastic church. The crossing, chancel and transepts are modern, rebuilt on ancient foundations, but the massive double-aisled nave is original 12th-century work. Its great circular pillars and simple arcade may be 'rude and plain' but they make effective architecture. Two 14th-century effigies lie in niches on the right-hand side of the chancel.

7
The Age of the Castle

The year 1066 is momentous in English history and, although William had no ambition to conquer Wales, the Norman advent soon shook the Welsh kingdoms too. To protect his own realms, William encouraged his barons to carve out semi-autonomous lordships for themselves on the borders (the Marches). The Welsh, weakened by dynastic quarrels, were an easy prey to the new Marcher warlords.

Hugh of Avranches, earl of Chester, and his cousin, Robert of Rhuddlan, were well established east of the river Clwyd by 1086. In the following four years they captured the Welsh ruler, Gruffudd ap Cynan, and founded castles at Degannwy (no. 117), Bangor, Caernarfon (see no. 128) and Aberlleiniog on Anglesey (see Appendix) and, less certainly, in Lleyn. These were of traditional Norman type: an earthen mound (motte) topped by a wooden keep, the main defensive unit, with less significant buildings below, defended by a bank and ditch (bailey). They were usually built within the Welsh *maerdrefi*, the administrative centres of the native rulers.

After initial success, Norman control in north Wales was short-lived. In 1094 Gruffudd ap Cynan regained his freedom and, with the help of his mother's Irish relations, drove out the Norman earls. The next seventy years, the reigns of Gruffudd (1094–1137) and his son, Owain Gwynedd (1137–70), mark the most peaceful period of Welsh independence, when the native princes absorbed many of the current European reforming ideas and adapted the more effective structures of both church and state to their own society.

Monastic foundations were encouraged, diocesan boundaries defined, and many new stone churches built. Earthwork castles identical to those built earlier by the Norman invaders were now erected by the princes at the centre of many of their personal estates. These estates were widely distributed because medieval rulers were continually on the move; they had to see and be seen in every part of their kingdom if they were to remain effective. They and their courtiers also needed the food which these estates produced. In theory there were two in each commote: a *maerdref* with the *llys* or court at the centre, where unfree labourers worked arable land and a tract of upland grazing or *ffridd* (see nos 126 and 127). In practice their distribution may not have been as regular as the law tracts suggest.

The economy of 12th-century Wales, described by Giraldus Cambrensis, depended very heavily on herding cattle. This pastoral economy was run from two bases, the *hendre* or main farm on the lower arable land and the *hafod* or summer base on the *ffridd*. Few medieval farms have survived, but their sites may be recognised in the common 'platform houses'. These earthworks represent the prepared base for a building with low stone walls, perhaps completed in timber. The narrow end is set into the hillside and protected from damp by a 'hood' to divert the water from the slopes above. Their social status may vary: some are substantial halls (the sites of which are often still occupied), others are quite roughly built and now abandoned (see no. 125). Most *hafodau* were on less carefully prepared sites since they were occupied only in summer. They can be distinguished from late prehistoric houses only by their preference for a rectangular plan.

After the death of Owain Gwynedd in 1170, southern Wales, under Rhys ap Gruffudd ('the Lord Rhys') in Dyfed, became dominant, but at the end of the century Gwynedd once again had a powerful prince. Llywelyn ap Iorwerth ('The Great') emerged as ruler in 1200, after a fierce family struggle. At his death in 1240 he was undisputed ruler of all 'pura Wallia', corresponded on equal terms with Phillip Augustus of France, and had hanged one of the most powerful Marcher lords for undue familiarity with his wife, the daughter of King John of England.

Llywelyn's reign saw the construction of the first sophisticated stone castles in Wales. Sited at strategic points peripheral to Snowdonia, often on his summer grazing lands, they guarded the store-cupboard of his kingdom. Simple towers, like that on Dinas Emrys (no. 110), may belong to this programme, but his best castles are much more sophisticated, and incorporate details of construction and advanced design being used by some of his friends – and enemies – among the Marcher lords. Dolwyddelan (no. 123), Dolbadarn (no. 124), Criccieth (no. 129) and Bere in south Meirionnydd (no. 134) still stand as witness to the energy and resources put into the defence of his kingdom after the disastrous attack which it suffered from his father-in-law, King John, in 1211. These castles were probably built between 1220 and 1230. The plans vary: towers are round, square or D-shaped – a ground plan especially characteristic of this series. The well-sited castle at Criccieth is undoubtedly the best designed, but it might have been surpassed by Degannwy (no. 117) had this crucial site not been destroyed by his son, Dafydd, as part of a 'scorched earth policy'.

At Llywelyn's death the kingdom and Gwynedd's pre-eminence were again threatened by a disputed inheritance and renewed interest from England. Only when his grandson, Llywelyn ap Gruffudd (Llywelyn II), overcame family rivals in 1255 could the political legacy of Llywelyn the Great begin to be rebuilt by a combination of raids and alliances. Llywelyn II's position as effective ruler of all Wales as far south as Caerphilly was eventually recognised by Henry III, in the Treaty of Montgomery (1267). This acknowledged the title 'Prince of Wales' and the concept of Wales as a unified state, never explicitly recognised before. The Prince of Wales was a vassal of the king of England but was, in effect, an independent political power.

His grandfather's castles still provided the main defence of the kingdom; Llywelyn II reinforced and enlarged them, but founded only one new castle, at Dolforwyn, near Welshpool, far outside his patrimony, begun in 1273 when clouds were already gathering on the horizon.

In 1272 Henry III was succeeded by his much more effective son, Edward I, and Llywelyn's brothers and uncertain allies soon began to make trouble for him with the new king. Llywelyn added to his own difficulties by refusing homage, and war was declared in 1276. This first campaign centred upon the Severn and Dee valleys, and Llywelyn was forced to retreat to the river Conwy, Edward consolidating his conquests by the construction of great new castles at Flint and Rhuddlan. At the Peace of Aberconway, concluded in 1277, Llywelyn lost almost all that he had gained 10 years before.

The peace did not last long. Llywelyn's brother, Dafydd, provoked Edward by an attack on Hawarden in March 1282, and war reopened. Llywelyn was killed in a skirmish near Builth Wells and Dafydd had to continue the fight alone. Edward swept down the Conwy valley from Rhuddlan, capturing Dolwyddelan in January 1283, breaking the defensive ring; the other castles fell in rapid succession, and Dafydd was captured and executed in the early summer.

This marked the effective end of Welsh resistance, but Edward intended to consolidate his victory. He planned one of the most ambitious and expensive campaigns of castle and borough building that Europe had ever seen. Over 12 years he spent £60,000 (about £33 million in today's terms), more than 10 times his annual income, on building castles and walled towns at Conwy (no. 118), Caernarfon (no. 128), Harlech (no. 132) and Beaumaris (no. 114) and the refurbishment of Llwyelyn's castle at Criccieth. This integrated programme – each borough defended by its castle, and each castle accessible by sea – has left Wales with a legacy of medieval military architecture of truly international importance.

The programme, financed by Tuscan bankers and executed by a chief architect from Savoy, was international from the start. The castles, each tailored precisely to its site, were designed within a matter of months by one man, Master James of St George, working under conditions of war. They reflected all the latest thinking in military science. The single, strong keep was no longer judged sufficient: defence lay in tactically designed walls – often two circuits – with optimum coverage and line of fire. The most perfect is the concentric castle at Beaumaris, an unencumbered site, but the others, such as Conwy, with a tandem arrangement of wards, are equally effective. The castle designs, with their imposing gatehouses, reflect a highly intelligent and informed attention to detail, as do all the incidentals, barbicans, portcullises, machicolation, arrowslots and hoard settings.

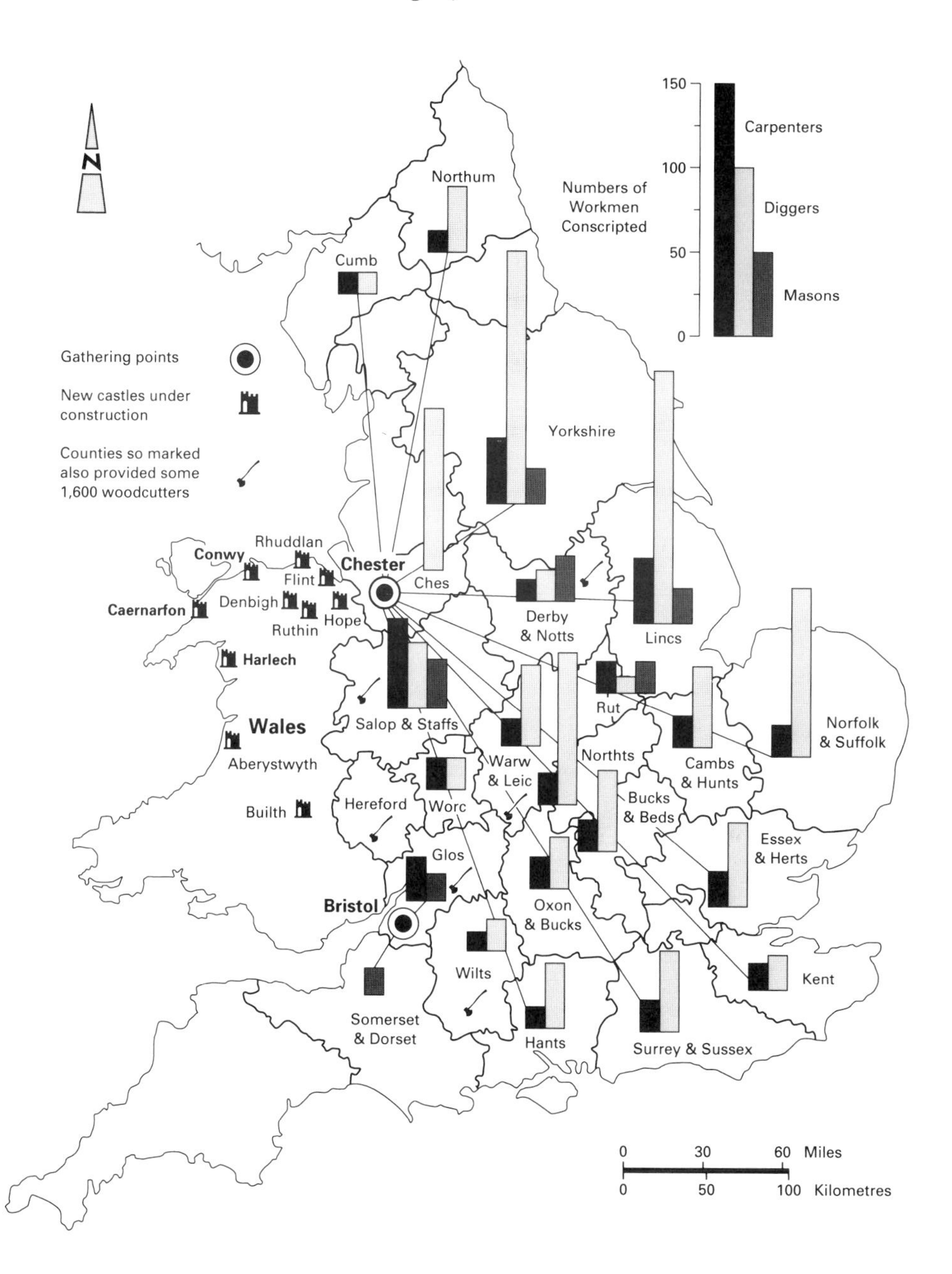

Organisation of labour for Edward I's castle building in Wales

Cutaway view of entrance defences, as exemplified at Harlech

Preparations for Edward's campaign entailed gathering not only a fighting force but also a building team. The organisational ability behind this programme would be impressive even with today's communications. One of the most fascinating aspects of these castles is that all the accounts survive, all the payments to masons, carpenters and ditch-diggers are listed, their names and origins known. Several of the master masons had come with Master James from Savoy, and their trademark, the spiral of putlog holes which supported their sloped scaffolding, can be seen on every castle wall.

Edward was unable to extend English governmental administration to north Wales as the semi-independent Marcher lordships lay between. The regime set up, therefore, was a quasi-colonial one: the Welsh could keep their own law of inheritance, but criminal law was to conform to that of England, and taxes were to be in money rather than kind. Extortionate taxation was one of the issues that led to a short-lived revolt in 1294.

The following century was dominated in Wales, as everywhere else, by the economic troubles caused by the Black Death. This plague is estimated to have killed a quarter of the Welsh population, bringing great social change to the countryside, where traditional laws of inheritance and labour dues could no longer be sustained in the face of the new reality. This enormous upheaval led to a climate of millenarianism, prophecy and unrest, spawning a number of threats to the English establishment.

The most serious was the revolt led by Owain Glyndŵr. In the early years it was a protest of the poor; as the revolt grew in momentum from 1402 onwards, Owain attracted to his banner some of the best brains and most experienced ecclesiastics in Wales, and the nature of his programme for an independent principality, with a parliament, two universities and an independent archiepiscopal province, developed an attractive maturity and a certain modernity.

For six years Owain was successful. He established a court and a chancellory in the castle at Aberystwyth, but in 1409 he was besieged in Harlech castle and his family was captured. He and his chief advisers escaped to the hills and maintained a guerrilla war until 1413.

Owain's gentry supporters quickly made their peace with the king, and during Henry VI's ineffective reign it was they who made the greatest gains. It was in the 15th century that the great estates were built up through the new freedom to buy and sell land. Despite intermittent warfare (the Wars of the Roses), this century was a period of economic and cultural revival. Contemporary poetry tells of aristocratic hospitality in newly built houses. Several of these hall-houses survive to this day (nos 122 and 130). With their great central halls rising the full height of the building, they were admirably suited to such entertainment and hospitality but provided little privacy; few survive unchanged by the fashions of later centuries.

The accession of Henry VII to the throne of England in 1485 had little immediate impact on Wales, but under the Tudors the social situation of the Welsh gentry was gradually transformed, for it gave them a new focus outside Wales for their ambitions. The demise of the unique Marcher jurisdiction facilitated the merging of English and Welsh government, and in 1536 the first Act of Union finally put an end to their formal distinction, though it could not eradicate from Wales an awareness of its own identity.

A reconstruction of Beaumaris Castle

114
Beaumaris Castle
Stone castle of Edward I

13th–14th century AD

OS 114 SH 607763 R1 Cadw–World Heritage Site

Castle is on eastern side of town, at end of main street (Castle Street). Parking nearby. Admission charge; standard hours

Official Guide; Taylor 1986

Beaumaris was the last of the ring of castles built by Edward I and his great architect, Master James of St George, to encircle the conquered kingdom of Gwynedd. The site was a new one, but stood close to the Welsh town of Llanfaes, whose role as a commercial centre and port was to be transferred to the English borough of Beaumaris.

At Beaumaris, Master James had an undeveloped site, and one without a rock foundation to dictate the plan. Consequently this is the most perfectly symmetrical of his concentric designs. It consists of two wards: the inner square in shape, the outer subtly angular with two gates offset from the inner ones. The whole structure was surrounded by a wide moat linked by a dock to the open sea. But, despite the perfection of plan, the castle as it stands lacks the impact of Conwy or Harlech (nos 118 and 132). It does not dominate, because it was never completed: the inner towers and walls have no battlements and the two gatehouses should have been a storey higher, with turrets rising above.

One can recognise many similarities between the castles built by Master James in Wales and in his homeland, Savoy, but each has certain unique features and refinements. Beaumaris is closest to Harlech, and the gatehouse blocks, with their suites of impressive apartments, are almost identical. Unique features at Beaumaris are the dock from which a 40-ton ship could unload directly into the castle, the plentiful and ingeniously designed groups of latrines on the inner curtain wall, and the mill beneath the Gunners' Walk which was powered by the tide and the moat sluice.

It is probable that the castle was planned and the site chosen in 1283, but work was not begun until 1295, after the crushing of a revolt led by Madoc ap Llywelyn, when the Welsh population of Llanfaes was expelled to Newborough. The building of the new castle was rapidly put in hand in the summer of 1295. Over two thousand men were employed there and the weekly bill for wages and supplies was in the region of £270 (about £135,000 in today's terms). By February 1296 the inner ward was sufficiently advanced for gates to be fixed and locked each night. Master James was becoming increasingly anxious about finances for the enterprise. A fascinating letter survives in which he details the work done and the resources needed for the next season, ending with a desperate plea to the treasury: 'And Sirs, for God's sake, be quick with the money for the works.' The workmen and soldiers guarding them had not been paid and the workforce was melting away.

During the war with Scotland (1300–6) work at Beaumaris ceased. It was begun again in 1306 and continued till 1330 but, even then, the full range of accommodation was never finished. The later work concentrated on completing the circuit of the outer walls and strengthening the gates. The new work can be distinguished from the old by the use of different stone. The junction on the outer curtain wall is best seen from across the moat, on the west side. The northern section was completely new in 1306, and the southern half was raised to full height.

A survey of the castle in 1343 showed that much still remained unfinished, but the defences were complete and the castle was strong – if not as comfortable as it should have been, since the residential suites had never been built.

Despite its strength the castle fell to Owain Glyndŵr's followers, who held it for two years. This episode caused a great deal of distresss to the English burgesses of the attached borough, which had never received its planned wall. This was not built until 1414 when the scare was over.

During the 16th century the castle began to decay. Like many others, it was used as a prison. One notable prisoner was the Catholic martyr Fr William Davies, who was held here before his execution in 1593. There is a tradition that he had the sympathy of the townspeople, said Mass in the castle chapel and that, when the time came for his hanging, no local man would do it and an executioner had to be summoned from Chester.

During the Civil War (1642–8) the castle was held for the king by Col. Richard Bulkeley, but the Royalist forces were rather more interested in private quarrels than the king's war. In 1648 it fell to the Parliamentarians, who garrisoned but did not repair it.

The modern visitor enters across a fixed bridge where there would once have been a drawbridge. Bear right through the barbican added in 1306 to enter the inner ward through the South Gatehouse. Though the outer gate had been lockable since 1296, the inner defences were never complete because the back of the gatehouse and the planned rooms there were never built.

The North Gatehouse, facing it across the inner ward, is more complete, and the suite of rooms on the first floor could have been occupied. The design of these apartments is very similar to those at Harlech, with a hall for public business in the front and bedchambers behind. The second floor was never built above the level of the window sills. Had the facade been completed it would have been extremely impressive, with side-towers rising to twice their present height. No floors survive, but these rooms may be seen from the west corner stair which gives access to the top of the north towers, which were completed to virtually full height.

The neat design of the back-to-back latrines can be appreciated from the wall-walk. These connect with others below, forming a triangular flue disgorging into the moat through pipes under the outer ward. The lower ones are reached from the wall-passages, designed like those at Caernarfon.

The chapel, now reached by an external stair, would originally have been entered from internal buildings, probably designed as royal apartments. This is a very beautiful room: empty and white-washed, it still has an atmosphere of prayer and repose. It is stone-vaulted and surrounded with a stone bench and an elegant triple blind-arcade, with deeply set lancet windows above.

Leave the inner ward by the North Gatehouse to see the offset landward gate. This gate (part of the later phase) seems to have become redundant even before it was finished. But the blocking of the gate itself may have been done during Glyndŵr's revolt or the Civil War. Several of the lower-level arrowslits and first-floor windows of the inner towers are similarly blocked.

The outer curtain wall has 16 towers, 10 built before 1296, the 6 on the north side not until 1306. This defensive wall was also a fighting platform providing over 300 shooting positions. The battlements were finished on this wall but not on the upper one.

Finally, examine the dock area and look for the masonry changes on the south-west wall as you leave.

115
Tudor Rose, 32 Castle Street, Beaumaris

Medieval hall-house

15th–17th century AD

OS 114 SH 606760 R2 (steps at entrance)

House stands in central section of main street and is now a shop. Visitors may look at it, without charge, whenever shop is open

This late medieval house has survived many vicissitudes and changes, and its present condition provides a fascinating exercise in architectural analysis.

The original building dates from the early 15th century, when the borough had just received its defensive wall. It consisted of an open-roofed central hall of three bays (8m or more by 5.4m) flanked by projecting wings to north and south. The hall had a fine roof with two elegantly carved and moulded arch-braced trusses; the original hearth was an open one in the centre of the floor, and the dais was at the southern end. The north wing has been entirely demolished but the southern one survives in an altered form (the front of the present shop). Such a hall on the main street of the town would have been the house of a wealthy citizen – perhaps a merchant who could have had his business premises in the south wing.

In the 17th century the building was radically altered by the insertion of a floor in the central hall and the extension of the southern wing towards the street front. In the 19th century it was used as a bakery, and a large oven was built into the corner of the hall. By the middle of the 20th century the house was fast becoming a ruin when it was bought by Henrik Lek, a Dutch Jewish refugee antique dealer, who restored the open hall by removing most of the 17th-century floor. The present owner has plans to replace half of this floor, which will diminish the impact of the open hall, though the architectural history will remain traceable.

Enter down two steps – a regular feature of Beaumaris, where road levels have been raised over the years. The front of the shop is a modern extension; the original wall line can be seen a little further in. Go through to the back, into the dais area of the original hall. The doorway is not original (notice the altered joists above), nor is the small fireplace in the corner of this narrow room, walled off in the 17th century and partly filled by the staircase built at that time to give access to the new room above.

Step up through a rough 17th-century wall

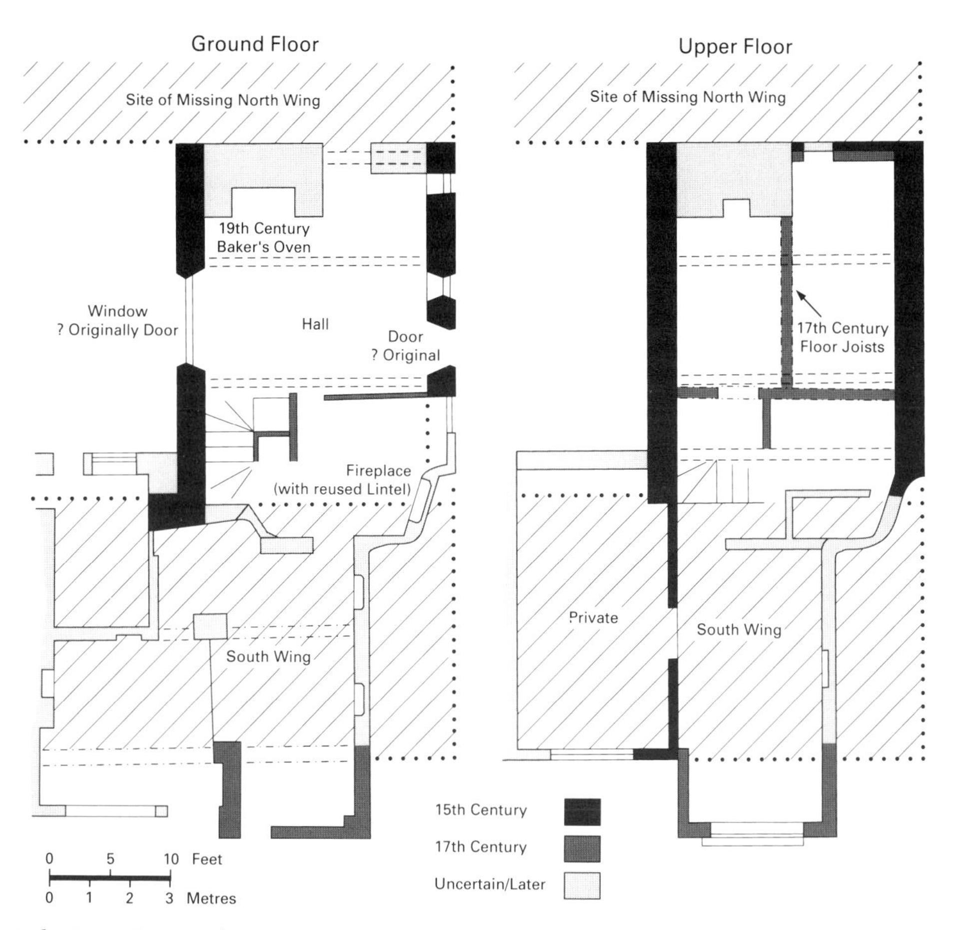

Tudor Rose, Beaumaris

beneath a large beam inserted to support the floor above. Two bays of the original hall remain open and it is possible to see the full height of the building. Two of the arch-braced trusses remain. They were originally supported on stone corbels but were cut when the 17th-century floor was put in, a sequence visible on the east wall. The quality of the elegant 15th-century woodwork contrasts very strikingly with the later work, though the main joist of the added floor has a 'broach stop' to the chamfer on the southern end, a difficult feat of carpentry which is normally indicative of expensive work.

The present staircase replaces a modest 17th-century well-stair which gave access to the upper floor which has been retained over the southern end of the hall. Upstairs the visitor is now confronted by a low beam, the original 15th-century head-beam of the dais canopy. Beyond is a 17th-century screen crudely pegged against the central hall truss whose carving can be conveniently examined from here. The windbraces of the 15th-century roof have been cut away at this point. The 17th-century stair would have entered the upper room from the south through a door in the screen, avoiding the low head-beam. Walls have been repositioned here, making it difficult to understand the earlier arrangement of this upstairs space.

The upper floor of the south wing retains its central truss, indicating the original width of the wing (4.5m). Both ends are visible: the northern one at the top of the stairs, and the southern one a few metres from the front wall, where the roof of the 17th-century extension has been given a north–south ridge. The central doorway is original.

Medieval farms and fields on the north side of the Great Orme. The farm buildings are just below and to the left of the summit café and rock, and the ridged strip fields stretch below them to the graveyard at the bottom of the picture. A mass of small mine shafts of uncertain date can be seen on the left

116
Great Orme Long Huts
Medieval or later farmsteads
12th–16th century AD
OS 115 SH 767837–SH 769834 U1

Site is on N side of Great Orme summit, below cable car terminal. By car, turn N off summit road towards church, leave car above cemetery and walk towards rocks and terminal

These two groups of long huts, the remains of substantial farm buildings, stand above an extensive area of lyncheted fields in which cultivation ridges can be very clearly seen. This evidence of agriculture extends across all the ground above the ancient church and its cemetery. The buildings – some undoubtedly contemporary with the farming, though their date cannot be pinpointed – are set into the hillside where it begins to rise steeply.

The eastern group lies just above a track which marks the edge of the field. Set behind a revetted platform is a long, rectangular building cut into the slope. Two large stones stand on the front wall of this building – or buildings: it may consist of two (6m by 3m), set along the slope, with a central one (perhaps later) built at right angles. At the west end of the platform is an L-shaped building. Entrances to both rooms are in the angle; another door on the west side may connect with a track leading down towards the western group.

The western farmstead stands just beneath the cliff; the walls and doorway of the small easternmost building are particularly clear. Close beside it is a longer building with a cross-wall. Both of these open on to a walled yard crossed by a track which disappears under the modern wall to the west. What may be another house (with rocks fallen in it) lies to the west, and there is another small structure beyond that. This group is aligned with a substantial lynchet bank running through the fields below, perhaps a boundary to the lands of this farm.

117
Degannwy Castle or Castle of Gannoc
Early medieval court and medieval masonry castle
6th–13th century AD
OS 115 SH 782794 U4

Twin hills are visible behind Degannwy town. From S on A496, just past Degannwy Castle Hotel, turn R up York Road which bends to R, then L; at top where road begins to curve R follow footpath between two gardens leading onto open land below castle rock. Bear R towards saddle. Beware nettles in summer and, especially, slippery grass on summits

Edwards and Lane 1988, pp 50–3; Lowe 1912, pp 169–85

The twin rocks of Degannwy have been the focus of settlement and warfare for more than a thousand years but, because they have been fought over so ferociously, little survives for the modern visitor to see. However, although the castle walls have been reduced to little more than rubble, the hilltop is still an evocative place.

During the post-Roman period the hill became a place of major political importance, the court of Maelgwyn Gwynedd, the foremost historical figure of the 6th century in

Degannwy Castle as it might have appeared in the time of Henry III

north Wales, patron of St Cybi and St Seiriol, but reviled as a drunken tyrant by the chronicler Gildas. Excavations on the western summit in 1961–6 confirmed occupation in the 5th and 6th centuries when broken amphorae show that wine was imported to the court, but no evidence of the buildings themselves survived. Tradition has it that Maelgwyn imprisoned his nephew, Elphin, here and that the first *eisteddfod* was held on the hill. Maelgwyn himself is said to have died in AD 547 of a 'yellow plague'. Degannwy may have remained a royal residence into the 9th century, when the *Annales Cambriae* record that it was destroyed by Saxons.

Documents show that the Norman, Robert of Rhuddlan, built a castle here in 1080, but nothing remains of it. It was later regained by the Welsh, and in 1191 Giraldus Cambrensis described it in the *Itinerarium Cambriae* as a 'noble structure'. However, it was soon to be destroyed as part of a 'scorched earth policy' in face of threats from King John. This was a tactic adopted more than once at this peninsular site, where it was possible to trap and starve an invading army.

When Llywelyn ap Iorwerth regained the castle in 1213 he rebuilt it in good style. Only a little of this castle survives today. In 1228 it is recorded that he imprisoned one of his sons here. After Llywelyn's death in 1240 his sons were not strong enough to resist the English advance and demolished the castle in anticipation of its loss. When the English arrived in 1245 they were forced to shiver in tents, so effective had been the Welsh destruction.

This campaign of Henry III saw the construction of the walls and towers, the ruins of which survive today. The castle, with towers on each hilltop and a bailey on the saddle between, had an associated borough which received a charter in 1252. It was under construction from 1245–54 but was never completely finished.

As Henry became more embroiled with his own troubles, the power of the Welsh prince Llywelyn ap Gruffudd was growing. In 1263, after a long siege, he captured this outpost of English power and systematically demolished it.

When Henry's son, Edward, advanced across this territory in 1283 he camped in the ruins of Degannwy, but, recognising the greater strategic value of a riverside site and also the political impact of a castle across the river Conwy, which up till then had been the frontier of the essential Gwynedd, he founded his new castle at Conwy. Degannwy was abandoned.

The ruins which are visible today belong mainly to Henry III's castle. The defences of the bailey – earth banks and ditches on the north side, the base of two D-shaped gatehouse towers and the curtain wall hastily rebuilt by Edward I on the south – can still be recognised. The mass of fallen masonry near the base of the gatehouse is a relic of the demolition of 1263.

Corbel from Llywelyn the Great's castle at Degannwy, believed to represent the king himself

The western summit, which was the scene of all the earlier occupation, has the more interesting remains. Having passed over the ruins of the gate to the bailey, turn left up a path on the line of the original access road, revetted and overlooked by a substantial round tower. It passes through the site of two narrow gates before turning up to the summit.

Henry III's wall continues along the west side of the summit, but just beyond the north-west corner it overlies the base of a round tower and a length of revetment wall which must belong to the castle of Llywelyn ap Iorwerth. Excavations showed that the earlier castle was better built than the later one and, to judge from a finely carved corbel (thought to portray Llywelyn himself), it was elegantly appointed. The quarry on the summit must have been the source of stone to build the castle; the wall foundations close by are thought to date from 1215, while the range of foundations and the great tower on the south side date from 1247–8 (Henry III).

The grass-grown foundations of a D-shaped tower (traditionally known as Mansell's Tower) on the east summit also belong to the later phase. There is no easy path to the top. The curtain wall was never completed round the north side of the bailey, which retains an earth bank and ditch defence. Surface irregularities around the castle belong to the abandoned borough founded in 1252. Cultivation ridges can be seen, but no house foundations. Practice trenches from the First World War are visible on the south.

118
Conwy Castle

Stone castle of Edward I

13th century AD

OS 115 SH 784774 R1 (with help) Cadw–World Heritage Site

Conwy town is by-passed by A55; visitors must turn into town off main road (adequate car parks). Entrance to castle is through Visitor Centre at E end of main car park inside walls; also accessible from street below. Exhibition on Edward I's castles in Visitor Centre, and on Castle Chapels in Chapel Tower inside castle. Admission charge; standard hours

Official Guide; Taylor 1986

Conwy, with its magnificent castle dominating the river estuary and standing high above its walled borough, epitomises the power and vision of Edward I and exemplifies the strategy of his conquest of Wales in both its military and political aspects.

The castle, completed in only four-and-a-half years, is judged to be one of the most impressive and interesting in Europe, the work of the foremost military engineer and architect of his day, Master James of St George. It stands on an elongated rock which has dictated the shape of the building, but the skill of the architect has produced on this restricted site a balanced, symmetrical and efficient plan: a castle which was both beautiful and effective.

The Welsh princes had a court at Conwy, where Llywelyn ap Iorwerth had founded a Cistercian abbey, but there was no castle. Edward had originally intended Conwy to be the county town and chief English base; that role was given to Caernarfon (no. 128), but Conwy did remain the administrative centre, and Edward himself lived in the completed castle for six months, celebrating Christmas there in 1294.

Building was extremely rapid between 1283 and 1287, but maintenance was probably neglected once English rule was firmly established. Within thirty years the roofs were becoming dangerous, but they were not leaded until 1346 when, to strengthen the roof structure, stone arches were inserted in the Great Hall range and the king's apartments – the only significant alteration the castle has seen.

Conwy became an important port for Ireland, and Richard II passed through on his return from that country in the dark days before his deposition in 1399. Its excellent design prevented its being taken by force, but on Good Friday 1401, during the Glyndŵr revolt, it was taken by surprise. While the garrison of only 30 men were in church, 45 Welsh rebels headed by Gwilym ap Tudur (an ancestor of Henry VII) entered, killed the two remaining guards, and held it for two months.

Charles I sold the dilapidated castle for £100 (about £7,500 in today's terms) in 1627, but during the Civil War its military role was revived. In 1645 it was brought back to a defensible state by John Williams, archbishop of York, a native of Conwy (see no. 122). He used his own money to repair the gates and defences, but he quarrelled with Sir John Owen, the king's commander, and eventually opened negotiations with the besieging Parliamentarian army. The castle surrendered in 1645 and the town was spared destruction, but John Williams's reputation was irretrievably damaged. After the war all fortifications were to be rendered unusable, and the process of destruction began.

The ruins were saved from total destruction by the lure of the 'picturesque' and the growth of tourism (encouraged by the road and railway just below the castle). In 1875 John Parker, keeper of the Ashmolean Museum in Oxford, repaired one of the towers at his own expense, for visitors to sit and sketch the scene.

A narrow rectangle dropped with deceptive delicacy over the bare rock of the riverside promontory, Conwy is in effect two castles in tandem, despite the external uniformity of towers and walls. The outer ward to the west is entered from within the town walls, but divided from the town by a deep ditch; the inner ward to the east could be cut off from the outer ward, and had an independent entry from the sea. The importance of this inner ward, housing the king's apartments, is emphasised architecturally by the addition of turrets to its four corner towers.

Conwy displays all the most characteristic points of military castle design particularly well. From the outside one can see the alternating arrowslits in the battlements, the ring of square beam-holes in the top of the towers to support a hoard, and appreciate the

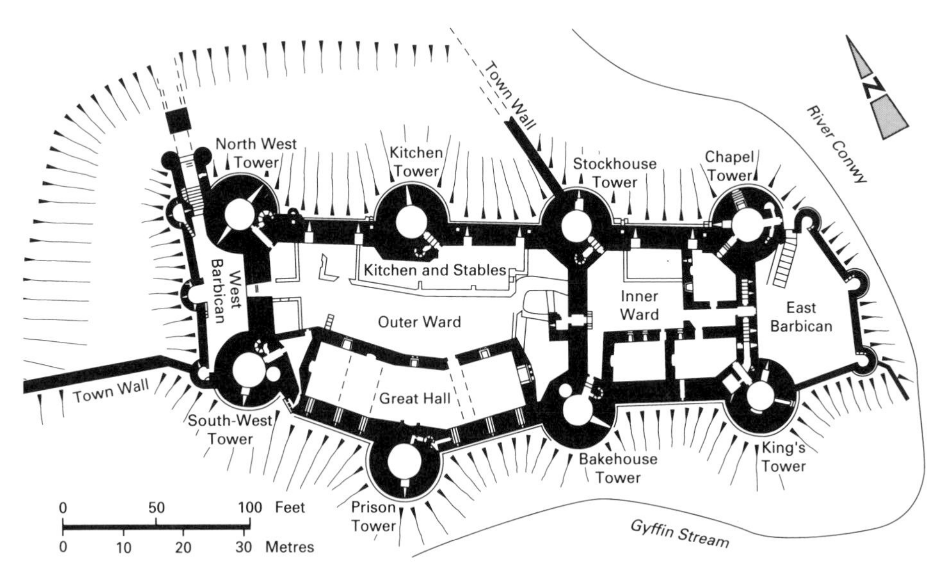

Conwy Castle

Conwy Castle, east end

siting of towers to maximise the field of fire. Inside, the attachment of gates, portcullis grooves, drawbridge pits and chains, machicolations and barbican design can be examined in detail. The West Barbican and the gate overlooking the original ramped entrance are especially rewarding.

Conwy, however, was not only a fortress, it was also a royal residence intended for lavish entertainment and serious political display. The suite of rooms in the outer ward, all with fine fireplaces and large decorated windows, must have been impressive, but the king's private apartments, including his Great Chamber in the inner ward, may have been even more splendid. The window tracery which survives there is unusually beautiful, as is the ornate chapel in the north-east tower.

The castle is divided from the town by a rock-cut ditch which visitors cross by a new bridge from the Visitor Centre to the site of the original drawbridge. Pause on the path below the walls to examine the battlement features, and also the patch of white plaster which confirms the record that the exterior was originally plastered, concealing the spiral of putlog (scaffold) holes. Rejoin the original gate passage and enter the West Barbican, with its display of military science.

The interior of the outer ward is long and narrow, bowed to the south to acccommodate the shape of the rock. Originally it would have appeared even narrower; several internal buildings have been reduced to footings. The chief building in the outer ward, now appearing as a single curved room, 38m long by 12m wide, housed the Great Hall in the central section with a large hooded fireplace backing onto the Prison Tower; beyond it was probably a smaller hall with its own fireplace and, beyond that, the Constable's Chamber. At the north end, entered from a cross-passage, was perhaps the Garrison Chapel with the altar beneath the splendid east window. The stone-arched roof was a 14th-century replacement. Just below the surviving arch is one of the grey stone corbels which had supported the original wooden roof trusses.

Behind the Great Hall is the Prison Tower, entered by a very inconspicuous doorway leading off a window in the hall. A narrow, tortuous passage ends in a 1.2m drop into what appears to be the basement room of the tower. Below was the true dungeon, a circular pit whose only access was a trapdoor, light and air coming only from a small, high shaft. The upper rooms of this tower were, by contrast, quite pleasant, with fireplaces, several good windows and convenient latrines. All the towers in this ward were similarly arranged and probably accommodated the constable, his family and the garrison. The range of fine rooms below represent the reception rooms of the castle's 'permanent staff' and are additional to the royal apartments in the inner ward. Visitors can go up the western towers and there gain access to the wall-walk.

The original defences between the inner and outer wards were reduced in the 16th century, the ditch partly filled, and the drawbridge removed; today one may be scarcely aware of what had been a major barrier between one fortress and another.

The inner ward contained the private apartments and offices of the king. The fine rooms on the first floor of this block communicated with the King's Tower, which probably housed the royal bedchambers. All the floors and the original wooden stairs have gone, so full appreciation of this suite of rooms is difficult, but the tracery in the windows overlooking the courtyard gives some hint of their original elegance.

The first floor of the north-eastern tower contained the royal chapel. The ravages of time and weather have scarcely dimmed the beauty of this tiny chapel; its ornate chancel, contrived within the thickness of the tower wall, is lit by three lancet windows and arcaded in seven bays which rise to form the ribs of the vaulted ceiling. It was in this chapel that Henry Percy, earl of Northumberland swore an oath of fealty to the doomed Richard II.

The Chapel Tower has been re-roofed and re-floored; visitors may climb to the top of the turret for a magnificent view of the estuary and mountains.

The final section of the castle is the East Barbican, designed as an independent entry to the inner ward giving access to and from the sea via a watergate (removed by Telford when he built the suspension bridge). It is designed much like the West Barbican, but does not seem to have seen serious military service. All records suggest that it was used as a garden from an early date.

119
Conwy Town Walls

Medieval borough defences

13th century AD

OS 115 SH 782776 U1

Walls encircle Conwy town (see no. 118). Whole circuit is visible from ground level and from north corner to Upper Gate it is possible to walk along the top. Mill Gate section is also accessible

Cadw Guidebook

The walls of Conwy are judged the finest in Britain. They are not only completely intact, but largely unencumbered by later building, and still give the impression of enclosing and protecting the town. Like the castle, their history is well documented, and they are sufficiently well-preserved in detail to demonstrate all the tactical features of their design.

The circuit of the wall is 0.75ml (1.3km), with 21 towers at regular intervals of about 46m. The wall is 1.68m thick and 9m high,

Bird's-eye view of Conwy town and walls as they might have appeared in the 14th century. Tower 5 is at the far end of the quay and 13 at the top left-hand corner

with towers rising to 15m. Externally it presented a continuous stone face, but the towers were open-backed, the wall-walk maintained across them by a series of removable wooden bridges. This ensured that each section, with its independent stair to ground level, could be isolated if it was attacked and scaled. At wall-walk level, each tower had a floor (set back from the bridge) which gave access to the lower arrowslits and to a stair to the battlements. They may not have been roofed.

The wall and towers provided 480 firing positions, the projecting towers covering the base of the wall to either side. Tower 13 at the highest point illustrates the tactic of the surveillance system: it is set forward of the wall-line to give a clear view of the approach to the Upper Gate and down the north side.

The wall was fronted by a ditch on the north and west sides, and was pierced originally by three double-towered gates and two posterns (the road archways on the northern side are modern). The only landward gate, on the north-west, was very heavily defended, but the others, fronting the two rivers, were less so. The town walls were linked to the castle by lengths of narrow walling, too narrow for attackers to run along.

The construction of the town walls went hand in hand with that of the castle, and they were essentially complete by 1286. The surviving accounts and a study of the different stones used show that, usually, the towers were built first, up to wall-walk level, then the curtain wall was built to link them, and finally the upper part of the tower and all the battlements were added. This sequence is particularly clear on Towers 5 and 6 at the seaward end of the north side. The town walls were still a useful defence during the Civil War. What is remarkable is their subsequent survival during 19th-century development. Both Telford (Tower 10) and the railway company (Towers 17/18) were careful to maintain their visual integrity.

From the quay, visitors may walk around the outside of the walls for the entire circuit, except at the south-western corner where they should re-enter by the Upper Gate; walk down Rosemary Lane and take the footpath beside the Catholic church to the site of Llywelyn's Hall and Tower 16; leave by the station and go through the new underpass to return through the Mill Gate. It is possible to walk along the top of the north wall; access points are at Tower 5 and the Upper Gate.

The wall fronting the quay is partially obscured. At the centre is a twin-towered gateway, and at the northern end there is a very thick spur wall projecting into the river from the corner tower. It had a small gate controlling access to the quay and ferry, and the wall formed a protective harbour. John Williams (see nos 118 and 122) fell off this wall as a boy, damaging himself for life.

Originally there were no openings in the northern wall. Even now, pierced by two roads, it is still one of the finest stretches of medieval town wall in Britain. The foreground has been cleared and part of the ditch redug, restoring the formal rhythm of the design. Examine the structural sequence displayed on Towers 5 and 6 and the tactical siting of Tower 13; also, if you wish, Telford's pseudo-barbican at Tower 10.

The main feature of the short western side is the heavily defended Upper Gate. The needs of modern traffic have caused the roadway to be lowered, but evidence for the original arrangements (barbican, drawbridge, portcullis and doors) can be seen in the south wall (beware traffic!). The gatehouse contained guardrooms and a porter's chamber above, closed with a wooden back wall built by Master Laurence of Canterbury.

The southern stretch of wall contains three features of particular interest. The first lies between Towers 15 and 16 (behind the new flats) where three large windows pierce the wall. These belonged to an earlier Welsh building known as Llywelyn's Hall, which may have been the setting of peace talks ending the first of Edward's wars against Llywelyn ap Gruffudd in 1277. This wooden building was incorporated into the town walls (notice roof corbels) and it was maintained up to 1315, when it was dismantled and taken to Caernarfon. The next tower (16) was modified for domestic use in 1305, when floors, windows and a fine fireplace were put in. The third feature may be seen from the outside, beyond the railway arch (1847). It is a series of 12 latrines corbelled out from the wall. Built at the cost of £15 (about £9,000 in today's terms) in 1286 – these must have been for the use of clerks of the King's Wardrobe (private secretariat) and the office of the Master of the King's Works (Master James of St George himself). The offices which these lavatories served would have been of timber, built against the wall.

The Mill Gate led down to the king's mill on the river Gyffin, a corn mill previously belonging to the abbey. The gate is unusual in that its towers contain domestic accommodation. This part of town, with the lodgings of the major officials and their record offices, was burnt in the revolt of 1401 – perhaps an indication that the bureaucratic burden, as much as the political frustration, had become unbearable.

120
Aberconwy House, Conwy

Late medieval merchant house

14th–20th century AD

OS 115 SH 782775 R2 NT

House is on corner of Castle Street and High Street in centre of Conwy. Open daily except Tuesdays, 1 Apr–31 Oct; admission charge

Official Guide

Aberconwy House

This is the best medieval town house to survive in north Wales, but some features of its original construction are puzzling, notably the absence of any original fireplaces, which must raise questions about its intended use. Its roof structure and the elaborate construction of the jettied or overhanging second floor are also unusual for this area, perhaps suggesting that it was built, probably in the later 14th century, by craftsmen from Cheshire or the West Midlands.

The building is an approximate rectangle, 14m by 5m, three storeys high. The lower walls are of stone, while the projecting upper floor is timbered. The ground floor is about 1m below the present road level. The original door (now a window) was at the street corner; the present entry is a 17th-century modification. This basement, in which the fireplaces are additions, was probably always a shop or store.

The original living quarters were on the first and second floors. On the first floor the room which contained the staircase would have been the main reception room. The present entry from an outside stair is a relatively recent arrangement necessitated by the rise in road level. The room beyond has a large fireplace, and was used as a kitchen in the 18th century but was not originally heated.

The rooms above, which are open to the high medieval roof, were described in a 17th-century inventory as 'The Great Loft' and the 'Cellar' (or store-room). The roof is unusual in having no ridge-pole. The present chimney in the 'Loft', which also serves the room next door, is a 16th-century addition.

Further alterations were made in the 17th century, when fireplaces and new doorways were added – probably during the occupancy of Evan David, whose probate inventory suggests that he was a merchant of some wealth and standing. It was then a standard merchant house with business premises below and living accommodation above. In the late 18th century it was the home of a sea captain, and between 1850 and 1910 it was a Temperance Hotel with a coffee shop on the ground floor.

During this century it has been owned and restored by the National Trust, who have a shop on the ground floor and have recently refurbished the rest of the building, displaying the house in its various transmutations.

121
Pen y Mwd, Abergwyngregyn

Medieval earthwork castle

11th–12th century AD

OS 115 SH 656726 U3/R2

Site is in Abergwyngregyn village, off A55 4.6ml (7.4km) SW of Penmaenmawr; on entering village go straight ahead, ignoring RH turn, and turn sharp R at end. Normally room for 1 car on R. The motte is on private land and permission to enter should be sought from Tyn y Mwd, the 1st (W) in a group of slate-hung houses on L

This is a very characteristic motte, standing close to the river and covering the point where travellers to Anglesey started their crossing of the Lavan Sands. The building of the castle is not recorded. It may belong to the aggressive campaign of Hugh of Avranches, the Norman earl of Chester, but it is not named in any document. The original Norman strategy was to build relatively few castles, but later they would build a castle at each conquered Welsh commotal centre. Alternatively, the mound may have been built later by the Welsh princes, who adopted the Norman style of castle building, copying the model so closely that the two styles cannot be distinguished unless there is documentation.

The mound is almost circular, more than 6m high and 40m in diameter at the base. The level top, where a wooden keep would have stood, is oval (19m by 16m). The top is very flat, with no sign of any masonry structure, so it was probably never refortified in stone once the original wooden castle had decayed. The mound is built largely of clay and has retained its sharp profile, but it is suffering erosion and damage from fallen trees. There is a hint of a protective ditch on the south side, but no sign of a bailey.

Abergwyngregyn was one of several royal *maerdrefi* or manors scattered across Gwynedd. Aberffraw was the chief residence,

View of Abergwyngregyn motte from the north

but Llywelyn ap Iorwerth is said to have preferred his *llys* or court here. Its exact location is unknown, but recent finds of stone foundations and 13th-century pottery suggest that it was close to the motte. Llywelyn's unfaithful wife, Siwan (see no. 139), died here in 1237, as did their unsuccessful son, Dafydd, in 1246.

122
Cochwillan, Tal y Bont

Medieval hall-house

15th century AD

OS 115 SH 607694 R1

In Tal y Bont village (2.5ml, 4km, SE of Bangor) go S under railway bridge and continue on this road, crossing bridge over A55; bear R where road turns to L, then immediately bear L to top of rise; turn R; house at end of track (200m). View by appointment at any time (tel: 01248 364608). Guided tour

Official Guide; Smith 1988, pp 100–2, 130–1

One of the largest and finest hall-houses in north Wales, Cochwillan has survived almost unchanged. Unlike so many important medieval houses, it has not been enlarged or developed since the 16th century, when the Williams family fell on hard times. The estate was eventually absorbed by the neighbouring Penrhyn estate, to which it still belongs.

The present house must replace a vanished predecessor, for the estate is mentioned in 13th-century records. The exact date of its construction is not recorded; although architectural style would indicate the mid-15th century, family history suggests a slightly later date, after the battle of Bosworth (1485) in which the Cochwillan family had been useful supporters of the winning side. Gwilym ap Gruffudd, subsequently made sheriff of Caernarfonshire for life, is most likely to have built the house, whose size and sophistication suggest wealth and status.

After his death in 1500, the family's power

Cochwillan, interior of the hall

and influence declined. Consequently, Cochwillan was not modernised during the 16th or 17th centuries, when concepts of domestic style and comfort were changing radically and many houses were completely rebuilt.

The most famous member of the family of Cochwillan was a cousin, John Williams, archbishop of York. He had risen to great power at the court of James I, and in 1622 he bought the bankrupt Cochwillan estate. His star waned under Charles I, but he rallied to the Royalist cause when war broke out, and refortified Conwy Castle at his own expense. An astute politician, he foresaw disaster for his native town and negotiated a treaty with parliament. After his death in 1650, Cochwillan descended to the status of a farmhouse, and by 1800 the two end compartments were probably occupied as separate cottages. When a new farmhouse was built, the old house became a haybarn, which it remained until 1969, when it was restored and returned to domestic occupation.

The hall is entered by two opposed doorways, a classic feature of the medieval house. The present approach is from the north, but the southern front was originally the major entry, with a gatehouse (now lost) across the courtyard. The walling of the south front is particularly impressive: massive blocks coursed with intervening small slabs, a technique which is characteristic of the 15th century in this area. The medieval walls stand perfectly vertical; later rebuilding has required buttressing!

The great hall survives intact, and almost all the fine timbers are original. The western end, containing serving rooms with a heated solar above, is essentially unchanged, but has been modified for modern use. The east end had been more seriously damaged, and has been reconstructed with modern accommodation on three floors. This end may have contained another solar and might, like Pennarth Fawr (no. 130), have extended southwards as a wing.

The hall is one of the largest in north Wales, 11.5m by 6.5m, with a hammer-beam roof of three bays, 9m high. The eastern screen where the dais has been reconstructed had been slightly damaged and some timbers have been replaced. The western screen is entirely original, and the carpenter's numbering on the post and panel wall and the uprights above it can still be seen. The hammer-beam roof (more strictly a 'false hammer-beam', since the weight is carried by the thick stone walls) is exceptionally fine. All the trusses and the main purlins are elegantly chamfered and the spandrels or corners under the hammer-beams are carved. The wall plate is hidden behind a battlemented moulding and a pierced frieze, much of which is original. The traveller, Richard Fenton, who visited the house in 1800, records shields on the ends of the beams, but, of the original heraldic decoration only the carving over the servery door – Marchudd ap Cynan's device, a Saracen's head – survives. The hall has a large lateral fireplace with a huge wooden lintel. This fireplace is integral to the building, which never had a smoky central hearth.

123
Dolwyddelan Castle, Dolwyddelan

Castle of the Welsh princes

13th century AD

OS 115 SH 722523 R3 Cadw

Castle is signposted on A470 0.9ml (1.4km) S of Dolwyddelan village (3.5ml, 5.6km, N of Blaenau Ffestiniog). Turn into car park; walk back and up to farm (where guidebooks, tickets and key to the keep are available); bear R around café and toilet block to stepped path up rock ridge to castle (c.10 mins). Admission charge; standard hours

Official Guide; Avent 1983

Dolwyddelan Castle, with its tall battlemented keep perched on a rocky ridge high above the valley floor, is everyone's idea of what a castle ought to look like. Indeed, it has often been used as the setting for costume dramas of high romance. This dramatic image is partly true and partly false, for the imposing keep was heavily restored in the 19th century.

This valley is the traditional birthplace of Llywelyn ap Iorwerth ('The Great'). The actual site was perhaps the vanished castle on the summit of the rocky knoll in the valley floor, for there is no evidence for any building at the present castle site earlier than the early 13th century, when the area came under Llywelyn's control. The site covers two routes into Snowdonia, and admirably demonstrates Llywelyn's scheme of defence and control.

Dolwyddelan remained an important stronghold for his grandson, Llywelyn ap Gruffudd (Llywelyn II), and its capture by the English, perhaps through treachery, on 18 January 1283 was a turning point of the Edwardian campaign. It was immediately repaired and garrisoned by Edward with a force kitted out with white tunics, camouflaged for a winter campaign in the mountains. The English maintained a military presence here until 1290, but their long-term strategy of control relied on military and administrative centres accessible by sea, and inland castles became increasingly irrelevant.

The castle was occupied again in the 15th century, when it was leased to Maredudd ap Ieuan, a local nobleman, who added an upper storey to the keep. In the middle of the 19th century it was extensively restored by the public-spirited Lord Willoughby de Eresby.

The castle consists of two rectangular towers linked by an irregular curtain wall set on the highest point of a narrow rocky ridge. It is isolated from the ridge by rock-cut ditches with counterscarp banks; access was originally by a wooden bridge at the north-east corner (present entry). The keep and the curtain wall are judged to be the work of Llywelyn ap Iorwerth. The keep was then only two storeys high: a basement accessible by trapdoor, and a great room heated by a large fireplace (now restored) and provided with a latrine in a narrow wall-chamber. This room had a steeply pitched roof; the gable line can be seen on the inner face of the south wall. Its doorway at first-floor level was strongly defended, with a drawbridge at the top of the outer stairs. The collapse of its defensive porch has exposed the drawbridge pit.

The curtain wall accommodates itself to the irregular outline of the rock. The entrance was very simple; there are no stone steps to the wall-walk, so wooden stairs must have sufficed. Two latrine chutes can be seen at the north corner. Though now reached from inside the west tower, they pre-date it.

The secondary nature of the west tower is proven by straight joints at each end where it abuts the curtain wall. This tower, a little larger but less seriously defended than the keep, is believed to have been built by Edward I. Its ground-floor doorway and windows have sandstone surrounds, the only instance of imported stone being used in the castle. It had an upper room with a large fireplace and its own latrines.

The alterations made by Maredudd ap Ieuan in 1488 increased the accommodation and convenience, but it must have remained an austere dwelling. He added a third storey

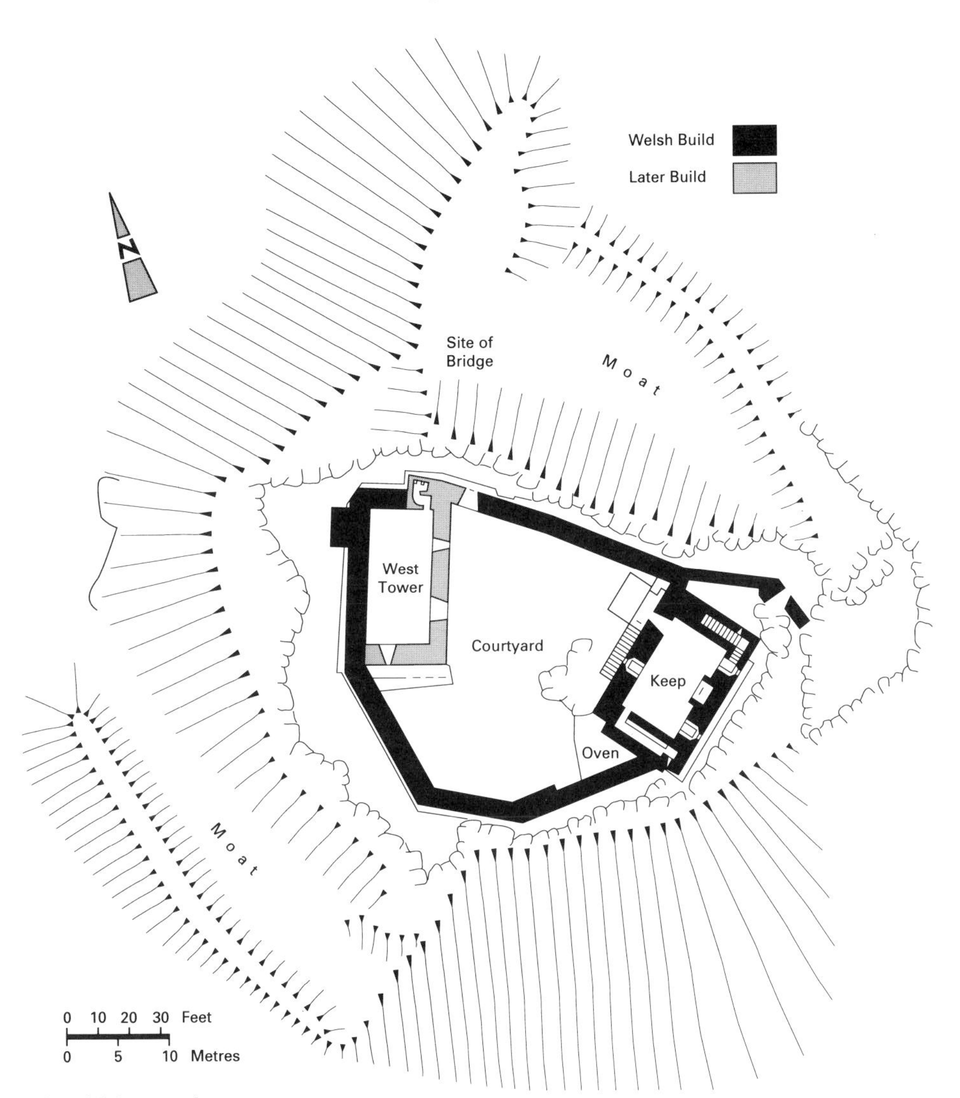

Dolwyddelan Castle

to the keep, providing another large, but unheated, room. The floor joists (not restored) were set on a rebated wall. In the west tower, Maredudd provided an external stair (now gone) to give more convenient access to the upper floor.

The 19th-century restoration concentrated on the keep. Floors, walls and battlements were recreated, together with a prominent series of projecting stone beams – supports for a fictitious hoard. Such supports should be of wood, and holes for their temporary emplacement are often found (see no. 118), but there was no evidence for them here.

124
Dolbadarn Castle, Llanberis

Castle of the Welsh princes

13th century AD

OS 115 SH 586598 R3 Cadw

Castle is at E end of Llanberis. Access on foot from public car park between the lakes; cross road and river to take steep path through wood. Alternative access from car park just beyond Royal Victoria Hotel, on N of road, at end of town; take narrow path around S end of castle rock. Neither approach is easy for those who have difficulty walking. Admission charge; standard hours

Official Guide; Avent 1983

A castle made famous by romantic painters, Dolbadarn boasts a tall keep standing high above the lake against a dramatic backdrop of rocks and mountains; its history, however, is surprisingly poorly documented.

The date of construction is not recorded, but it was almost certainly built by Llywelyn ap Iorwerth ('The Great') between 1216 and 1240 to command the route through the mountains towards the rich lands of Anglesey, the power base of the princes of Gwynedd.

The castle is traditionally the setting of some notable and tragic events in the history of the kingdom of Gwynedd. It is believed that Llywelyn ap Gruffudd (Llywelyn II), who came to power in 1255 after a family struggle, imprisoned his brother, Owain, here for twenty years. This imprisonment, though long and irksome, may not have been too uncomfortable if he was accommodated in the upper floor of the keep, with its private lavatory and warm bedroom. The contemporary poet Hywel Foel ap Griffri refers to Owain as '*Gŵr ysydd yn nhŵr yn hir westi*' ('A man in the tower, long a guest'). During this time Llywelyn's power increased, surpassing even that of his grandfather, Llywelyn ap Iorwerth, but in 1277 he was defeated by Edward I, who – to muddy the Gwynedd waters – demanded the release of

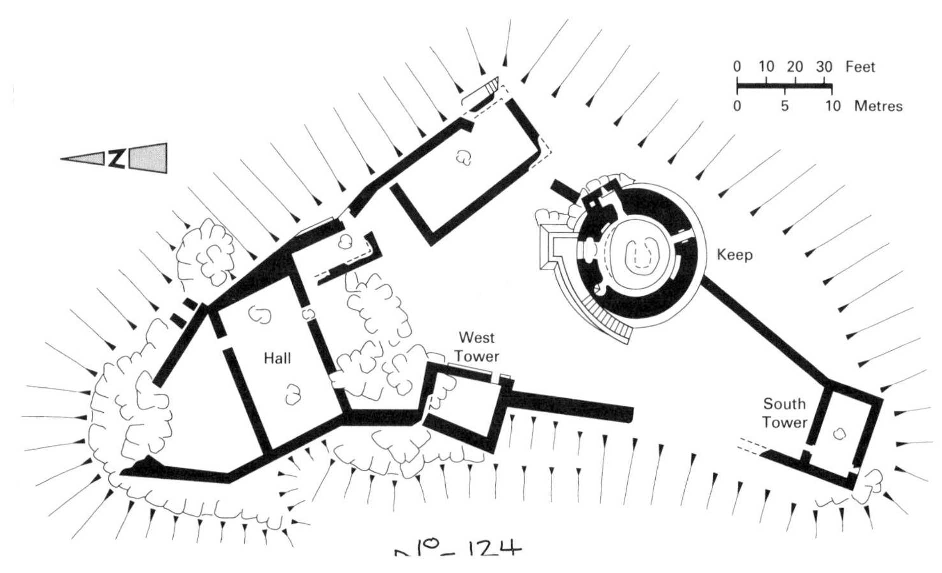

Dolbadarn Castle

Owain. Five years later, war was renewed; Edward swept through north Wales and, after Llywelyn II's death in a minor skirmish near Builth, Dolwyddelan (no. 123) capitulated on 18 January 1283. Dafydd, Llywelyn's other brother, tried to maintain the struggle, but by the spring he was encircled and trapped. In May 1283 he issued two deeds from the castle at Dolbadarn, but within a month he was captured and was led away to execution in Shrewsbury.

There is little evidence that the castle was maintained as a military base for long after 1283, but it did remain a royal manor for the new king, for there are records of repairs in 1303–4.

The buildings on the rocky knoll form two groups, perhaps of slightly different dates. They certainly differ in construction. The curtain wall and associated buildings (surviving only as footings) are unmortared, while the round keep (still standing 14.6m high) is built of well-mortared masonry. A rectangular building to the north-east of the keep is certainly a late addition (perhaps part of the Edwardian manor), since it overlies the line of the curtain wall and blocks what was possibly the original entry to the courtyard.

The round keep is a very substantial and sophisticated building, modelled on those being built by the English Marcher lords in south Wales. Entry was at first-floor level, and was protected by a portcullis, a rare device in Welsh castles. The present stone stairway is secondary, possibly late medieval; it replaces a removable wooden stair. The first-floor room covered a basement reached by trapdoor; it contained a fireplace, and had a latrine in a projecting rectangular turret. On the floor above, this projection contained a small bedroom, tucked in behind the fireplace, with its own adjacent latrine – the suite which may have been used by Owain during his long captivity. There is no modern access to these rooms.

The unmortared curtain wall is not well preserved, and the site of the main entrance is uncertain. Two small, angular towers cover the south and west sides and in the northern point of the rock there is a large hall (15m by 7.5m) with opposed doorways, the main public building of the establishment. Possibly it was from this hall that beams were removed for reuse in Caernarfon Castle (see no. 128) – the symbol of Edward's victory over the Prince of Wales and Lord of Snowdon, as Dafydd had styled himself in his last letters from Dolbadarn.

125
Platform Houses, Llanberis Pass

Medieval house sites

12th–14th century AD

OS 115 SH 626566 U4

Site is 1.3ml (2km) NW of Pen y Pass on S side of A4086. Lay-bys nearby; parking space is at a premium in summer. Cross river at Pont y Gromlech and walk W for c.500m to top of low spur projecting from valley side; or cross river to Climbing Club Centre (Ynys Ettws) and skirt S around nose of spur by shorter, steeper route behind house. Site is on top of shoulder of ridge

Gresham 1954

There are two stone houses standing on the top of this ridge, about 60m apart. Both are close to freshwater springs and set within a relatively well-drained area partially cleared of stones. The stone clearance ends on an artificially straight line at the west, but no cultivation ridges are visible. These houses are probably *hafodau*, occupied only while the cattle were on upland pastures. Other ruined sites exist in this central section of the pass, where the valley widens a little, providing adequate agricultural land.

The western house is a particularly good example of a 'platform house' – a level house site set across the contour, cut into the hillslope at one end and built up at the other. Only the narrow gable end is against the

Western house in Llanberis Pass

hillslope, and water is channelled away to either side by a 'hood', or bank and ditch, at the upper end. This medieval system contrasts with the later practice of building the house along the contour – a position which frequently results in damp walls.

The western house is about 10m by 5m, the normal proportions for such a house. The door is on the east side in the lower end. The cross-wall may be a later addition to convert the ruin to a sheep shelter. The hood around the north end is especially well preserved.

The eastern house is smaller; built on a more level site, the platform element is less marked. The hood is just recognisable around the southern end, more a ditch than a bank.

126
Cwm Brwnynog, Llanberis
Hafodau

14th century AD

OS 115 SH 594568 U4

Walk 2.75ml (4.5km) from Llanberis, taking road opposite Royal Victoria Hotel which joins path to Snowdon running alongside Snowdon Mountain Railway track as far as Halfway House; branch off down slope alongside wall. Hafodau *are immediately below second, ruined, cross-wall on narrow ridge between two streams*

Some seventy years after the victory in 1282, the English king made a thorough inventory of his new lands, paying particular attention to the estates which had belonged to the Welsh princes. The *Record of Caernarfon* (1352) notes four royal *hafodau* or summer grazing bases in Dolbardarn. These are listed as Combroinok Hir (Cwm Brwnynog Hir), Helvaylgayth, Vayshcom and Havot Grynwothok. Despite phonetic rendition by English-speaking officials, all four sites can be identified in the upland valleys to the south of Llanberis. The great boundary banks on Moel Eilio (see no. 127) and across Bwlch Maesgwm SH 573560 may mark the edge of these summer pastures.

The establishment of *hafodau* was part of a cattle economy. In Wales the summer pastures were not far from the *hendre* or main farm, but far enough to warrant the building of simple houses at the summer base, where younger members of the family would guard and milk the cows and make butter and cheese. With the growth of sheep farming, occupation of *hafodau* declined, though many became permanent farms as population increased.

The structures in Cwm Brwnynog are in two groups, both on the same narrow ridge, close to the river. They stand within a large enclosure formed by a revetted bank, which is probably contemporary.

There are three rectangular houses visible in the upper group, two of them levelled into the hillside. They are single-roomed, 7–8m by 4.5m, with walls about 1m thick. They lack the

Reconstruction drawing of a platform house like those in Cwm Brwnynog or Llanberis Pass

hood at the upper end (see no. 125), perhaps because they were designed only for summer living. Two of them can be seen very clearly as you approach from above – they are just below the enclosure bank. A third stands to the north, isolated by a small ravine. The lower group consists of three buildings: two, side by side, have walls still almost 1m high; the third, just up the slope from them, is set askew. Other ancillary buildings may be recognised under the turf.

Many *hafodau*, perhaps the majority, are single, isolated buildings. The presence of eight or nine structures here may be due to royal ownership.

127

Bryn Mawr Boundary, Llanberis

Medieval land boundary

12th century AD

OS 115 SH 558595–SH 557582 U4

Various roads and footpaths lead up from Llanberis and Waunfawr. Simplest route by car is to go SE from roundabout on A4085 E of Caernarfon; after 1.3ml (2.1km) take 2nd turn L (signposted Ceunant), go straight across Groeslon crossroads and persevere for 1.6ml (2.6km). Park in quarry where tarmac ends and walk to road gate; turn up R following wide path to crest of ridge (c.15mins)

This well preserved boundary is a stony bank, 2.5m wide and about 0.7m high, with a slight ditch on the west side. The path to the top of Moel Eilio follows it for most of its length. It starts where the steep valley sides level out into moorland grazing, and it follows the crest of the ridge for about 1ml (1.5km) ending where the slopes change to a rocky cliff. Further south, another length of similar bank continues what may be the same boundary, closing off Bwlch Maesgwm (SH 573560).

The bank is a parish boundary, but its substantial nature indicates that it had a serious agricultural function but pre-dates the normal 18th- and 19th-century stone walls which divide modern sheep-walks. It is likely to be medieval in date and to mark a division between summer grazing lands. The scale of the work suggests that it relates to the lands of the kings of Gwynedd in this area. Welsh castles, like Dolbadarn (no. 124), were often built within royal grazing lands, since summer was the campaigning season and herds needed protection in the hills.

128

Caernarfon Castle

Stone castle of Edward I

13th–14th century AD

OS 115 SH 477626 R1 (with help) Cadw–World Heritage Site

At SW corner of town, nearest car park on slate quay, entrance on opposite side of castle. Exhibitions; audio-visual presentation in Eagle Tower; Royal Welsh Fusiliers Museum in Queen's Tower (no extra charge). Admission charge; standard hours

Official Guide; Taylor 1986

The greatest of Edward I's castles in north Wales, Caernarfon was designed from the start to be the centre of the new government and to house the royal household or that of the viceroy. Its unusual angular towers and coloured banding were also to evoke echoes of Constantinople and to reawaken memories of the glorious past of Segontium, the legend of Macsen Wledig and the 'many-towered fort at the mouth of the Seiont' (see no. 92). This castle, above all others, had a multi-layered role in the power politics of the English conquest: it was to be a fortress, a palace and a symbol.

Caernarfon was not a new site. The legacy of the Roman fort (no. 92) made it central to later administrative geography, a position reinforced by the Normans in 1090. Their motte remained at the centre of the Welsh

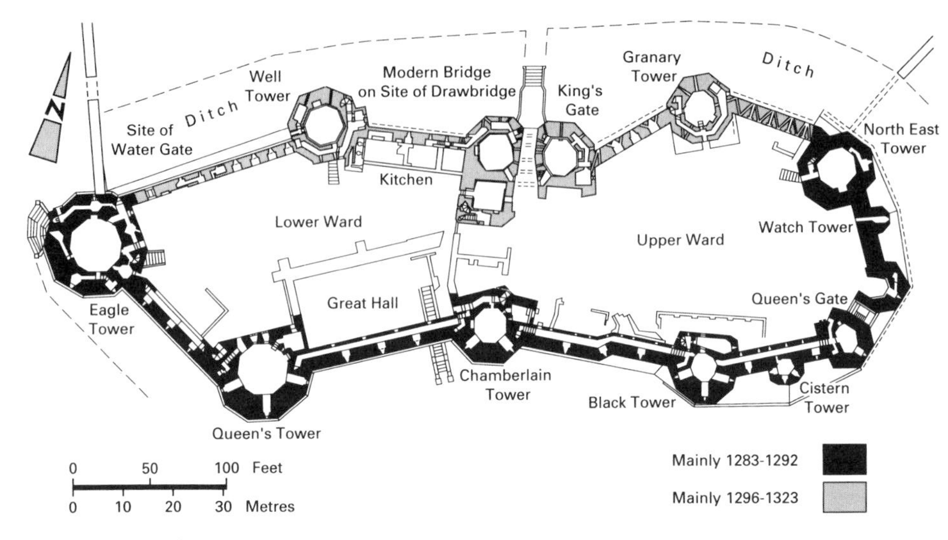

Caernarfon Castle

maerdref, and, when the fall of Dolwyddelan (no. 123) exposed the heartland of Gwynedd to English power in 1283, the motte still stood. The presence of this mound explains the shape and height of the upper ward and especially the height of the Queen's Gate.

The building of Caernarfon – the castle, the town walls and the quay – was begun in the early summer of 1283 under the direction of Master James of St George, and continued apace. At this early stage the north side of the castle was defined only by a ditch and a wooden palisade. The priority was to establish a large protected area within which work could proceed in safety. By 1292 part of the Eagle Tower, the southern circuit with its banded masonry, and the town walls were built, but the north wall of the castle was only a few metres high. Its vulnerability was demonstrated in 1294, when the town walls were breached and the incomplete castle stormed during Madoc ap Llywelyn's rebellion.

Repairs and completion of the north wall and main gate of the castle were undertaken immediately. Work concentrated on additional defences, and the refinement of banded masonry was abandoned. Expenditure on reconstruction continued at a high level for six years, stopped during the Scottish Wars but began again in 1304 and continued under Edward II until 1327. However, even by then the full plan was not achieved. The two gatehouses, especially the Queen's Gate, were never completed, the barrier between the upper and lower wards was never built and the Watergate beside the Eagle Tower, designed to bring supplies directly to the Well Tower and the kitchens, was never begun.

The fact that the castle was never finished is an indication of its diminishing strategic and political importance. It never became the base for a ruling Prince of Wales or viceroy, and its administrative functions became routine, though it was still officially the capital of north Wales. The garrison here withstood two sieges during the Glyndŵr Rebellion, in 1403 and 1404, when both Harlech and Conwy were taken. Even in decay the castle was successfully held for the king during the Civil War (1642–8), when Lord Byron was thrice besieged inside the still-formidable walls.

The castle and town walls survived the 18th

and 19th centuries as the town grew around them (see exhibition in Chamberlain Tower). The castle was rescued from quiet decay by a local businessman and deputy constable, Sir Llewelyn Turner, who employed the architect Antony Salvin to replace battlements, stairs and roofs; their work can be recognised by the use of a buff sandstone. This refurbishment and the advocacy of the local MP, David Lloyd George, combined to revive memories of its past political potency, and it became the setting of modern Investiture Ceremonies (exhibition in the North East Tower).

Like Conwy (no. 118), Caernarfon has an elongated ground plan with two wards in tandem, but there are several differences. The defence of the entrance is not through the use of barbicans, like Conwy, but is concentrated into the twin-towered gatehouse and its series of internal obstacles. In its more low-lying position, the fire-power from the walls is organised differently. It does not rely only on wall-top battlements but has two levels of enclosed wall-passages and, at the north-east end, an exceptionally ingenious system of triple arrowslits which maximise fire-power at a particular point of attack. Caernarfon is a single stronghold, not a hierarchy of strong points: its strength lies in the thickness of the entire circuit, which may explain why the barrier between the two wards had a low priority and was never completed.

Caernarfon does not have the crowded interior of Conwy. Apart from the Great Hall, most of the domestic and official accommodation was concentrated into the towers. They contain an exceptional number of small rooms within the thickness of the walls. Several chapels and small private kitchens may be identified, suggesting that a number of independent households could be accommodated. Large decorated windows show that the top floors of both the King's and the Queen's Gate were designed to form large and splendid halls, though neither was built.

Because of the multiplicity of wall-passages

Caernarfon Castle

and small rooms, Caernarfon is a complicated castle to visit. The official guidebook provides a tour which covers every accessible nook and cranny. Here, just the highlights will be mentioned.

Before entering by the stone bridge which replaced the original wooden drawbridge, look up at the statue of Edward II (born here in 1284) and the traceried windows of the never-completed hall. The narrow entrance passage was punctuated by five doors and six portcullises. A drawbridge and another portcullis barred entry to the lower ward, but the planned defences here were never completed. A stair leads to the first floor of the gatehouse and the chapel above the gate passage.

The main kitchens lay between the entrance and the Well Tower. Several interesting details survive relating to the collection and heating of water for the kitchens (explained on an information panel). Behind the kitchen was a meat-smoking room and the Well Chamber, which was also accessible from a small room, perhaps a private kitchen, on the floor above. In the basement of the Well Tower is a door leading from the ditch, planned as an entry for sea-borne supplies.

The Eagle Tower was the main residence of the castle. It was probably the first to be built and roofed, but its top storey and the turrets were not added until 1316, when records show a final payment for fixing a stone eagle in place on the battlements. Visitors may climb to the top of this tower and stand beside this eagle on the western turret.

The basement provided direct access to the sea through a small and strongly defended door. The main rooms above were probably designed for Sir Otto de Grandison, the first justiciar of north Wales, but would have been used by the king and queen when in residence. It is believed that Edward II was born in one of the rooms here. The two main chambers are presently occupied by exhibitions and the audio-visual theatre, but it is possible to examine the numerous intra-mural chambers. The octagonal rooms beside the spiral stair are thought to be private chapels (one has a holy water stoup).

A small door at the right-hand side of the Queen's Tower leads, via a spiral stair, to the roof and to the wall-passages and wall-walk. The two covered wall-passages with the open wall-walk above provided three tiers of defenders who could be mustered at any point. The passages continue around the front of each tower and give access to the entire south wall overlooking the river. At present the only exit at the Queen's Gate end is from the lower wall-passage, so descend to this level at the Chamberlain Tower.

The Black Tower (reached from the lower passage, but not from the courtyard) and the Cistern Tower were never completed to full height, and their lower levels are solid because they were built against the earlier motte. The castle wall crosses the ditch of the motte at this point, hence the kink.

The Queen's Gate, suspended above the town, is now more like a huge window than a gate. It was originally approached by a sloping ramp and a drawbridge like that at Conwy. This high position made it less vulnerable than the King's Gate; the defences are less elaborate and were, in fact, never finished.

The upper level of the wall-passage would have continued round the back of this gatehouse, past the small Watch-tower and around the North-east Tower, but in 1295 ideas were changed. Only the open wall-walk was continued, and the lower arrowslits were designed in a different way. These complex triple arrowslits, unique to Caernarfon, are explained in a wall panel near the Granary Tower.

The town walls of Caernarfon have never been as famous as those of Conwy (no. 119) because, although still complete, they have been engulfed by later building. During the 20th century they have been partly cleared, and the external circuit is visible. There are eight half-round towers and two double-towered gates, one opening on to the medieval quays and the other, on the landward side, covering the bridge over the now-culverted Cadnant river. It is possible to walk on the walls for a short distance near St Mary's Chapel – the borough (not parish) church in the north-west corner.

129
Criccieth Castle

Welsh castle with English alterations

13th–15th century AD

OS 123 SH 499376 R2 Cadw

Criccieth is on S coast of Lleyn peninsula, between Porthmadog and Pwllheli, and can be approached via A497, or B4411 S of A487. Castle is on coastal promontory and is signposted from centre of town. Admission charge; standard hours

Official Guide

Criccieth Castle, on its great rock lapped by the sea, its high towers silhouetted against the sunset, makes a romantic and dramatic picture; a direct statement, it appears, about the imposition and maintenance of power. But, in reality, the interplay of native and invader on this site is unusually complex. Details of its history are still a matter of debate.

The castle was founded by Llywelyn ap Iorwerth ('The Great'), and was extended by his grandson, Llywelyn ap Gruffudd (Llywelyn II). After its capture, Edward I refurbished it, and accounts show that Edward II also did some rebuilding here in the 14th century, when the castle was used as an English prison. It was finally destroyed during the revolt of Owain Glyndŵr in 1404 and never rebuilt.

The broad outline of this history is not in doubt, but controversy has raged over the date of the individual towers. A close study of the surviving remains provides an object lesson in historical reconstruction from architectural and archaeological observation, but to follow the argument in detail readers should purchase the guidebook which lays it out very fully and clearly. Today, visitors approach the castle by a modern path, diverging from the medieval one to run up the slope behind the inner bank and come into the castle by a break in the outer curtain wall. It is then best to turn sharply left through the narrow passage (originally roofed) between the curtain walls to the front of the inner gatehouse, the focus of a good deal of the chronological argument.

Four periods of building have been distinguished, based upon variations in building stone, masonry style, type of mortar and straight joints and buried wall-faces. It was originally thought that the English kings had spent very little on the castle, so nearly all the surviving buildings were credited to the Welsh princes. Subsequent documentary research, however, has shown that English expenditure was, in fact, substantial. So it was then suggested that the whole of the inner ward was English work, constructed within a sprawling Welsh castle. But this could not be reconciled with the archaeological observations, and a more subtle disentanglement of historical events is now proposed.

The castle built by Llywelyn ap Iorwerth in the early 13th century was a small but imposing structure on the very summit of the hill, protected on the landward side by two banks and ditches. It was the administrative centre for the commote of Eifionydd, and also a prison for distinguished prisoners, usually close relatives of the prince. This castle consisted of two D-shaped gatehouse towers and a large rectangular tower on the south-east, linked by a curtain wall enclosing a relatively small courtyard. The gatehouse is most imposing, and some think the design smacks more of the work of Edward's great architect, Master James of St George, than that of Llywelyn's castle builders. However, Beeston Castle in Cheshire, built in 1220 by a friend of Llywelyn ap Iorwerth, could have been the model for the Criccieth gatehouse.

The masonry of this period – the lower part of the gatehouse, the curtain wall, etc. – is characterised by the use of local stone and a

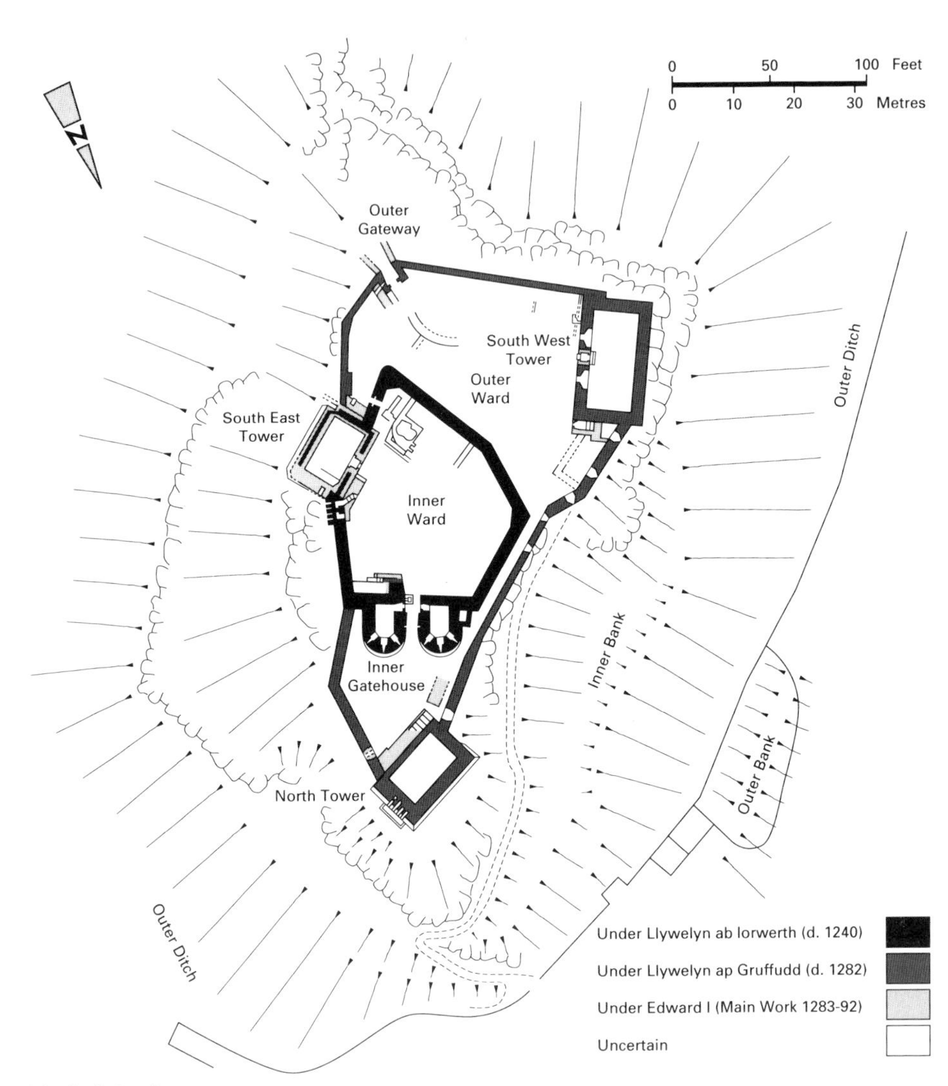

Criccieth Castle

grey mortar. The distinction between this first Welsh work and that of Edward I and Edward II, who both heightened the gatehouse towers, can be easily seen on the outer face.

The castle was greatly enlarged by Llywelyn II, who built the outer ward using a different style of masonry with a different mortar. The new castle covered the whole of the hilltop, and two new towers were built on the south-west and northern corners. Carved stone from the south-west tower suggests that this was the prince's apartment. A new entrance to the castle at the southern corner had quite a simple gate. Only very minor alterations were made to the original castle, now the inner ward.

Criccieth was captured by English forces some time before 14 March 1283. As a strongly built castle with access to the sea, it accorded with Edward's strategy for controlling his newly conquered lands, and the accounts show that he spent £500 (twice the cost of the high western towers at Harlech (no. 132)) on works at Criccieth. Yet it is difficult to identify sufficient building of this period to account for the cost.

A third phase can be distinguished easily enough in the masonry – once more using local stone, but in squarer blocks. This masonry can be identified in the gatehouse, where the towers were raised and given battlements. It is also seen in the south-east tower, which seems to have been extensively rebuilt and probably heightened. This work involved refacing the earlier walls, and the details are difficult to disentangle. The best evidence is at the north-western corner, where the new wall abuts Llywelyn ap Iorwerth's curtain wall. The outer gate also saw some additions, but in order to find £500 worth of building it is necessary to postulate the addition of an extra storey to both residential towers and the strengthening of the north tower, perhaps for a siege engine. The provision of new stairs is the best evidence for all this. Interior buildings may also have been constructed.

Edward II had to spend a good deal of money on more repairs between 1307 and 1327. The only visible alteration is the further raising of the gatehouse. New stonework blocking Edward I's battlements can be clearly seen on the front of the towers.

The castle was in its heyday from 1359 to 1381, when a local Welsh hero of Crécy, Syr Hywel y Fwyall ('Sir Howel of the Battle-axe') was constable. During the Glyndŵr revolt when the sea was held by the rebels, the small garrison in Criccieth surrendered, and the castle was burnt. With the loss of the castle the adjacent borough declined and in 1545 it was described as 'clene decayed'.

130
Pennarth Fawr, Pwllheli

Medieval hall-house

15th century AD

OS 123 SH 419376 R1 Cadw

House is signposted from A497 3.1ml (5km) E of Pwllheli and is on R, 0.5ml (0.75km) along road. Large vehicles should approach from N (off B4354). Open without charge during daylight hours

Official Guide (with Criccieth Castle); Smith 1988, pp 96–9, 113a–b

Pennarth Fawr is smaller than Cochwillan (no. 122) and has been more extensively altered, but both houses should be visited because so many features are complementary and mutually illuminating.

They are approximately contemporary, and their social status was similar. The overall plan is identical, a central hall open to the roof, a cross-passage between two opposed doorways, with private and service rooms at either end on two floors. There are some significant differences, notably the presence of a spere truss (see below) at Pennarth Fawr, where the original hearth was in the centre (the lateral fireplace being a later addition). Pennarth Fawr suffered 17th-century alterations (now removed), whilst Cochwillan, where poverty and benign neglect came earlier, was spared these.

Like Cochwillan, the actual date of building is not recorded, but recent tree-ring dating of the spere truss (see below) has shown that the tree from which it is made was felled shortly after 1476. This means that the builder must have been Howel ap Madog, not his father, as suggested in the information panel. In 1615 the open hearth was replaced by a lateral chimney with a stone arched fireplace and a shield recording Hugh Gwyn, great-grandson of the builder. In 1656 a floor was inserted and small rooms created in the upper part of the hall. A joist from this floor (now lying by the north wall) carries an inscription

Artist's impression of the dais end of the hall at Pennarth Fawr as it might have appeared in the late 15th century

which records this remodelling with astonishing precision. An 18th-century drawing shows the northern end with a projecting wing, demolished in the 19th century when a new house was built against the south-eastern corner. In 1937 the owner, William Evans of Broom Hall, undertook major restoration work, dismantling the inserted floor and returning the hall to its spacious medieval appearance.

The house is now essentially as it was in the early 17th century, but lacks the northern compartment which would have contained the solar. The southern compartment containing buttery and pantry has survived, but the post and panel screen separating these service rooms from the hall has gone. The open stair leading to the room above is a modern replacement.

The hall is of three bays, 10m long, 6m wide and 6m high. Decoration is concentrated on the spere truss which faced the high table and divided the hall proper from the cross-passage. The spere truss was a device to extend the width of the building by providing aisle-posts to support the roof. The moulding of the aisle-posts, the carving of foot and capital beneath the windbrace and the cusping on collar and arch braces, all indicate the quality of this carpentry, even though the rest of the roof is relatively plain. Recent examination has revealed a mortise hole in the 'arcade plate' (purlin set vertically) south of the spere truss, which suggests that the passage screen might also have incorporated an aisle-post. The small louvre truss remaining in the first bay supported an opening in the roof and indicates the original presence of an open hearth.

131
Dolbenmaen Motte, Porthmadog

Medieval earthwork castle

12th century AD

OS 124   SH 506430   U1

Site is on A487, 5ml (8km) NW of Porthmadog, visible on R (N) at new bridge over river Dwyfor. A better view is gained by turning immediately R towards Cwm Pennant; park between motte and church

Gresham 1973, pp 370–80

The castle mound, 36m in diameter and some 6m high, can be clearly seen from the road despite the trees; its flat top preserves a hint of vanished buildings in stone. A substantial ditch survives on the west, but on the other sides the base has been damaged by later walls. Had there been a bailey, it has been lost under later farm buildings and the 16th–18th-century house, Plas Dolbenmaen.

The mound is on private land, and visitors cannot climb on it, but it is worth visiting because the grouping of church, castle and manor house is both attractive and unusual for Wales, where such nucleated villages are rare. The history of the motte, built at a fordable crossing of the river Dwyfor, is not well documented. It could be a Norman base, or the product of the revival of Welsh power in the early 12th century. It later formed the administrative centre (*maerdref*) of the commote of Eifionydd and a royal seat until about 1230, when Llywelyn the Great moved the court to Criccieth (no. 129). A village of bondmen would have been attached to the court to work the lord's fields, hence the tight cluster of houses around it to this day.

132
Harlech Castle

Stone castle of Edward I

13th century AD

OS 124 SH 581312 R3 Cadw–World Heritage Site

Castle is in centre of Harlech town; limited parking available at upper (eastern) entrance. Also accessible from below, near railway station, during summer months. Admission charge; standard hours

Official Guide; Taylor 1986

Because of its spectacular position, outlined against the sky and the mountains of Snowdonia, this is one of the best known of the Welsh castles. Of all the great castles, it is the one with the most significant post-Edwardian history. Major episodes of the Glyndŵr revolt (1404, 1408) the Wars of the Roses (1468) and the Civil War (1647) took place here.

Despite the natural impregnability of the rock on which the castle stands, there is no evidence that the site was occupied or defended prior to the building of the Edwardian castle. The only references to Harlech in Welsh documents are literary; in the stories of the *Mabinogion* it is identified as the court of Bendigaid, but no historical figure had a *llys* or court here.

Recognition of the strategic importance of the site must be credited to Sir Otto de Grandison, marching north from his capture of Castell y Bere (no. 134). The architect, as always, was Master James of St George, already, in 1283, working on two other major castles. It is fitting that when the castle was finished, after seven years of intense activity, Master James was made constable, and would have lived in the fine apartments which he had designed in the Gatehouse.

The castle was built very rapidly, but two phases of construction may be recognised. The concentric design was established from the start: a narrow outer ward surrounding an almost square inner ward with round towers at each corner, and an enormous Gatehouse bestriding the eastern wall and dominating the only landward access. The primary concern was to establish a safe base for the garrison and workmen, so work started with cutting the rock ditch and building the outer circuit of walls. The inner circuit was established, but was not completed to full width or height until 1289. A change in masonry all round the inner ward about 4.5m from the ground represents a temporary stopping point in the work, probably during the first winter, 1283–4.

Like all the other Edwardian castles, Harlech had sea access; the sand dunes are recent. A Watergate was built right down at the bottom of the rock and a long stairway was constructed, protected by a seaward wall and two artillery positions. The revolt of Madoc ap Llywelyn in 1294 tested the castle. It was entirely cut off by land, but survived on rations shipped from Ireland. The rebellion caused sufficient anxiety to prompt the enclosure of the rock slopes. Apart from the reinforcement of the eastern bridge in the 14th century, this was the only alteration made to the original plan.

Although Harlech had withstood the Welsh rebels in 1294, in 1404 it fell to Owain Glyndŵr. Owain held the castle for more than four years. It became the residence of his court and family, and it was perhaps here that he was formally crowned as Prince of Wales. Together with Aberystwyth, it was the centre of his power at the time when his bid for independence had every prospect of success. The castle was eventually regained by the future Henry V, who laid siege to it with heavy artillery – perhaps the occasion when the outer curtain wall was destroyed.

Harlech also played a significant role in the Wars of the Roses. In 1468 it was the last Lancastrian stronghold to fall, after a long siege conducted by William Herbert, earl of Pembroke, while Margaret of Anjou, the wife of Henry VI, was taking refuge inside.

In the 16th century most royal castles were ruined, but Harlech was sounder than some because the assizes continued to meet in the Gatehouse. During the Civil War, Royalists were able to hold the castle during a prolonged siege and Harlech was, once again, the last castle to be lost. Its fall on 15 March 1647 signified the end of the war. In 1660 the government ordered the demolition of all defences, but nothing was done and the robust shell of the castle has withstood the years.

From the rising ground to the east of the castle it is possible to appreciate the sequence of defences that focus upon the great Gatehouse. First the rock-cut dry moat linking two ravines and isolating the rock from landward attack; then a double drawbridge (reinforced in the 14th century) where the modern stair enters between two solid turrets elegantly corbelled out from the apron wall.

The outer ward is very narrow, and one is immediately confronted by the double towers of the Gatehouse. The design and workmanship of these great towers is very characteristic of Master James and his compatriot masons. The entrance passage is very strongly defended with a series of three solid doors and three portcullises, as well as

Harlech Castle and rock from the air

arrowslits through which to threaten any intruder caught between the lowered barriers. All the details of these mechanisms are well preserved here.

The ground floor of the Gatehouse contained guardchambers and porters' rooms, but on the floors above were two suites of very fine, heated, well-lit rooms designed as accommodation for the constable and for visiting dignitaries. These apartments, repeated in the unfinished gatehouse at Beaumaris (no. 114), are one of the points of special interest at Harlech. They were reached by spiral staircases in the western turrets or, when the last portcullis was closed, by an outside staircase which linked them directly to the inner ward. No floors survive, but the rooms may be seen from the platform at the top of this outside stair.

The accommodation was the same on both floors. There were two rooms of unequal size on the west, with fine fireplaces and large windows overlooking the inner ward. The southern one, extending over the entrance passage, was a hall or public chamber, the smaller one to the north perhaps a more private office. Doors at the corners gave on to the turret stairs and to unheated bedrooms in the main towers. On each side, convenient latrines had been built into the thickness of the wall. Between the two bedrooms, over the front end of the passage, was a small, square room with a lancet window, almost certainly a private chapel or oratory. As a convenient and comfortable apartment these rooms can scarcely be bettered; moreover, their western facade, as originally designed, with high traceried windows, is a structure of surpassing symmetry and elegance.

The north-east tower, the Prison Tower, containing a dungeon in the basement, with two comfortable heated rooms above, has a staircase which gives access to the wall-walk on which it is possible to walk round to the south-east tower with a corresponding staircase. The western towers, in which stairs have not survived, belong to the second construction phase and were built by an Irishman, Master William of Drogheda, who

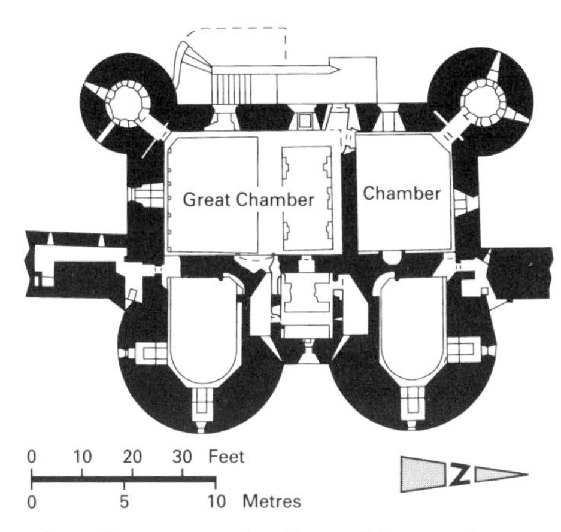

Plan of rooms on first floor of the gatehouse, Harlech Castle

was paid £228.7s.6d (about £120,000 in today's terms) in 1289.

The inner ward was surrounded on three sides by large buildings set against the curtain wall. On the west, with large windows overlooking the sea, was the Great Hall with buttery and kitchens. On the south there was a building referred to as the Ystumgwern Hall. This name is puzzling; it may have been a hall-house transported from Ystumgwern, not far from Harlech, and re-erected in the castle. Such reuse of timber halls is recorded on other occasions (see, for example, no. 119).

Access from the inner to the outer ward is through a narrow door in the north wall leading to a minor gate on to the castle rock, or through a modern break in the west wall. On the southern side of the outer ward is a fine turret elegantly corbelled out from the wall. It was a rubbish chute and latrine!

An English borough was founded alongside the castle at Harlech, but no walls survive and there may never have been any. Nor is there any regular grid of medieval streets on this constricted site.

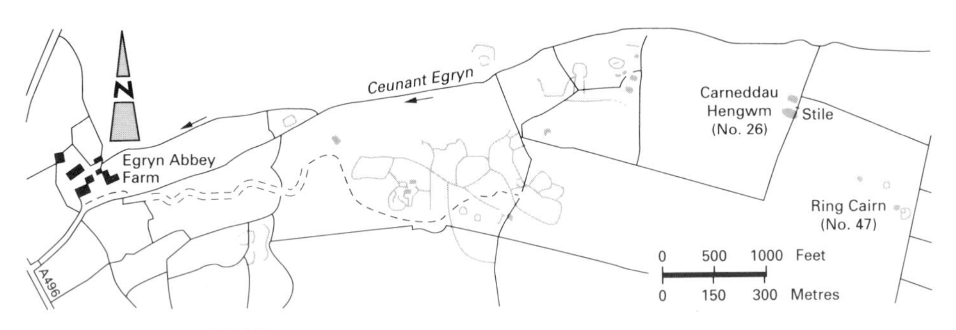

Egryn long huts and fields

133
Egryn Long Huts, Tal y Bont

Medieval and earlier settlement

1st millennium BC and 12th–16th century AD

OS 124 SH 605204 U4

See Carneddau Hengwm (no. 26). Huts and fields cover the hillside between 120m and 240m above sea level. They are easier to see on way down; remains begin at gate from open land. Keep dogs on lead; respect livestock. Bracken can obscure walls in high summer

Hooke 1975

This is an exceptionally intact ancient landscape, which here seems to be essentially of one date. The houses are all rectangular, belonging to the later medieval period or even the 16th century, when population expansion led to occupation of marginal lands.

The remains consist of irregular fields defined by walls of large boulders. Among the fields are enclosures containing two or three long huts. Several of these huts are divided into two or three rooms, but the plans are not standard. Two small enclosures with houses attached lie to the south of the path on level land just through the upper gate. The largest cluster, with a double yard, is midway down the slope to the north of the track, and other well preserved houses are below it.

From the track there is a good view of Pen Dinas hillfort, a prominent landmark on the north side of the stream. A strong stone wall surrounds the natural rock boss which forms the basis of the fort; outside that is a wide ditch. There is an embanked outwork on the west, the path to it blocked by late medieval walls associated with a platform house. Minor excavations here in 1919 produced no datable finds but fuelled debate about whether the defences were prehistoric, post-Roman or medieval (Crawford 1920). The massive in-turned entrance on the west is the most notable feature.

Also on the north side of the stream is an Iron Age farmstead of concentric circle type. The central house is set on a shelf overhanging the valley, so close to the ravine that its enclosing wall is incomplete. From the last leg of the track another settlement of this type is visible, in rough ground just south of the stream. It may have had two outer enclosures like Maes y Caerau (see no. 46).

134
Castell y Bere, Llanfihangel y Pennant

Castle of the Welsh princes

13th century AD

OS 124 SH 669086 U3 Cadw

From Tywyn take B4405 to Abergynolwyn (7ml, 11.3km) where castle is signposted. Follow signs for 2ml (3.2km) along narrow road with passing places. Car park at site. Alternative access from A493 via Llanegryn or Bryn Crug (signposted Craig yr Aderyn, see Appendix) is equally narrow

Avent 1983; Butler 1974

This is a romantic castle, its walls and towers appearing to grow naturally from the narrow spur of rock which rises dramatically from the level floor of the Dysynni valley.

The site must have attracted attention from an early date but little evidence of pre-medieval occupation survives, and the present castle belongs essentially to the early 13th century. In 1221 it is recorded that Llywelyn ap Iorwerth ('The Great') took back control of Meirionnydd from his son, Gruffudd, 'and began to build a castle in it for himself'. Bere is undoubtedly that castle, and several points of design link it to other castles built by Llywelyn the Great, notably the D-shaped towers at the north and south ends. The isolation of the South Tower, then separated from the rest of the castle by a rock-cut ditch, is, however, a unique feature.

The castle is on the southern border of Gwynedd, and in the war of 1282–3 it was besieged by the central English army from Montgomery under Edward's lieutenant, the Savoyard Sir Otto de Grandison. The castle fell on 25 April 1283. The English took over the castle; a small garrison with some masons and carpenters was left behind. The only obvious alteration made is the construction of the walled yard linking the South Tower to the rest of the defences. The internal buildings along the north wall, however, show a bewildering series of straight joints, and some may belong to this period, when Edward envisaged maintaining the castle as a centre

Artist's impression of Castell y Bere

of English power. Documents show that he planned to found an English borough close by, as he did at Beaumaris and his other major castles.

These plans came to nothing. The town never flourished, and the castle was captured by the Welsh during Madoc ap Llywelyn's revolt in 1294. Despite the king's urgent desire to regain it, Bere does not appear again in the royal accounts, which suggests that it was abandoned.

The modern entrance path runs under the south-eastern side of the rock and turns around the southern end of the spur. Notice the rock-cut ditches which isolate the castle, as at Dolwyddelan (no. 123). The entrance is on the west, defended by two ditches and two drawbridges, separated by a steep flight of steps overlooked by a small square tower and a large round tower standing astride the main curtain wall. This barbican is well defended but rather haphazard in plan, a response to the constraints of the narrow site. The layout can be well seen from the modern path beside the rectangular Middle Tower.

Just inside the entrance is a large well, essential for such a castle under siege. The footings of the buildings along the north side of the courtyard have many butt joints, suggesting a complex building history. The duplicated staircase leading to the upper floor or floors of the D-shaped North Tower is puzzling. The discovery of several pieces of carved stone in the rubble which filled the basement of this tower suggests that it housed the royal chapel. The very stoutly built Middle Tower was probably the main defensive point, and the South Tower, originally separate from the rest, may have housed the private apartments of the prince. It was a large two-storey structure, with a latrine and other features which suggest domestic accommodation. Access to it must have been by a wooden stair from the upper floor of the Middle Tower and a wooden bridge over the rock-cut ditch.

135
Tomen y Bala, Bala

Medieval earthwork castle

11th–12th century AD

OS 125 SH 928361 U3

At NE end of Bala, S of High Street. Immediately visible at 1st L turn from E end of town. One car can be parked but easier on foot. Access to top may be locked

The geological fault which contains Bala Lake and the Dee and Wnion valleys is a significant feature of north Welsh geography which came to play an important role in movement and control within the country. The presence of three or more Roman forts down the valley, and the concentration of no less than four earthwork castles at the north end of the lake, emphasise the anxiety of rulers to control this area.

Bala from the air. Note the grid of parallel streets in the medieval town. The motte is covered in dark trees in the foreground, to the left of the High Street

An unusual ringwork was built at Llanfor (SH 938368 – just behind the church) and more traditional mottes were raised further up the valley (SH 950373) and lower down, at a point where the river Dee leaves the lake (SH 930350) as well as at Bala. None of these is documented. They might be the products of the late 11th-century Norman campaign or the later Welsh revival.

Although Llanfor may originally have been the more important site, Tomen y Bala, which at 40m diameter and 9m high is the largest, eventually outstripped it. Bala is likely to have been the *maerdref* or administrative centre of the commote of Tryweryn, and it was still fortified in 1202, when Llywelyn ap Iorwerth, who was extending his power towards Powys, drove out Elis ap Madog, Lord of Penllyn. Llywelyn reduced the defences and very probably built the more modern stone castle at Carndochan (see Appendix), but Bala must have retained its importance, because an English borough was established beside it in 1310.

From the top of the mound it is possible to appreciate the typical grid pattern of the streets and the regular burgage plots (original property units in the later medieval borough), which still dictate the layout of the centre of the town.

8
The Medieval Church

The Christianity brought or restored to north Wales by the saints of the 5th and 6th centuries was, in theology and dogma, the religion of the universal Catholic church. The training of the monks and scholars was an international one, and for many laymen the culmination of a successful political and diplomatic career was to make the pilgrimage to Rome, to be acknowledged as a powerful brother in the family of Christ.

In organisation, however, there were differences between Rome and the Celtic west. In the Celtic lands – where urbanism and Roman government structures had been less firmly entrenched, or even non-existent – the church was more personal, more individualistic, and relied for support on family loyalties rather than formal offices. It was a church of monks and anchorites whose spheres of influence were defined within family and educational networks and not marked by clear territorial boundaries.

In the course of the 7th and 8th centuries this loose Celtic system of church organisation came into conflict with the formalising tendencies of the Roman church and the missionaries sent out from the centre to evangelise the pagan Saxons and Germans. The long-drawn-out dispute over the date on which Easter should be celebrated is but the most famous symptom of these differences which divided not so much the Celts and St Wilfrid, but the leaders of the western churches themselves. It was only in 768, a hundred years after the Synod of Whitby, that Bishop Elfoddw was able to bring the church in north Wales into line with Roman observances. In 786 the region was visited by a papal legate, and in the following century the court of Gwynedd became a centre of culture and European learning, where visitors were expected to know not only Latin but Greek. It is sad that the Viking raids of the 10th century have wiped out the visible evidence of this civilised period. Raids on all the major centres are recorded: on the cathedral at Bangor, the monastery at Penmon and on the court of Aberffraw itself.

Hugh of Avranches, earl of Chester, and his cousin, Robert of Rhuddlan, tried to extend Norman power into Gwynedd at the end of the 11th century. Though they did not succeed politically in the north, as they had in the south, the social and religious influence of the new rulers of England was soon felt in north Wales. Church affairs were reorganised on a more clearly defined territorial footing; dioceses were established at some of the old monastic foundations, such as

View of Penmon church with the prior's house and conventual buildings. The transformation from Celtic monastery to Augustinian priory is typical of many such establishments in Gwynedd

Bangor, and parishes with recognised geographical boundaries were created. In south Wales these changes were brought in by the new Norman overlords and the bishops whom they appointed. In north Wales it was the native princes who instituted these reforms.

In Anglesey there is a good deal of evidence for widespread rebuilding of churches in the 12th century, when the new parish organisation was established. Unfortunately, in most cases only fonts and architectural fragments survive (see, for example, no. 99) but the monastic church at Penmon (no. 103) is almost intact. On the mainland, Bangor Cathedral and Aberdaron (no. 108), another monastic church, retain some evidence from this period, but it is obvious that Anglesey was much wealthier than other parts of Gwynedd at this time. There are some notable churches from the following century in Meirionnydd, where it became traditional for monastic churches like St Cadfan's, Tywyn (see no. 113), to be cruciform in plan and parish churches to be rectangular, important ones like Llanaber, near Barmouth (see no. 111), being aisled.

In the early 13th century there were a great number of changes to the monastic life of Gwynedd. The old Celtic monasteries – where discipline and routine had been personal and individualistic, if not lax – were persuaded to adopt more regular practices, to become colleges of canons following one of the standard European rules, often that of the Augustinians.

European orders such as the Cistercians, who had come over to Whitland in Dyfed in 1140, were invited by the princes to found new monasteries; some, like Aberconwy, were very richly endowed. Sadly, only Cymer Abbey (no. 149) is still standing today. All trace has been lost of the very grand abbey church which Edward I built for the community from Aberconwy when he moved them down the river to Maenan, and also the Franciscan friary which Llywelyn the Great built at his port at Llanfaes, Anglesey.

Friars, whose philosophy and mission differed from that of the more contemplative monks, settled close to the major centres of population, and their friaries have seldom survived redevelopment of these towns. This is certainly true of Bangor, where the only trace of the Dominican friary is the series of impressive gravestones now in the museum. A school of very fine memorial sculptors flourished in north Wales at this time (see nos 139, 143 and 144), and their work is indicative of the high standard of decoration which might have been found in the richer churches that we have lost.

The 14th century, the period of the Black Death and the economic chaos which succeeded it, did not see much new building. But at the end of the following century, after the lengthy Wars of the Roses and the accession of the Tudor Henry VII in 1485, considerable regeneration took place. The lead in this revival was taken by the bishops of Bangor, who embellished the cathedral with new arcades and a fine west tower. Both these features were copied at other churches being rebuilt and enlarged at this time, for example, Llanidan (no. 140), Aberdaron (no. 108) and Clynnog (no. 145). The money which sustained this burst of religious activity may be connected with the accession to power and influence of many local cousins of the new king, whose father's family had come from Anglesey.

The monastic communities, however, did not share in this revitalisation, and when, for political rather than religious reasons, Henry VIII decided to examine their viability, none in Gwynedd could be found to be flourishing. All had been reduced to a small handful of monks, whose religious observance – if not scandalous – was no longer the beacon to the faithful that it had once been.

136
St Gwenfaen's Well, Rhoscolyn

Holy well

Uncertain date

OS 114 SH 259754 U2

Turn S to Rhoscolyn off B4545 between Trearddur Bay and Valley (either road); park car carefully near Rhoscolyn church (small building on rise); take road to R (W) of church, then follow footpath to R of farmyard; continue L (SW) on to spectacular stretch of coastal footpath. Well is about 15 mins walk from farm; also accessible by coastal footpath NW from Rhoscolyn beach (slightly longer)

This is one of the most complex and well preserved of the well chambers in Anglesey, but the date of the stonework is unknown, perhaps even 18th century. There are many 'holy' wells on the island, most with healing powers, but some with more sinister reputations as 'cursing wells', into which it was customary to throw a stone or a piece of paper carrying the name of the victim. Pins were very often used in these rituals: straight ones for beneficial effects, bent for evil doing. This well at Rhoscolyn is traditionally said to cure mental disorders, and it was customary to throw white quartz pebbles into the water.

It consists of a sunken antechamber with a stone paved floor and four seats across the corners. Beyond is an enclosed pool with seats at either side, and in front of that an open pool approached by three steps on each side. The water is held behind a vertical slab and spills over a notch into a narrow stone-lined channel and thence over the cliff.

Gwenfaen's Well

Old church at Llanfihangel Esceifiog

137
Llanfihangel Esceifiog Church, Gaerwen

Early medieval cross-slab and medieval church

9th century and 15th–17th century AD

OS 114 SH 478734 U2

0.5ml (0.8km) NW of Gaerwen, turn R (N) off A5 opposite Holland Arms Hotel; 0.5ml (0.8km) along, park carefully just before or after cottage. Take lane bearing L, through kissing gate, over stile at end (5 mins). Overgrown churchyard to R, passable to those in thick trousers

This is a site for those who like their ruins ivy-clad. Its setting on the intensely quiet edge of the marsh is another of its romantic attractions.

The parish church of St Michael was abandoned when the village found a new centre along Telford's road (A5).

The early date of the foundation is shown by a 9th–11th-century gravestone now lying broken on the ground within the roofless chancel. It is a thick, slightly tapered stone, about 1.5m long, bearing an outline cross with barred ends and a point at the bottom. Several of the contemporary gravestones at Llangaffo (see no. 102) are similar.

The surviving parts of the church were built in the 15th and 17th centuries. The most notable feature is the badly eroded inscription in raised Gothic letters around the reset west door. This inscription, and another on the east wall, are in Welsh. It is rather unusual to find Welsh used in a church context in the late 15th century. The inscription around the door reads: OETTA Y ADRODD YN Y DRWS / PADER A GWEDDI DROS ENAID [*WILLIAM*] AP [*HOWEL*] AP [*DAFY*]DD AC ENEIDIEU ME/[*I*]RW [*A C*]HRISTNOGION Y BYD, or: *Stop to recite in the doorway a paternoster, and a prayer for the soul of William ap Howel ap Dafydd and the souls of the dead and the Christians of the world.* The other inscription, even more difficult to read, seems to be a warning against brawling in church!

138
Capel Lligwy, Moelfre

Medieval chapel

12th–16th century AD

OS 114 SH 499863 U3 Cadw

See no. 79 (Din Lligwy), which is in next field

This is a small, roofless chapel with no recorded history or architectural pretension; but a surprisingly complex sequence of building may be read in its walls.

The southern doorway and the base of the

Capel Lligwy

walls are 12th century. In the 14th century the nave and chancel were reconstructed and the walling of this date can be recognised by a change in masonry, particularly clear on the outside of the walls. Notice the straight joint between the church and the south chapel which was added in the 16th century. This chapel has a small crypt and was presumably built as a memorial chapel. The windows have been blocked but can be seen from the inside.

Grave cover of Siwan, wife of Llywelyn the Great, in Beaumaris church

139

Gravestone of Siwan, Beaumaris

Carved medieval gravestone

AD 1237–40

OS 114 SH 604761 R1

Coverstone and coffin are in south porch of Beaumaris parish church, in centre of town. Church is open daily, 9.30am–3.30pm

Gresham 1968, pp 63–5

This is one of the finest of the memorials made by the north Welsh school of carvers during the 13th century. Other fine examples may be seen at Vale Crucis Abbey, near Llangollen (Clwyd), and in Bangor Museum, where several examples from the destroyed Bangor Friary are preserved. This one is unusual in that the upper part is a portrait, an interesting combination of the effigy and floriated cross traditions. A moulding down only one side of the slab shows that it was designed to be set into a niche in a south wall.

The slab is traditionally identified as that which covered the grave of Siwan (Princess Joan), the wife of Llywelyn ap Iorwerth, who died in 1237. She was the illegitimate daughter of King John of England and, though their marriage had not been without troubles, Llywelyn buried her in style in the Franciscan friary at Llanfaes. When the friary was dissolved in 1538 many of the monuments there were destroyed, but this one was brought to Beaumaris. The coffin, however, had been thrown out, and was only rescued from use as a horse trough in the 19th century.

The effigy shows the head and shoulders of the princess, wearing a wimple and a coronet, with hands raised in prayer. The rest of the slab is covered with more conventional floriated decoration. The foot of the stem is held in the mouth of a wyvern, a mythical heraldic bird whose tail is knotted and intertwined with the foliage.

Beaumaris church is very fine, and worthy of a visit in its own right.

Ruined arcade, Llanidan Old Church

140
Llanidan Old Church, Brynsiencyn

Later medieval church
14th–15th century AD
OS 114 SH 495669 U1

From Brynsiencyn on A4080, just beyond present church (0.5ml, 0.8km, NE of pub on sharp corner) turn L at lodge, drive 0.4ml (0.6km) down lane; space to park. From NE, turning is 1.6ml (2.6km) from crossroads beyond Plas Newydd

This church was abandoned in 1844, declared to be in bad condition, too expensive to maintain and awkwardly situated; a new one was built on the main road. The controversy which this decision raised (published in *Archaeologia Cambrensis* 1846) has a very modern ring, especially the economic argument that a new building would be cheaper than repairing the old – which proved, not surprisingly, to be untrue!

This church, on an old foundation, was one of those which was radically altered in the late 15th century in emulation of the work being done at the time in Bangor Cathedral. Here the church was doubled in size by building a second nave to the north of the first, linked by a central arcade, almost identical to the one in Bangor. The door, with its flanking heads, and the window of the surviving end on the north nave are of 15th-century type, and the door to the southern nave is 14th century. Beside it is a holy water stoup, always full of water. Claimed to be a miraculous phenomenon, it is probably due to seepage from the wall.

When the church was abandoned, the western end was retained as a mortuary chapel and a closing wall was built, leaving most of the central arcade free-standing within the churchyard. This churchyard, overhung with yews and partly choked with luxuriant vegetation, has a Gothick air which adds a romantic *frisson* to the visit.

In the 18th century, Henry Rowlands, the author of *Mona Antiqua Restaurata* (published 1723) was vicar of this parish. His work not only preserved a great deal of archaeological information but also fed numerous Druidic fantasies.

141

St Dwynwen's Church, Llanddwyn Island

Medieval church and well

5th–16th century AD

OS 114 SH 387627 U4

From centre of Newborough, take road to beach (3ml, 4.8km). Park in Forestry Commission car park (£1.20 at automatic barrier); church is on island, 30 mins walk to R along beach. Exhibition in Pilot House

The church is badly ruined, but the peace and beauty of the island, which is a nature reserve renowned for its geology and natural history, make the long walk worthwhile, especially on a summer's evening – or even on 25 January, St Dwynwen's feast, the Welsh equivalent of St Valentine's Day.

The church stands in a circular churchyard (now grazed by Soay sheep) and only the 16th-century chancel, with two dressed windows, stands to any height. It is possible to make out the wall footings of the transepts and a rather short nave. The chancel was rebuilt in the 16th century, evidence of the sustained popularity of the 5th-century patron saint of lovers.

The ruins of St Dwynwen's Church

The legendary St Dwynwen was a 5th-century princess, in love with a man of her own choice, but promised by her father to another. She prayed to be released from the pangs of love and to be allowed to live unmarried, which she did in a hermitage on the island. Her dying wish was to be carried up to watch the sunset through a cleft rock which still stands to the north-west of the ruins (look through the north window of the chancel). Since her death (traditionally in AD 465) her shrine has become a pilgrimage centre for those afflicted by unhappy love affairs.

St Dwynwen's 'well' is simply a freshwater spring emerging from the cliff on the north side of the island below the cleft rock. It has been used as a divination well, in which women could read their prospects of happiness in the movement of a handkerchief thrown into the water. It can be reached from the northern path; go down the steep grassy slope, with care, just opposite the obtuse angle of the grazing enclosure.

142

Llangelynin Well, Conwy

Medieval holy well

14th century AD and later

OS 115 SH 751737 U3

Leave Conwy by Upper Gate Street, bear R off St Agnes Road (signposted Hendre); persevere for 3ml (4.8km); road becomes steep and narrow; at telephone box, bear L and continue for 700m. Ample parking through gate; cross stile on L. Bear R to another stile; turn L to churchyard (c.200m). Church open in summer, otherwise key kept at Carnedd Wen nearby

View of Langelynin Old Church. The well is in the corner of the churchyard under the trees

The well is in the southern corner of the churchyard (on left as you enter). It is a rectangular pool surrounded by a paved ledge with seats on either side. These may be recent additions, since the well house (first roofed in 1622) had become derelict, and its walls and those of the churchyard have been rebuilt within the last decade. The well was particularly renowned for its power to cure sick children.

The church in this remote upland spot is a building of great simplicity and charm with a surprisingly complex history. The nave is the oldest part, to which the present chancel was added in the 15th century. In the following century, north and south chapels, a south porch and a new east window, which cut through the 15th-century one, were added. In 1800 the south chapel and the gallery were demolished, but the church has remained essentially unchanged since then.

This is a beautiful place, more than worth the effort of reaching it. Several footpaths converge on this spot, where there used to be an inn for those crossing the mountain. The footings can be seen close to the churchyard gate. There is also an early round hut which it might be tempting to associate with St Celynin, believed to have lived in the 6th century AD.

143
Coffin of Llywelyn the Great, Llanrwst

Medieval stone coffin without lid

AD c.1240

OS 115 SH 797616 R1

In Gwydir chapel attached to Llanrwst parish church. Church is beside river, reached from SW corner of Ancaster Square, and is kept locked. Contact vicar at Rectory, Llanddoget Road, Llanrwst, tel: 01492 640223

Hemp 1956

Llywelyn ap Iorwerth, who reigned as Prince of Gwynedd from 1201 to 1240, is rightly known as 'The Great'. He restored the dominant position of north Wales after the troubles which had followed the death of his grandfather, Owain Gwynedd, and by 1216 he had made himself overlord of all Wales. During his reign castles were built, churches were restored and abbeys and friaries were founded. He established the Cistercians at Aberconwy, where he ended his days – some say, as a monk. He was certainly buried there, and his coffin was probably brought to Maenan, close to Llanrwst, when the community was moved by Edward I. Unfortunately, the lid has been lost and there is no record of what it looked like, but this coffin (traditionally identified as his) is unusually elaborate. Most Welsh examples (such as that of his wife Siwan, or Joan, see no. 139) are plain, with just a carved lid. This decorated coffin may be of English workmanship, perhaps prepared well in advance, because the style of carving is early rather than mid-13th century.

The chapel contains the early 15th-century effigy of a descendant of Llywelyn, Hywel Coetmor, one of the victors of Agincourt. The splendid Gwydir chapel itself was built in 1633 by one of the Wynns of Gwydir, the family which dominated the Conwy valley for many generations.

144
Eva Stone, Bangor Cathedral
Medieval gravestone

AD 1380

OS 115 SH 580720 U1

Cathedral is in Bangor High Street, and is normally open during daylight hours. The stone is grouped with other historic fragments in a 'museum corner' in N aisle

Cathedral Guide; Gresham 1968, pp 230–7

This is one of a group of three remarkable monuments which were all carved by the same hand and commissioned by the same landowner in the years around 1380. The other two are images of the legendary figures, St Iestyn and King Pabo (see no. 99), and their memorials are set up in the churches dedicated to them in Anglesey. This monument is the gravestone of a contemporary woman and, though there is a problem with the damaged identification inscription, it is almost certain that it commemorates Eva, the mother of Gruffudd ap Gwilym and sister-in-law of Gwenllian ferch (daughter of) Madog, who are named as

Llywelyn's coffin, as shown by Thomas Pennant in 1783

donors of the Iestyn stone. The family came from near Prestatyn, the source of the fine sandstone from which the slabs were carved. In about 1375 Gruffudd ap Gwilym inherited land in Anglesey from his father and uncle, and married an heiress from the Llanbabo area. It seems that he made the generous gifts to churches on his new lands when he took up this inheritance, bringing the stone and the sculptor from his old home. Other examples of this school can be found in Clwyd.

The slab is carved in low relief; it shows a woman wearing a wimple and a square 14th-century headdress. She has a tight-fitting dress with a finely pleated skirt. Eighty-five buttons and buttonholes are worked down the front. She holds a set of praying beads, not quite a rosary since the beads are differently arranged. She is lying with her head on a pillow and flowers are strewn around her. The damaged inscription in which she was identified runs around the edge of the slab.

The 'museum corner' contains six fragments with 10th-century fret decoration, pieces of crosses and other monuments, which are all that remain to indicate the wealth and importance of the monastery of St Deiniol, raided by the Vikings in 1073. It was rebuilt under Gruffudd ap Cynan, but very little remains of the 12th-century cathedral in which he and Owain Gwynedd were buried. Most of what is visible today belongs to the 13th–15th centuries. Noteworthy are the unusual 14th-century tiles and the fine nave arcades and tower which provided the model for so much other late 15th- and early 16th-century rebuilding in the diocese.

The 'Mostyn Christ' is a rare survival of a pre-Reformation 'Bound Rood'. It is believed to have come from Rhuddlan Priory and was preserved by a Catholic family, eventually passing to Lord Mostyn.

The Eva stone

Twelfth-century sundial in Clynnog churchyard

145
Clynnog Sundial, Clynnog

Free-standing sundial

10th–12th century AD

OS 123 SH 413497 U1

Clynnog is 9.5ml (15km) SW of Caernarfon on A499. Sundial stands in churchyard at SE corner of Capel y Bedd attached to E side of church. Parking is difficult in village but there is usually space in hotel car park opposite

Hughes 1931; Thomas 1989

Sundials are rare survivals anywhere in these islands and, until the recent discovery of another in Tywyn (no. 113), a monastic site like Clynnog, this was unique in Wales. A sundial, which marks the regular division of the day, is not to be confused with a 'Mass clock', which only indicates the time of the offices of the church. Mass clocks are usually later in date and more casually cut, with only one or two lines to show the time of the services.

The sundial is cut on a free-standing rectangular pillar almost 3m in full height. The hole for the gnomon or needle which cast the shadow is at the top of an incised semicircle which projects beyond the width of the stone, giving it an unusual shouldered outline. The semicircle – the half-day of 12 hours – is divided into four equal parts. The division of the day into eight 'tides' or three-hour periods is a Saxon system, but Saxon sundials in eastern England are all designed to be built into church towers and are not free-standing pillars. However, pillars of this kind can be found in Ireland, where the Saxon system was no doubt introduced by the Vikings, who had become familiar with it in northern England. The presence in north Wales of this Irish timepiece is probably due to the close connections between the two countries during the reign of Gruffudd ap Cynan in the early 12th century.

The sundial first came to light in the early 19th century, being used as a bridge over a mill stream; then it was used in a dairy, and it was only returned to the churchyard, where it is assumed to belong, in 1930.

The church at Clynnog, the main shrine of St Beuno, is one of the most important in north Wales. Capel y Bedd is his traditional burial place, and excavations in 1913 discovered much earlier, perhaps even 7th-century, foundations beneath the present 16th-century chapel. Because of the fame of the shrine, the church and its college of canons were very wealthy, and the large, beautiful, airy church which stands today, with its perpendicular windows and well-proportioned tower, is the result of extensive rebuilding in the 15th and 16th centuries. It was a centre of pilgrimage right up to the Reformation.

146
St Cybi's Well, Llangybi

Medieval holy well

Medieval and 18th century AD

OS 123 SH 427412 U2 Cadw

Monument signposted off A499, 2ml (3.2km) S of Llanaelhaearn. In village, official path wet in winter; drier but steeper alternative through Llangybi churchyard, over stile in far corner and down field to cross river by footbridge

Cadw Guide (with Criccieth Castle)

This is an idyllic spot, the beauty of the setting alone being enough to effect many cures!

The well is traditionally associated with St Cybi, a Cornishman who was one of the major saints of the 6th century in north Wales. He is best known for his monastery at Holyhead (see no. 89) and his *Life* mentions no sojourn in Lleyn, but perhaps he might have been here at some time, seeking patronage from the warlord who lived above, in Carn Pentyrch (see Appendix). There are two early cross-inscribed stones from near the church which give credence to an early foundation.

The origin of the tradition of pilgrimage at this well is therefore obscure, but it had probably become firmly established by the Middle Ages, and was reinforced at the end of the 18th century when – following the fashionable success of Bath – a report was commissioned on the curative properties of the water. The vicar of Llanystumdwy was so

A cutaway reconstruction of St Cybi's Well as it might have appeared in the late 18th century

impressed by the stories of cures – of blindness, fevers and lameness – that he persuaded the landowner, William Price of Rhiwlas, near Bala, to provide conveniences and amenities for the sick.

The present buildings, therefore, probably date from the middle of the 18th century, though the main well-chamber, the earliest structure on the site, might be a good deal older.

The spring emerges in the well-chamber at the back. The water then flows through a culvert into the main well-chamber, which has a wide ledge all round it with seats in niches. Steps lead down into the water. The water flows out through a canalised stream, under a small latrine building set at a discreet distance, and thence into the river.

Adjoining the main well-chamber is a small cottage which used to have a connecting door. The cottage is undoubtedly part of the amenities built by Mr Price. It housed the custodian of the well, and was used by those taking the cure. The treatment here involved both drinking the water and bathing in it. After each bath the patient was put to bed in the cottage. The course of treatment might last a week. The cottage has been enlarged, and was occupied until 1870.

147
'St Mary's Church', Uwchmynydd

Settlement, traditional pilgrim embarkation point

?Later medieval

OS 123 SH 139253 U4

Site is 3ml (4.8km) W of Aberdaron along narrow twisting road; NT car park at end before ascent of Mynydd Mawr. Leave car and

St Mary's Church, as shown by Thomas Pennant in 1783

turn towards sea, taking footpath along L side of enclosed field, bearing R around promontory; site visible below. Bracken partially obscures site in summer

There is a tradition that the building at this beautiful spot is a church in which pilgrims to Bardsey prayed on the mainland for the last time before making the dangerous crossing to the holy island, which is directly opposite this narrow cove.

At the cliff foot is a freshwater spring known as St Mary's Well. There is no man-made structure, but it is reputed to have been used by pilgrims assembling before the voyage.

However, it is unlikely that even the most pious would risk this embarkation point, and both the visible foundations and the earliest drawing of the building (1783) suggest that it was a large house rather than a church. It is surrounded by a broad enclosing bank and an extensive area of cultivation ridges. This evidence for prolonged medieval farming is astonishing in view of the exposure of the site. It is notable that the evidence is confined to the south-facing slopes of this broad gully.

148
Wleder Stone, Llanfihangel y Traethau

Medieval gravestone

Mid-12th century AD

OS 124 SH 595354 U1

Stone is in Llanfihangel churchyard (off A496 between Talsarnau and Harlech). From N, church is signposted, 1st R shortly after sharp corner. Steep and narrow road leads to gate of churchyard (0.2ml, 320m). Adequate parking

Nash-Williams 1950, no. 281

This stone carries a rare, late inscription of particular interest because of the style of lettering and the reference to Owain Gwynedd, the king who reigned from 1137 to 1170.

Wleder Stone

It is a tall, narrow stone with a Latin inscription reading vertically downwards on each face. It starts with an initial cross and reads HI(*C*) EST SEPULCRV(*M*) WLEDER MAT(*R*)IS / ODELEV Q(*U*)I P(*R*)IMV(*M*) EDIFICAV(*IT*) / HANC EC(*C*)L(*ESI*)A(*M*) / IN TE(*M*)P(*O*)R(*E*) EWINI REG(*IS*), or: *Here is the tomb of Wleder, mother of Odeleu, who first built this church in the time of King Owain.* Unfortunately, no more is known of Wleder or Odeleu, and nothing survives of the 12th-century church.

Although the stone is a difficult schist and the carver does not seem to be especially skilled, the epigraphy reflects very accurately the new fashions in lettering which had originated in the court of Charlemagne and been brought over to Britain by the Normans. Particularly characteristic are the enclosed letters (as in the abbreviated QUI and SEPULCRUM), the pointed oval O, the W, and the N, where the diagonal does not reach the ends of the uprights.

149
Cymer Abbey, Dolgellau

Cistercian abbey

12th–16th century AD

OS 124 SH 721195 U1 Cadw

Abbey is signposted off A470, between Dolgellau and Barmouth 0.5ml (0.8km) N of turning to Fairbourne. Turn R and R again towards caravan park. Park car in 2nd car park on L

Official Guide

The Cistercian abbey of Cymer was founded in 1198–9 under the patronage of Maredudd ap Cynan, a grandson of Owain Gwynedd. The first monks came from Abbey Cwmhir in Powys, which was a daughter house of Whitland in Dyfed, itself founded by monks from Clairvaux, the mother house in Burgundy.

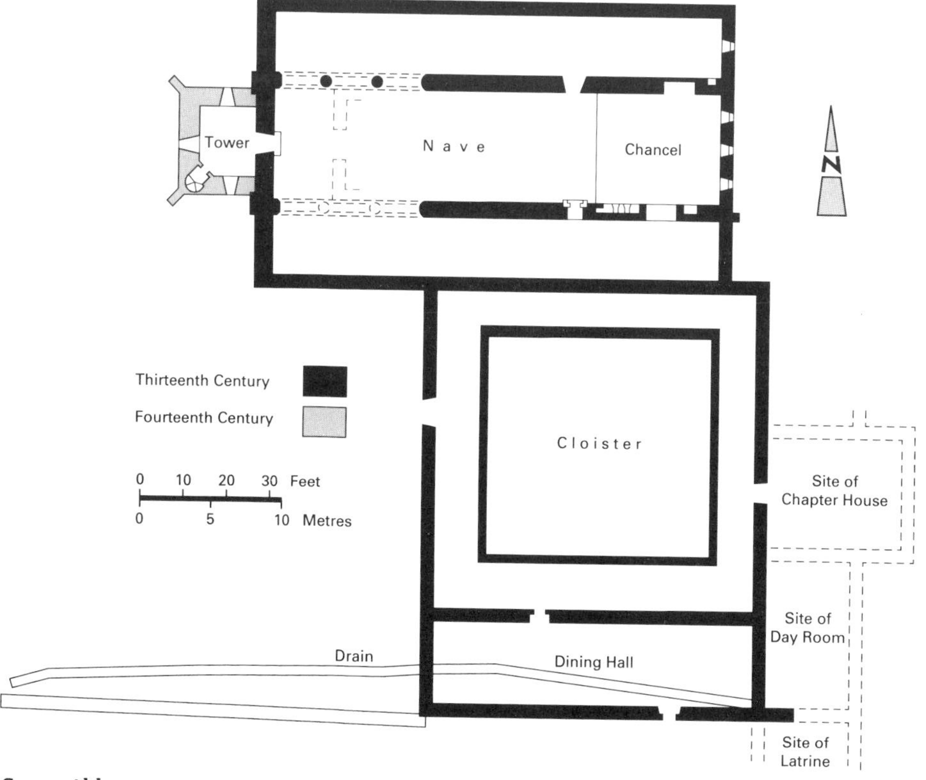

Cymer Abbey

The monks farmed sheep on the local hills and on lands in Lleyn, and were involved in mining and metallurgy. They also kept a notable stud, rendering high-quality horses to Llywelyn ap Iorwerth. But the abbey was never especially wealthy, and after the wars of the 13th century its economic position declined further. However, it did possess a very large and fine silver gilt chalice and paten (dish on which the consecrated host is laid), which must have been hidden on the mountainside at the Dissolution. They were rediscovered in the 19th century and are now in the National Museum of Wales in Cardiff. At the Dissolution in 1536 the abbey was worth only £51 (roughly £16,500 in today's terms).

This poverty is reflected in the abbey buildings. Only the church survives to any height. It consists of an aisled nave just over 30m long. The monks probably intended to build the normal crossing with two transepts and a chancel to the east, but this was never done and the present east wall (not bonded into the side walls) and chancel area seems to be a compromise arrangement. In a normal Cistercian church the tower would have been over the central crossing, but since no crossing was built, when the tower was added in the 14th century, it was put at the west end.

Cistercian churches were normally beautifully proportioned but not richly decorated. This one is especially plain, but there is some attractive carving on the sedile on the south wall of the chancel, and a little survives on the severe east window. The small putlog holes to support scaffolding would have been covered by plaster.

The monastic buildings to the south were never extensive, and it is possible that some of the domestic quarters around the cloisters might have been timber. Monasteries were laid out to a standard pattern, traditional to each order. The cloister, chapterhouse and dining hall are in their normal positions around a square on the south side, and their planning anticipates the unfulfilled enlargement of the church. It is possible that the present farmhouse incorporates part of the monastic guesthouse, and there may have been sheds and wharves on the river associated with the monks' industrial and agricultural businesses.

150
St Derfel's 'Horse', Llandderfel

Medieval shrine

Probably 14th century AD

OS 125 SH 982371 R1

Llandderfel is 3.5ml (5.6km) E of Bala at B4401/B4402 junction; 'horse' is in porch (visible through window) of parish church in centre of village. Parking for 1 car beside gate to churchyard. Key kept at Tirionfa Home, 50m above church on R

Evans 1991

This strange seated animal, probably a stag rather than a horse, is all that remains from the celebrated shrine of Derfel Gadarn, the centre of large pilgrimages in the later Middle Ages. Virtually nothing is known of the 6th-century St Derfel, but he is reputed to have been a warrior who took part in the notorious battle of Camlan. He was associated with the healing of animals, especially cattle.

Unfortunately, there is no surviving description of the shrine and its famous statue, except that it was said to be very large, and Derfel is assumed to have been shown as a knight – hence the identification of the animal as a horse, though a recumbent one would be inappropriate. There is a rectangular recess on its back which might have held a palanquin or some kind of box-like shrine for relics, but the documents always refer to Derfel's image, not his bones, and imply a life-size statue. The back of the animal's body is hollowed out to make a sort of coffer, perhaps for the shrine offerings, but there is no sign of a lid or lock.

The image of Derfel Gadarn (Derfel the Warrior) had a particularly dramatic end, the subject of one of the most memorable

St Derfel's 'Horse'

incidents of the Reformation in north Wales. In 1538 Dr Ellis Price of Plas Iolyn – 'one of the greatest of our knaves' in Thomas Pennant's opinion – was appointed commissionary-general for the diocese of St Asaph to root out superstitious practices. He arrived at Llandderfel while a pilgrimage was in progress, and was offered a large bribe by the villagers to allow them to keep their valuable statue of the saint. But he reported to Thomas Cromwell that he had resisted the bribe and was sending the statue to London. It was finally burnt on the pyre in Smithfield on which John Forrest, the Franciscan confessor of Queen Catherine of Aragon, was martyred. It was said that there had been a local prophecy that the image would at the end set a forest alight.

The animal is not mentioned by Price, but it remained a notable feature of the church in later centuries. There is a tradition that on Easter Tuesday it used to be taken to a hill behind the church, near St Derfel's Well, set up on an axle and ridden as a rocking horse.

Appendix: Sites of Further Interest

This is a list of sites which lie on private land, or which are on open ground but remote and difficult of access and marginally less rewarding than the others covered in this guide. The 1:25,000 OS maps will be a great help in finding these and many other sites which have had to be omitted for reasons of space. Permission should be sought before visiting sites marked R. It is often difficult to trace the owners of sites, and it is usually best to seek help and information from the nearest house.

Palaeolithic Period

Kendrick's Cave, Great Orme
OS 115 SH 780828 R3

A limestone cave in a private garden, used as a workshop in the 19th century. A decorated horse jawbone and a necklace of teeth have been found.

Neolithic Period

Bryn yr Hen Bobl, Llanfairpwll
OS 114 SH 518690 R2

Ask at Plas Newydd Gardens. A small rectangular chamber with a pierced closing stone beneath the original kidney-shaped cairn; a unique narrow 'terrace' is appended to the cairn on the west. A contemporary settlement was in the vicinity. Excavated in 1927.

Rhoslan (Cefn Isaf), Criccieth
OS 123 SH 483408 U3

A rectangular chamber with a large capstone; probably a portal dolmen, but it lacks height. Footpath nearby.

Fourcrosses, Pwllheli
OS 123 SH 399384 R2

A small, square chamber with a capstone, reconstructed in 1934, probably a portal dolmen. Fine view.

Ystum Cegid Isaf, Dolbenmaen
OS 123/124 SH 498413 U2

An unusual tomb, possibly a passage grave or perhaps a Severn–Cotswold cairn, with a 'thin' flat capstone; the passage stones are incorporated into a field-wall. Footpath nearby.

Cist Cerrig, Borth y Gest
OS 124 SH 543384 R2

Three tall stones form the portal structure of this fine dolmen; a very beautiful monument, despite its denudation. Cup-marks can be seen on the sloping rock just south of the tomb (compare no. 19).

Gwern Einion, Llanbedr
OS 124 SH 587286 R2

Ask at Brwyn Llynau (SH 585296, tel: 01766 780625). A very fine high portal dolmen with a sloping capstone; one sidestone has been moved back. It is incorporated in the walls of a sheepfold behind the field byre.

Bronze Age

Tregwehelydd Standing Stone, Llanddeusant
OS 114 SH 340831 U4 Cadw

This fine and typical standing stone is rather awkward to reach despite its Guardianship status. It has been mended with splendid bronze bands.

Carreg Leidr, Llanerchymedd
OS 114 SH 446843 R1

Tradition says that Carreg Leidr ('Thief Stone') is the thief who stole a Bible from the parish church, and turned to stone as he carried it away on his shoulder.

Cremlyn Stones, Beaumaris
OS 114 SH 571774/SH 571776 R2

Two tall standing stones, 250m apart, both well over 2m high. Excavation showed that the southern one had replaced a wooden post, so the position must have been significant.

Cefn Llechan Stone Circle, Henryd
OS 115 SH 747753 U4

A ring of stones, probably originally nine. Three still stand, three others have fallen, one split by blasting. The tallest was 2m high and the circle had a diameter of about 12m. A footpath crosses the circle.

Maen Llwyd, Glynllifon, Pontllyfni
OS 123 SH 444541 R1

This 3m-tall standing stone (visible from gate) was excavated in 1875, when cremated bone and a broken urn were found close by. This association of a standing stone and a burial is surprisingly rare.

Carnguwch, Tre'r Ceiri
OS 123 SH 375428 R4

(See no. 67.) An exceptionally fine hilltop cairn (visible from distance), 6m high and more than 30m across. It is founded on a large boss of natural rock, and the added stone has been revetted with a well-built wall. There has been debate about whether it is a burial cairn or a motte. There has been no excavation.

Penllech Cup-marked Stone, Tudweiliog
OS 123 SH 224345 R1

This stone (1.1m by 0.65m) has 17 or 20 shallow cup-marks on its flat face. The origin of the stone is unknown; it has been used as a gate-post but is now standing against the hedge on the inside of the first field on the left of the lane. It may have come from a megalithic tomb or a Bronze Age cist.

Bedd Gurfal, Llanbedr
OS 124 SH 613311 R2

A beautiful ring cairn with eight tall stones standing in a circle 5.5m across. It is beside a path (not public). An Iron Age settlement site (concentric circle) can be seen a short distance to the east.

Cerrig Arthur Stone Circle, Barmouth
OS 124 SH 631188 U4

A badly damaged circle cut into the mountainside at the junction of tracks from Bwlch y Rhiwgwr. Two tall (*c.*1m) stones which may be an entrance are the most conspicuous features of the site, but the stumps of other stones can be seen forming an oval about 14m across. It might be a settlement enclosure, rather than a ritual monument.

Settlements: Later Prehistoric and Early Medieval

Pant y Saer Hut Group, Benllech
OS 114 SH 513824 U2

An oval enclosure wall surrounding two round huts at east and west. The eastern one has two small, rectangular buildings adjoining it on either side of the entrance. Excavated in 1933, it produced Iron Age, Roman and post-

Roman finds. This site is rather awkward to find, and obscured by bracken in summer.

Dinas, Plas Cadnant, Menai Bridge

OS 114 SH 552733 U2

A group of round huts and rectangular buildings occupying the top of a rocky promontory. The settlement was defended by a rampart on the gentle eastern slope. Accessible from public footpath, but obscured by bracken in summer.

Pant y Griafolen, Dolgarrog

OS 115 SH 708667 U4

The footpath from Pen y Gaer (no. 63) to Llyn Dulyn passes through a long straggle of 28 huts, cairns and field-walls on the slopes running down to the river.

Hafotŷ Wernlas, Rhostryfan

OS 115 SH 500584 R2/U2

The slopes above Rhostryfan are covered with early fields and huts but they are all liable to be obscured by bracken. The group behind Hafotŷ was excavated in 1922 and revealed round and rectangular huts within a rectangular enclosure. Evidence of iron-working was found. The area is crossed by many footpaths, but the fields are private.

Caerau Huts and Fields, Pantglas

OS 123 SH 469488 R3

The slopes north of Caerau Farm and east of the main road are covered in early terraced fields which can be picked out easily by those who are familiar with the 'staircase' effect that they produce. Among them are several hut groups (farms). Two on the lower slopes were excavated in 1935. The southern one has an unusually compact plan, in which the various chambers might be considered rooms rather than independent buildings.

Braich y Cornel, Cwmystradllyn

OS 124/115 SH 552446 R4

A spread of settlement evidence – huts, fields and burnt mounds – covers the slopes above Llyn Cwmystradllyn. Not all are easy to see but the walk is rewarding because the valley contains particularly interesting industrial archaeology.

Erw Wen, Moel Goedog

OS 124 SH 606323 R2

(See nos 44 and 73.) Ask at Tyddyn Siôn Wyn, tel: 01766 780468. An Iron Age settlement cut into the slope. The initial phases of the large central house were in wood, later replaced in stone (visible). The house is surrounded by a circular enclosure ('concentric circle' settlement) and a small medieval house stands within it on the south, with two others outside to north and south. Excavation produced a 6th-century BC date.

Homestead below Moel Goedog

OS 124 SH 617321 U4

Two hut groups lie 130m apart close to the footpath running south of Moel Goedog. Both consist of compact groups of round huts with a rectangular building facing the small yard. Associated field-walls can be seen.

Muriau Gwyddelod, Harlech

OS 124 SH 586303 R2

Two neighbouring compactly planned hut groups with field-walls emanating from their enclosure walls. The stone walls are exceptionally well preserved, and the district epitomises 'ancient landscape'. It can be very well seen from the air and from vantage points in the vicinity, but there is no public access to the huts themselves. Ask at Brwyn Llynau (SH 585296, tel: 01766 780625).

Hillforts

Din Silwy (Bwrdd Arthur), Llanddona

OS 114 SH 586814 R3

A prominent flat-topped hill surrounded by a broad stone wall. The simple entrance is at the south, 90m east of the trig. point. There are no signs of buildings in the interior, though finds suggest occupation during and perhaps before and after, the Roman period.

Twyn y Parc Promontory Fort, Bodorgan
OS 114 SH 369650 R4

A long, narrow arm of rock projecting into the sea, defended by two banks at the neck; the inner one is very high.

Castell Crwn, Cemlyn
OS 114 SH 332908 R2

This is a small, very precisely circular enclosure with a sharp bank and ditch, possibly Viking in origin.

Carn Fadryn, Botwnnog
OS 123 SH 280352 R4

A stone-walled hillfort with stone huts like Tre'r Ceiri (no. 67). There is a large sloping annexe on the north side and a small citadel, similar to Garn Boduan (no. 69), on the very top. The construction of the citadel in the 12th century by the sons of Owain Gwynedd is recorded by Giraldus Cambrensis. This is one of the earliest Welsh castles, but very prehistoric in style.

Carn Pentyrch, Llangybi
OS 123 SH 424417 U4/R4

A stone-walled fort on the hill above St Cybi's Well (no. 146). The triple defences are probably of different dates. The innermost ring with its thick, high stone wall may be early medieval; the other two lines consist of walls and banks and are probably prehistoric, with later alterations and additions. The fort is divided by a modern wall; the more interesting western side is on private land.

Castell Caerau, Dolbenmaen
OS 124 SH 509439 U4

Consisting of a small, very strongly defended boss of rock, this fort, possibly dating from the early medieval period, is similar to the inner defence at Carn Pentyrch (see above). Field-walls and sheep pens obscure it.

Moel Offrwm, Llanfachreth
OS 124 SH 749210 and SH 747206 R4

There are two stone-walled forts on this hill. The larger one, on the summit, has two walls on the south; an entrance on the north-east with guardchambers, and contains several house platforms. An annexe occupies a spur on the south-east.

Cefn Pared, Gregennan
OS 124 SH 664150 U4 NT

This very striking ridge has some minimal defences on the south-west end.

Craig yr Aderyn, Dysynni Valley
OS 124 SH 644069 R4

The eastern slope of the famous Craig yr Aderyn ('Bird Rock') is defended by two lines of earth and stone ramparts. The outer one has an impressive in-turned entrance at the south-east corner.

Roman Period

Caer Llugwy (Bryn y Gefeiliau), Betws y Coed
OS 115 SH 745572 R2

An auxiliary fort on flat land close to the river, the ramparts can just be recognised and stone buildings (possibly a *mansio* or guesthouse) in the annexe to the west have been exposed. Excavations in 1920–2 revealed occupation and industrial activity (lead-working) in the 1st–2nd centuries AD. Many broken wine amphorae were found near the guest house.

Caer Gai, near Bala
OS 125 SH 877315 R1

A farm stands inside the characteristic rectangle of a Roman auxiliary fort. The ramparts can be seen from the road below. There is evidence of a cemetery and civil settlement outside the fort, which was garrisoned from AD 75/80–130.

Early Medieval Period

Bangor Museum
OS 115 SH 580721 R1

The museum contains two notable exhibits of this period: the inscribed lead coffin from Rhuddgaer (5th century AD) and the longest obituary notice in post-Roman Britain, the Trescawen Stone. Both were found in Anglesey.

Gravestones, Llangeinwen Church
OS 114 SH 439658 U1

Four broken gravestones of 9th–11th-century date have been built into the north-west and south-west buttresses of the nave of this largely rebuilt medieval church. The best one, on the north-west, is very like the spiral-decorated one at Llangaffo (no. 102).

Cross-inscribed Stone, Pistyll
OS 123 SH 319418 U1

This small 8th–9th-century stone with a cross inside a circle is built into the southern wall of the main road almost opposite a lay-by. It has a lintel over it, and stands midway between two telegraph poles, but is difficult to find.

St Mary's Abbey, Bardsey Island
OS 123 SH 120222 R4

Only the 13th-century tower of the abbey, the goal of so many medieval pilgrims, remains standing. One of the early gravestones is in the tower, and part of a cross is in the Wesleyan chapel. The island is private and visits should be arranged in advance with the Bardsey Island Trust Officer, Dafydd Thomas, Stabl Hen, Tyddyn Du, Llanystumdwy, Criccieth, tel: 01766 514774. All trips may be delayed unexpectedly at either end by bad sea conditions.

Medieval Period – Fortifications

Castell Trefadog, Llanfaethlu
OS 114 SH 291859 R2

A very heavily-defended coastal site. Recent excavation revealed the foundations of a 14th-century stone house inside the enclosure. An unusual site, perhaps akin to Penmaen Castle, Gower. Some have suggested a Viking origin for the site.

Aberlleiniog Motte, Penmon
OS 114 SH 616794 R2

A fine motte with a hint of a bailey to the south. This one is a documented Norman castle, built by Hugh of Avranches. It is surmounted by a square stone keep used, and possibly built, during the Civil War (1642–8) as a base for gun-running, originally Royalist, then Parliamentarian.

Castell Prysor, Trawsfynydd
OS 124 SH 758369 R3

This natural boss of rock is strengthened and topped by a stone mound which was originally revetted with drywalling, now badly ruined. Edward I wrote a letter from here on 1 July 1284, but it is obviously an earlier Welsh castle.

Carndochan, Bala
OS 125 SH 847306 R4

A ridgetop castle, probably built by Llywelyn ap Iorwerth. A poorer version of Castell y Bere (no. 134), with a D-shaped tower at the south end, a round one at the north, and a square building in the centre, all badly ruined.

Castell Cynfael, Tywyn
OS 135 SH 615016 U3

This is a castle motte formed by cutting a deep ditch around the upper part of a small hill. It is known to have been constructed by Cadwaladr in 1147. The histories of other mottes in this neighbourhood, Tomen Las, near Pennal, and Tomen Ddreiniog, beside the Dysynni, are not known.

Medieval Period – Houses

Hafotŷ, Llansadwrn

OS 114 SH 563783 R2 Cadw

An exceptionally interesting house with a complex building history beginning in the 14th century. When repair and conservation work are finished it will be open to the public and have its own guide. Enquire at Beaumaris Castle.

Fedw Deg, Penmachno

OS 115 SH 789534 R1 Cadw

Visit by appointment only. An interesting farmyard with buildings of many dates. The 16th-century house overlies earlier foundations, and has itself been downgraded by the building of a later farmhouse. The old house has a fine doorway with an impressive stone lintel, windows with good lintels and some original pre-glazing bars, a huge fireplace, and original coarse slates on the roof.

Cwm Ciprwth Platform Houses, Cwm Pennant

OS 115 SH 527477 U4

Two house foundations with associated fields may be seen on the way to the Cwm Ciprwth mine. The western one is a very good example of a platform house with hood; the other is on flat ground and would be called a 'long hut'. They would have resembled each other when occupied.

Cefn y Fan, Dolbenmaen

OS 124/123 SH 506421 R4

Grass-grown remains of a 15th-century hall notable for having been burnt down by Owain Glyndŵr in 1403. It had belonged to Ieuan ap Maredudd ap Hywel, whose other house at Gesail Gyfarch was also destroyed then. That was rebuilt, this one was abandoned.

Summary of Dates

Prehistoric monuments in this book are ascribed to archaeological periods based on the conventional three-age system of Stone Age, Bronze Age and Iron Age. This system of classification has served archaeology well through the years, but has recently been criticised for giving too much emphasis to materials and too little to society. Our study of settlements and burial places now shows that periods of greatest change and upheaval in society do not necessarily coincide with the adoption of new technologies.

Accordingly, archaeologists now tend, when they can, to use absolute chronology for descriptive purposes. This has been made possible by the use of radiocarbon dating. Every living thing contains carbon 14, which, after death, decomposes at a known rate. This dating technique measures the amount of carbon 14 remaining in an organic substance, such as charcoal from a burial mound, to give a date for its death – the felling of the tree, for instance. Unfortunately, we now know that radiocarbon dating gives results that are too young, and dates are therefore corrected or 'calibrated' on a set calculation to give a 'calendar' rather than a 'radiocarbon' date.

But the calculation for correcting radiocarbon dates is by no means accepted by all archaeologists, and the very accuracy of radiocarbon dating itself has received criticism in recent years. For this reason, it was decided to retain the conventional three-age system for the basic classification of the monuments in this book. The date given for each monument in the site heading is designed only to be a rough guide. When a radiocarbon date is given in the text, it is specifically described as a radiocarbon date, is given uncorrected in years BC and is therefore too young in calendar years. From the Roman period onward, radiocarbon dating is not normally appropriate, and calendar years are always given.

The following table is designed to outline the basic chronology over the time-span covered by the book, and may help explain some of the terms used in the text.

Approximate Date	Archaeological Period	Characteristic Features
225,000 BC	Lower Palaeolithic (Old Stone Age)	Warm interglacial within Pleistocene Ice Age. First evidence of man in Wales.
100,000 BC	Middle Palaeolithic	Mousterian hand-axes in south Wales, little evidence in north.
26,000 BC	Early Upper Palaeolithic	First evidence of *Homo sapiens* in Gwynedd; Kendrick's cave, Llandudno occupied. Onset of final glaciation.
15,000 BC	Late Upper Palaeolithic	Ice retreats; man returns to south Wales.
10,000 BC	Early Mesolithic (Middle Stone Age)	Nomadic hunter-gatherers in Anglesey and Lleyn use finely worked microlithic flints to tip arrows and spears for hunting.
6000 BC	Late Mesolithic	Seasonal settlements established in upland and lowland areas by regionalised groups of peoples. Some evidence for manipulation of environment.
3500 BC	Early Neolithic (New Stone Age)	First farmers arrive. Megalithic tombs built in fertile, low-lying parts of Gwynedd. Pottery first used; stone axes of Graig Lwyd microdiorite from Penmaenmawr used. Much forest clearance.
2500 BC	Late Neolithic	Communal tombs decline in importance. Ceremonial henges built. Farming activity spreads to marginal uplands. Beaker pottery becomes fashionable.
2000 BC	Early Bronze Age	More individualistic society. Burial mounds, cairns, stone circles and standing stones erected, especially in the upland areas of Gwynedd. Settlements elusive unless represented by burnt stone mounds. First evidence of metallurgy, mining of copper and manufacture of bronze tools.
1100 BC	Late Bronze Age	Population pressures, deterioration of climate and soil degradation lead to abandonment of upland farming. Defensive settlements first appear in Gwynedd.

Approximate Date	Archaeological Period	Characteristic Features
600 BC	Iron Age	Hillforts, concentric circle farms and less distinctive hut groups built in increasing numbers. Iron tools first appear. Consolidation of tribal groups, including Ordovices in Gwynedd.
AD 43	Roman Period	North Wales conquered by Romans (AD 77). Auxiliary forts (e.g., Segontium) established and roads built. Industry and agriculture flourish under *Pax Romana*.
AD 410	Early Medieval Period	Roman withdrawal. Irish raids. Emergence of kingdom of Gwynedd. Spread of Christianity. Viking raids. Power fluctuates between the Welsh kingdoms, but short-lived unity is achieved by Rhodri Fawr (844–78), Hywel Dda (942–50) and Gruffudd ap Llywelyn (1055–63).
AD 1066	Medieval Period	Normans invade Gwynedd (1086–94) but are repulsed by Gruffudd ap Cynan (1081–1137). Reigns of Gruffudd and his son, Owain Gwynedd (1137–70) mark high point of Welsh independence; monasteries founded, churches built and social and economic life developed. Expansion of Gwynedd under Llywelyn ap Iorwerth ('The Great') 1195–1240.
1276–83		Gwynedd, again expanding under Llywelyn ap Gruffudd (Llywelyn II, 1255–82), is crushed by Edward I of England.
1283–92		Major castle building programme by Master James of St George for Edward I.
1400–10		Owain Glyndŵr leads Welsh rebellion.
1485	Post-Medieval Period	Henry VII becomes first Tudor monarch.
1536–40		Dissolution of monasteries by Henry VIII.
1536–43		Acts of Union passed, whereby a unified Wales is merged politically with England.
1642–8		Civil War between Royalists and Parliamentarians brings many medieval castles back into use for the last time.

Glossary

Amphora A large jar for the bulk transport of wine or other liquids.

Antechamber Room used as entrance to a more important one.

Apsidal Round-ended or apse-shaped.

Arcade A row of arches usually supported on columns.

Archaeo-magnetic dating System of dating using the shift in the position of the earth's magnetic pole through time.

Augustinian Communities of clerics, often known as 'Canons Regular', who adopted the rule of St Augustine.

Bailey The defended outer courtyard or 'ward' of a castle.

Barbican An outer defence protecting a gateway.

Barrow A mound of earth or earth and stones used, most often during the Bronze Age, to cover burials.

Bay The space between roof trusses. A three-bay hall has two gable walls and two trusses.

Berm A strip of ground between the base of the curtain wall or rampart and the ditch.

Blind arcade A solid wall decorated with arches.

Bog-ore Iron concentrations in peat, a source of iron ore.

Burgage plot A plot of land, usually long and narrow, forming the unit of property in a medieval borough.

Burgess A property owner in a medieval borough who usually held certain rights in that town.

Buttery A store-room for wine and other beverages.

Cairn Mound of stones; may cover burials of Neolithic or Bronze Age date and often had additional ceremonial functions. Clearance cairns are non-sepulchral, and result from clearing stones from fields.

Cantref 'A hundred townships' – the main Welsh administrative unit of land division, used in pre-Norman and later times (plural: *cantrefi*).

Chamfer A bevelled edge on a beam or joist.

Chapterhouse The room in which monks met daily to discuss business and hear a chapter of the monastic rule.

Chi-rho A monogram formed from the two initial letters X (*chi*) and P (*rho*) of the name of Christ written in Greek.

Cist A stone-lined or slab-built grave.

Cistercian A movement of reformed Benedictine monks, established at Cîteaux in 1098. The 'White Monks', named from their white habits, were particularly successful in Wales.

Clas A community of clergy in the pre-Norman Welsh church (plural: *clasau*).

Clerestory Upper part of the nave wall, containing a row of windows.

Cloister A four-sided enclosure, usually at the centre of a monastery, with a covered walk along each side, used for study.

Commote A Welsh administrative unit of land (*cymwyd*), a subdivision of a *cantref*.

Constable The governor of a castle.

Corbel A projecting stone used for support of floor or roof timbers.

Counterscarp bank A small bank outside a defensive ditch.

Crossing The central space at the intersection of the east–west axis and north–south transepts of a church. The tower often stands above it.

Cross-slab A shaped stone slab on which is carved a cross; often, but not always, a grave cover.

Cultivation ridges Parallel ridges normally created by ploughing with a fixed mould-board plough which always turns the sod in the same direction. Some ridges (lazybeds) may be due to spading up. Normally indicative of medieval farming, but some may be prehistoric.

Cup-marks Man-made depressions about 50mm across and 20mm deep cut into natural rock exposures or, occasionally, the capstones of Neolithic tombs. Purpose unknown, but assumed ritual or magical. Date: Neolithic/early Bronze Age.

Cursive hand Lower case lettering.

Curtain wall The wall, often strengthened with towers, which encloses the courtyard of a castle.

Ffridd Mountain pasture (plural: *ffriddoedd*).

Gaul Roman and post-Roman France.

Genitive case Grammatical case indicating possession.

Hafod Summer grazing base on the *ffridd* (plural: *hafodau*).

Half-uncial script A manuscript hand popular in the 7th–10th centuries; also used in stone-carving.

Hall The main public room of a house or castle, used for administration of estates and justice, entertaining and eating.

Hendre/Hendref The main farm; compare *hafod* (plural: *hendrefi*).

Henge A non-defensive circular earthwork with a bank and ditch and one or more entrances, apparently used for ceremonial purposes during the late Neolithic period.

Hoard A temporary fighting platform of timber projecting from the top of a tower, allowing defenders to get directly above attackers.

Hollow way Ancient trackway cut deeply into a hillside through long and heavy use.

Interpolation An inserted phrase.

Intra-mural chamber A small room in the thickness of a wall.

Lancet A plain, slender window with a pointed arch.

Launder A raised wooden water channel.

Leat A channel dug for conveying water.

Llys **The house or court of the prince, situated in his *maerdref* (plural: *llysau*).**

Lordship The area ruled by a lord under the supremacy of the king.

Louvre The opening in the roof to allow smoke to escape.

Lynchet The edge of a 'terraced' field; the step created by a combination of soil creep against a barrier and undercutting by ploughing.

Mabinogion A collection of traditional Welsh stories set down in their present poetic form in the 12th century, but of earlier origin. The central core, the 'four branches', are the stories of Pwyll, Branwen, Manawydan and Math; to them have been added other stories from oral tradition, based on quasi-classical as well as native sources. Amongst these are the stories of Culhwch and Olwen and the 'Dream of Mascen Wledig'. In addition there are some later 'romances' – the stories of Owain and of Peredur. An accessible modern version is that of Kevin Crossley-Holland and Gwyn Thomas, *Tales from the Mabinogion* (London, 1984). The standard full translation is that in the Everyman Library, G. Jones and T. Jones, *The Mabinogion* (new edn, London, 1974).

Machicolation Openings in the floor of a projecting structure, often in front of a castle gate, through which missiles could be dropped on to attackers.

Maerdref The prince's manor or personal lands (plural: *maerdrefi*); there was normally one in each commote administered by a *maer* or steward.

Marcher lord A baron with special legal status, based on the Welsh border or Marches.

Megalith Large stone (from the Greek *mega* (large) and *lithos* (stone)); used of structures, such as Neolithic tombs, made of large slabs (often known as megaliths).

Motte A mound of earth constructed to support a tower and palisade. A type of castle introduced by the Normans.

Mullion The vertical bar between window openings.

Nucleated village Houses clustered around a manorial centre.

Ogam A system of writing invented in Ireland before the 5th century AD, comprising 20 letters represented by groups of notches, and often used for early medieval inscriptions on stone.

Portcullis Wood and iron defensive gate which could be raised or lowered in grooves in the wall of a castle gate-passage.
Postern A small gateway, subsidiary to the main entrance.
Purlin A horizontal beam in a roof.
Putlog holes Small square voids left in a wall face to receive horizontal supports for scaffolding.

Rafters The minor vertical timbers of a roof.
Revetment Timber- or stonework built to give support to the side of a bank or ditch.
Ring cairn A circular bank of stone with a hollow centre. Ceremonial monument of Bronze Age date.
Ringwork A type of early castle consisting of an earthen bank, usually circular, with external ditch.
Romanesque A style of architecture, 12th-century and earlier, with round arches and thick walls (called 'Norman' in England).

Scarp A steep slope, often artificially cut.
Sedile The seat for the clergy, normally set into the south wall of the chancel.
Serif Short line at the top or bottom of letters.
Solar The drawing room of a medieval house.
Syntax Rules regulating the order of words in a sentence.

Tenon A projection on stone or timber to provide a join by insertion into a mortise hole (as 'mortise and tenon' joint).
Tracery Decorative stonework in the upper parts of windows or on walls.
Transept The portion of a cruciform church crossing the main axis at right angles, orientated north–south.
Truss Main framework of beams supporting a roof. Designs differ regionally and through time.
Tympanum A semicircular or triangular wall space over a door or within a pediment, usually decorated.

Vault An arched stone roof.
Vernacular languages Native speech of the people; the predecessors of our modern languages developing away from Latin.
Villa Roman-style farmhouse with rooms arranged around a central court; a rural estate, 1st–4th centuries AD.

Ward A courtyard within the walls of a castle.
Well-stair A staircase of several flights arranged around a central space or well.
Wheel-cross A type of cross on which the head has an inset wheel joining the arms; it may be solid or pierced.
Wimple A linen veil covering the head, side of face and neck; 13th–14th-century.

Bibliography

Guidebooks

The monuments in the care of Cadw and other conservation bodies often have guidebooks for sale at reception areas which give a more detailed history and tour of the site. R Avent's combined guide to the Welsh castles, *Castles of the Princes of Gwynedd*, and A J Taylor's study, *The Welsh Castles of Edward I* should also be on sale in some castle shops, and these books and the guidebooks covering the great Edwardian castles are highly recommended.

Aberconwy House Guide to refurbishment, National Trust (1992).
Anglesey L Macinnes, *A Guide to Ancient and Historic Sites in the Isle of Anglesey*, Cadw Guidebook (Cardiff 1994).
Bangor Cathedral E P Roberts, Official Guidebook.
Beaumaris Castle J A Taylor, Cadw Guidebook (Cardiff 1988).
Caernarfon Castle J A Taylor, Cadw Guidebook (Cardiff 1993).
Cochwillan J Douglas-Pennant (1972).
Conwy Castle and Town Walls J A Taylor, Cadw Guidebook (Cardiff 1990).
Criccieth Castle, Pennarth Fawr and Llangybi Well R Avent, Cadw Guidebook (Cardiff 1989).
Cymer Abbey D M Robinson, Cadw Guide leaflet (Cardiff 1990).
Dolwyddelan Castle, Dolbadarn Castle R Avent, Cadw Guidebook (Cardiff 1988).
Dyffryn Chambered Tomb M J Yates, Cadw Guide leaflet (Cardiff 1989).
Harlech Castle J A Taylor, Cadw Guidebook (Cardiff 1988).
Segontium Roman Fort J L Davies, Cadw Guide leaflet (Cardiff 1990).

Further Reading

This is a very selective list of general books which give further information about aspects of Welsh history and archaeology.

Prehistory

Bowen, E G and Gresham, C A, *History of Merioneth*, vol. 1 (Dolgellau 1967).
Bradley, R, *The Prehistoric Settlement of Britain* (London 1978).
Burl, A. *The Stone Circles of the British Isles* (London 1976).
Cunliffe, B, *Iron Age Communities in Britain*, 3rd edn (London 1991).
Darvill, T, *Prehistoric Britain* (London 1987).
Forde-Johnston, J, *Hillforts* (Liverpool 1976).
Hogg, A H A, *Hill-forts of Britain* (London 1975).
Lynch, F M, *Prehistoric Anglesey*, 2nd edn (Llangefni 1991).
Megaw, J V S and Simpson, D D A (eds), *Introduction to British Prehistory* (Leicester 1979).

Powell, T G E *et al.*, *Megalithic Enquiries in the West of Britain* (Liverpool 1969).
Taylor, J A (ed.), *Culture and Environment in Prehistoric Wales* (Oxford 1980).

Roman

Burnham, B and Davies J L (eds), *Conquest, Co-existence and Change* (Lampeter 1991).
Frere, S S, *Britannia: A History of Roman Britain*, 3rd edn (London 1987).
Jarrett, M G and Nash-Williams, V E, *The Roman Frontier in Wales*, 2nd (revd) edn (Cardiff 1969).
Margery, I D, *Roman Roads in Britain* (London 1973).
Todd, M, *Roman Britain 55B.C.–A.D.400* (London 1981).
Webster, G, *The Roman Imperial Army*, 3rd edn (London 1985).

Early Medieval

Chadwick, N, *Studies in the Early British Church* (Cambridge 1958).
Davies, W, *Wales in the Early Middle Ages* (Leicester 1982).
Edwards, N and Lane, A (eds), *Early Medieval Settlements in Wales AD 400–1100* (Bangor and Cardiff 1988).
MacCana, P, *The Mabinogi* (Writers of Wales Series, Cardiff 1992)
Nash-Williams, V E, *Early Christian Monuments of Wales* (Cardiff 1950).
Wade-Evans, A W, *Vitae Sanctorum Britanniae et Genealogiae* (Cardiff 1944) (Latin texts and translations).

Medieval

Butler, L and Given-Wilson, C, *Medieval Monasteries of Great Britain* (London 1979).
Carr, A D, *Medieval Anglesey* (Llangefni 1982).
Davies, R R, *Conquest, Coexistence and Change: Wales 1063–1415* (Oxford 1987).
Geraldus Cambrensis (Gerald of Wales), *The Journey through Wales and The Description of Wales* (ed. Lewis Thorpe, Harmsworth 1978).
Kenyon, J R, *Medieval Fortifications* (Leicester 1990).
King, D J C, *The Castle in England and Wales* (London 1988).
Knowles, D and Hadcock, R N, *Medieval Religious Houses: England and Wales* 2nd (revd) edn (London 1971).
Renn, D, *Norman Castles in Britain*, 2nd edn (London 1973).
Smith, P, *Houses of the Welsh Countryside: A Story in Historical Geography*, 2nd edn (London 1988).
Williams, G, *The Welsh Church from Conquest to Reformation*, 2nd edn (Cardiff, 1976).

General

Davies, J, *A History of Wales* (London 1993).
Dodd, A H, *A Short History of Wales*, reprint of *Life in Wales* (1972) (London 1990).

General Reference

The Royal Commission on Ancient and Historical Monuments in Wales has published county volumes or 'inventories' which give detailed descriptions of all monuments known at the time of publication. All three old counties of Gwynedd

have been covered, but the Meirionnydd volume is very old, requires revision and is difficult to find. For prehistoric sites it is superseded by Bowen and Gresham's *History of Merioneth*.

An Inventory of the Ancient Monuments in Anglesey (London 1937, reprinted with additions 1960).
An Inventory of the Ancient Monuments in Caernarvonshire: I – East (London 1956).
An Inventory of the Ancient Monuments in Caernarvonshire: II – Central (London 1960).
An Inventory of the Ancient Monuments in Caernarvonshire: III – West (with general survey of the county) (London 1964).
An Inventory of the Ancient Monuments in the County of Merioneth (London 1921).

Gazetteer References

This is the full list of references added to the relevant site entry in the gazetteer. They are designed to help the interested visitor find out more about a specific monument.

Alcock, L, 1960, 'Castell Odo: an embanked settlement on Mynydd Ystum, near Aberdaron, Caernarvonshire', *Archaeologia Cambrensis, CIX*, pp 78–135.
Avent, R, 1983, *Cestyll Tywysogion Gwynedd – Castles of the Princes of Gwynedd*, Cardiff.
Baynes, E N, 1908, 'The Excavations at Din Lligwy', *Archaeologia Cambrensis*, 6th series, *VIII*, pp 183–210.
Baynes, E N, 1909, 'The Excavation of Lligwy Cromlech in the County of Anglesey', *Archaeologia Cambrensis*, 6th series, *IX*, pp 217–31.
Baynes, E N, 1909a, 'The Excavation of Two Barrows at Ty'n-y-Pwll, Llanddyfnan', *Archaeologia Cambrensis*, 6th series, *IX*, pp 312–32.
Bowen, E G and Gresham, C A, 1967, *The History of Merioneth*, vol. 1, Dolgellau.
Butler, L A S, 1974, 'Medieval Finds from Castell-y-Bere, Merioneth', *Archaeologia Cambrensis, CXXIII*, pp 78–112.
Casey, P J and Davies, J L, 1993, *Excavations at Segontium (Caernarfon) Roman Fort 1975–79*, CBA Research Report 90, London.
Clough, T H M and Cummins, W A, 1988, *Stone Axe Studies*, vol. 2, CBA Research Report 67, London.
Crawford, O G S, 1920, 'An Account of Excavations at Hengwm, Merionethshire, August and September 1919', *Archaeologia Cambrensis*, 6th series, *XX*, pp 99–133.
Crew, P, 1981, 'Interim report: Watch tower on Holyhead Mountain', *Archaeology in Wales, 21*, pp 35–6.
Crew, P, 1985, 'The Excavation of a Group of Mountain-top Cairns on Drosgl, Llanllechid, Gwynedd', *Bulletin of the Board of Celtic Studies, XXXII*, pp 290–325.
Crew, P, 1986, 'Bryn y Castell – a late prehistoric iron-working settlement in north-west Wales' in B G Scott and H Cleere (eds), *The Crafts of the Blacksmith*, Belfast, pp 91–100.
Crew, P and Crew, S, 1990, *Early Mining in the British Isles*, Plas Tan y Bwlch Occasional Paper 1, Maentwrog.
Davies, R W, 1968, 'Roman Wales and Roman Military Practice-Camps', *Archaeologia Cambrensis, CXVII*, pp 103–20.

Edwards, N M and Lane, A, 1988, *Early Medieval Settlements in Wales AD 400–1100*, Bangor and Cardiff.

Evans, W G, 1991, 'Derfel Gadarn – A Celebrated Victim of the Reformation', *Journal of the Merioneth Historical and Record Society, XI*, pp 137–51.

Fox, C, 1946, *A Find of the Early Iron Age from Llyn Cerrig Bach, Anglesey*, Cardiff.

Gresham, C A, 1938, 'The Roman Fort at Tomen y Mur', *Archaeologia Cambrensis, XCIII*, pp 192–211.

Gresham, C A, 1954, 'The Platform House in North West Wales', *Archaeologia Cambrensis, CIII*, pp 18–53.

Gresham, C A, 1968, *Medieval Stone Carving in North Wales*, Cardiff.

Gresham, C A, 1973, *Eifionydd: a study in landownership from the medieval period to the present day*, Cardiff.

Gresham, C A, 1985, 'Bedd Porius', *Bulletin of the Board of Celtic Studies, XXXII*, pp 386–92.

Griffiths, W E, 1950, 'Early Settlements in Caernarvonshire' *Archaeologia Cambrensis, CI*, pp 38–71.

Griffiths, W E, 1958, 'The Excavation of a Romano–British Hut-group at Gors y Gedol in Merionethshire', *Bulletin of the Board of Celtic Studies, XVIII*, pp 119–29.

Griffiths, W E, 1960, 'The Excavation of Stone Circles near Penmaenmawr, North Wales', *Proceedings of the Prehistoric Society, 26*, pp 303–39.

Hemp, W J, 1927, 'The Capel Garmon Chambered Long Cairn', *Archaeologia Cambrensis, LXXXII*, pp 1–44.

Hemp, W J, 1930, 'The Chambered Cairn of Bryn Celli Ddu', *Archaeologia, LXXX*, pp 179–214.

Hemp, W J, 1956, 'Presidential Address', *Archaeologia Cambrensis, CV*, pp 1–6.

Hogg, A H A, 1956, 'The Hillfort on Conway Mountain, Caernarvonshire', *Archaeologia Cambrensis, CV*, pp 49–80.

Hogg, A H A, 1960, 'Garn Boduan and Tre'r Ceiri, Excavations at two Caernarvonshire Hillforts', *Archaeological Journal, CXVII*, pp 1–39.

Hogg, A H A, 1975, *Hill-forts of Britain*, London.

Hooke, D, 1975, 'Llanaber: A Study in Landscape Development', *Journal of the Merioneth Historical and Record Society, 7*, pp 221–30.

Houlder, C H, 1961, 'The Excavation of a Neolithic Stone Implement Factory on Mynydd Rhiw in Caernarvonshire', *Proceedings of the Prehistoric Society, 27*, pp 108–43.

Hughes, H H, 1931, 'An Ancient Sundial at Clynnog', *Archaeologia Cambrensis, LXXXVI*, pp 181–3.

Jarrett, M G and Nash-Williams, V E, 1969, *The Roman Frontier in Wales*, 2nd (revd) edn, Cardiff.

Jones, J Ellis, 1985, 'A Roman Milestone Re-exhibited', *Transactions of the Caernarvonshire Historical Society, 46*, pp 151–60.

Kelly, R S, 1983, 'A Pre-afforestation Survey at Cyfannedd, Arthog, Gwynedd', *Bulletin of the Board of Celtic Studies, XXX*, pp 441–52.

Lowe, W Bezant, 1912, *The Heart of Northern Wales*, vol. 1, Llanfairfechan.

Lynch, F M, 1971, 'Report on the Re-excavation of two Bronze Age Cairns in Anglesey: Bedd Branwen and Treiorwerth', *Archaeologia Cambrensis, CXX*, pp 11–83.

Lynch, F M, 1984, 'Moel Goedog Circle I, a Complex Ring Cairn near Harlech', *Archaeologia Cambrensis, CXXXIII*, pp 8–50.

Lynch, F M, 1986, 'Excavation of a Kerb Circle and Ring Cairn on Cefn Caer Euni, Merioneth', *Archaeologia Cambrensis, CXXXV*, pp 81–120.

Lynch, F M, 1991, *Prehistoric Anglesey*, 2nd edn, Llangefni.

Morris, J, 1980, *Nennius, British History and the Welsh Annals*, London and Chichester.

Morris-Jones, J, 1918, 'The Stone of Cingen', Appendix to *Taliesin*, in *Y Cymmrodor, 28*.

Morris-Jones, J, 1921, *Inventory of Ancient Monuments: Merioneth*, pp 171–4.
Nash-Williams, V E, 1950, *The Early Christian Monuments of Wales*, Cardiff.
Phillips, C W, 1936, 'An Examination of the Tŷ Newydd Chambered Tomb, Llanfaelog, Anglesey', *Archaeologia Cambrensis, XCI*, pp 93–9.
Powell, T G E, 1973, 'Excavation of the Megalithic Chambered Cairn at Dyffryn Ardudwy, Merioneth, Wales', *Archaeologia, CIV*, pp 1–49.
Powell, T G E and Daniel, G E, 1956, *Barclodiad y Gawres: the Excavation of a Megalithic Chamber Tomb in Anglesey*, Liverpool.
Powell, T G E *et al.*, 1969, *Megalithic Enquiries in the West of Britain*, Liverpool.
Reynolds, P K Bailie, 1938, *Excavations on the site of the Roman fort of Kanovium at Caerhun, Caernarvonshire*, Cardiff.
Savory, H N, 1960, 'Excavations at Dinas Emrys, Beddgelert, Caernarvonshire, 1954–56', *Archaeologia Cambrensis, CIX*, pp 13–77.
Scott, W L, 1933, 'The Chambered Tomb of Pant y Saer, Anglesey', *Archaeologia Cambrensis, LXXXVIII*, pp 185–228.
Smith, C A, 1987, 'Excavations at the Tŷ Mawr Hut Circles, Part IV: Chronology and Discussion', *Archaeologia Cambrensis, CXXXVI*, pp 20–38.
Smith, C A and Lynch, F M, 1987, *Trefignath and Din Dryfol: The Excavation of Two Megalithic Tombs in Anglesey, Cambrian Archaeological Monograph 3.*
Smith, P, 1988, *Houses of the Welsh Countryside: A Study in Historical Geography*, 2nd edn, London.
Stanley, W O, 1846, 'Towyn y Capel and the ruined chapel of St Bride on the west coast of Holyhead Island with notices of the curious interments there discovered', *Archaeological Journal, III*, pp 223–8.
Stanley, W O, 1867, 'On the remains of Ancient Circular Habitations in Holyhead Island called Cyttiau Gwyddelod', *Archaeological Journal, XXIV*, pp 229–42.
Stanley, W O, 1869, 'Ancient Circular Habitations at Tŷ Mawr, Holyhead Island with notices of other remains found there', *Archaeological Journal, XXVI*, pp 301–22.
Stanley, W O, 1876, 'Notices of Sepulchral deposits with Cinerary Urns found at Porth Dafarch in Holyhead Island in 1848; and of recent excavations in the sand mounds adjacent in 1875–6', *Archaeological Journal, XXXIII*, pp 129–43.
Taylor, A J, 1986, *The Welsh Castles of Edward I*, London and Ronceverte (revised reprint of *The History of the King's Works in Wales*, 1974, now out of print).
Thomas, W G, 1989, 'An Early Sundial from the Towyn Area', *Archaeologia Cambrensis, CXXXVIII*, pp 111–13.
Wainwright, G J, 1962, 'The Excavation of an Earthwork at Castell Bryn Gwyn, Llanidan Parish, Anglesey', *Archaeologia Cambrensis, CXI*, pp 25–58.
Warren, S Hazzledine, 1922, 'The Neolithic Stone Axes of Graig Lwyd, Penmaenmawr', *Archaeologia Cambrensis, LXXVII*, pp 1–36.
White, R B, 1978, 'Excavations at Trwyn Du, Anglesey, 1974', *Archaeologia Cambrensis, CXXVII*, pp 16–39.
Williams, I, 1949, 'Presidential Address: The Towyn Inscribed Stone', *Archaeologia Cambrensis, C*, pp 161–72.

Acknowledgements

My first thanks must go to Sian Rees, the series editor, for her invitation to write this book and for her encouragement and help during its gestation, not to mention her painstaking work on the final editing, without which many readers might have become lost on byways and backroads. Further thanks must go to the copy editor, Huw Jones, and to Ruth Bowden of HMSO who saved me from many slips and foolish errors.

Many friends have given advice on particular monuments, but special thanks must go to Peter Crew for much companionship on fieldwork over the years, for guiding me through the fascinating maze of Tomen y Mur and generally putting me right about Meirionnydd's Roman sites, as well as his kindness in allowing me to use unpublished plans. I am grateful to Dr Jeffery Davies for help with the Roman monuments; to my colleague, Dr Nancy Edwards, for discussions about the Early Christian stones and churches, and to Richard Avent for his generous help with the castles where he saved me from several errors. I have been instructed on medieval architecture by Tony Parkinson of RCAHM and by Jeff St Paul, the Gwynedd Conservation Architect, who helped me understand the Tudor Rose (no. 115). The book has also benefited from discussions with my colleagues in the School of History and Welsh History at the University College of Wales, Bangor, with Tomos Roberts, the university archivist, and with David Longley and his colleagues at the Gwynedd Archaeological Trust, especially David Thompson who has generously provided many photographs and Helen Flook who drew the reconstuction of early Bangor. Sian Spink, of the National Monuments Record in Aberystwyth, has been most helpful and efficient in providing photographs. I am especially grateful to Chris Musson of the Air Photographic Section of the NMR for finding me such splendid photographs and to Mary Aris of Gwynedd Archives Service for the loan of some of her air views.

Several of the monuments are on private land and I am grateful to the owners for their ready agreement to their inclusion in this guide. I hope they will never have cause to rue their generosity and openness.

I am particularly grateful to Antonia Eastman for reading the entire manuscript and 'test driving' many of the entries. Her comments, reactions and advice have been invaluable. I have also benefited from similar help from my students and members of field courses at Plas Tan y Bwlch who have been most constructive critics.

The publications department of Cadw, especially Diane Williams and Christine Kenyon, have been of great assistance with illustrations and advice on production;

Peter Lawrence has produced the line drawings with great good humour, efficiency and panache.

Finally, I should like to thank my husband, Peter Llewellyn, for his continued understanding, support and, as the deadline drew close, forbearance – not to mention his enormous help with the inevitable task of cutting, cutting and yet more cutting!

Sources of Illustrations

Most of the illustrations were produced by staff of Cartographic Services, Welsh Office; many redrawn with amendments using plans published elsewhere: nos 8, 118, 123, 124, 128, 129, 132, 149 (Crown copyright plans from Welsh Office or Cadw guidebooks); nos 38, 40, 61, 62, 63, 69, 82, 83, 84, 93, 111, 115 (Royal Commission on Ancient and Historical Monuments, Wales); nos 1, 2, 4, 8, 16, 17, 21, 23, 29, 44, 56, 58, 77, 78 (Lynch 1969, 1976, 1984, 1986, 1991); no. 22 (Houlder 1961); no. 94 (Gresham 1938). I am particularly grateful for permission to use unpublished plans: nos 86, 87 and 96 (Peter Crew) and no. 133 (Martin de Levandowicz). I am grateful to the editors of *Archaeologia Cambrensis* and the *Archaeological Journal* for permission to reproduce early engravings (nos 3, 5, 7, 9, 10, 19, 25, 33, 97); to the Caernarfonshire Historical Society for no. 91 (Jones 1985); to the National Library of Wales for no. 112 and to the Welsh Librarian, University College of North Wales for giving me access to the copy of Pennant's *Tours in Wales* with additional illustrations (nos 143 and 147).

Early Christian inscribed stones (nos 100, 106, 109, 111, 148) have been reproduced, some (nos 105 and 113) with amendments, from Nash-Williams, 1950 with the permission of the National Museum of Wales and University of Wales Press. I am also grateful to the National Museum for permission to use the reconstruction drawings used in the introductory sections of chapters 1, 2 and 3. The reconstruction drawings used in chapters 4, 5 and 7 and for entries 114, 119, 130, 134 and 146 are the copyright of Cadw: Welsh Historic Monuments. The drawing of Bangor in chapter 6 was specially made by Helen Flook of Gwynedd Archaeological Trust to whom the copyright belongs. The reconstruction of Degannwy castle (no. 117) was first published in Lowe 1912.

Copyright acknowledgements are due to the following photographic sources: National Monuments Record collection in the Royal Commission on Ancient and Historical Monuments in Wales (nos *53, *67, *70, *88, 98, 101, 107, 108, 136, 139, 140, 141, 144, 145, 150 (* indicates photographs from the Aerial Photography section of the NMR); Cadw: Welsh Historic Monuments (nos 6, 89, 92, 103, 117, 118, 128, 132, 138); Gwynedd Archaeological Trust (nos 14, 34, 59, 64, 66, 68, 72, 73, 74, 79, 80, 81, 90, 109, 121, 135, 137, 142); Clwyd-Powys Archaeological Trust (nos 76,

95); Peter Crew (nos 35, 41, 46, 110); UCNW collection (nos 11, 12, 13, 43); National Museum of Scotland (no. 32); Richard Kelly (no. 47); Antonia Eastman (no. 55); Cambridge University Collection (no. 57); Mary Aris (no. 99); Mick Sharp (no. 109 and the photograph of Penmon church in the introduction to chapter 8); Ministry of Defence (no. 116); National Trust (no. 120); Penrhyn Estate (no. 122); Stephen Gilligan (no. 125).

Index

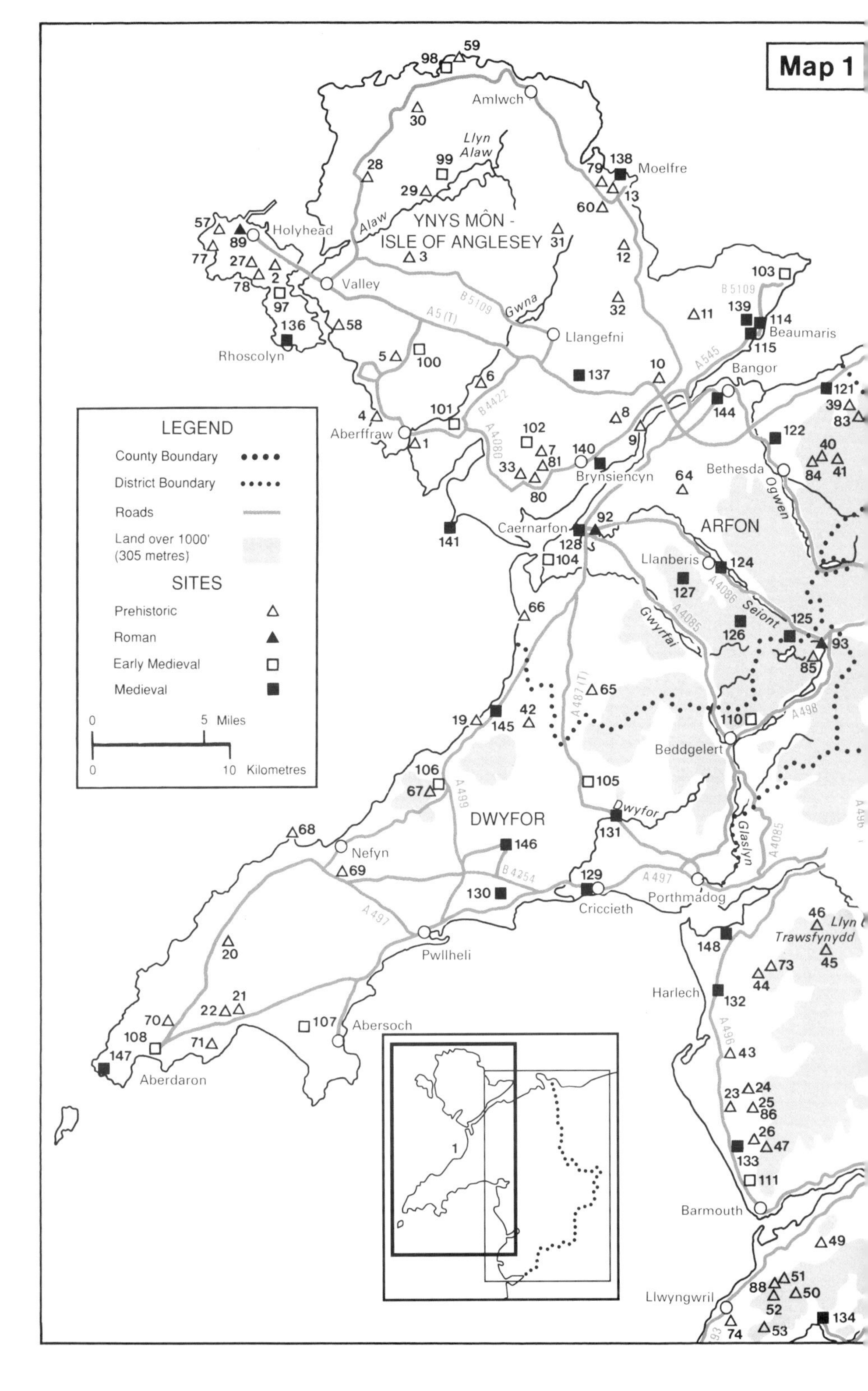
Map 1
YNYS MÔN - ISLE OF ANGLESEY
ARFON
DWYFOR
LEGEND
County Boundary
District Boundary
Roads
Land over 1000' (305 metres)
SITES
Prehistoric
Roman
Early Medieval
Medieval
0 5 Miles
0 10 Kilometres
Amlwch
Moelfre
Holyhead
Valley
Llangefni
Rhoscolyn
Aberffraw
Beaumaris
Bangor
Bethesda
Brynsiencyn
Caernarfon
Llanberis
Beddgelert
Nefyn
Pwllheli
Criccieth
Porthmadog
Harlech
Barmouth
Llwyngwril
Abersoch
Aberdaron
Llyn Alaw
Alaw
Gwna
Ogwen
Seiont
Gwyrfai
Dwyfor
Glaslyn
Llyn Trawsfynydd

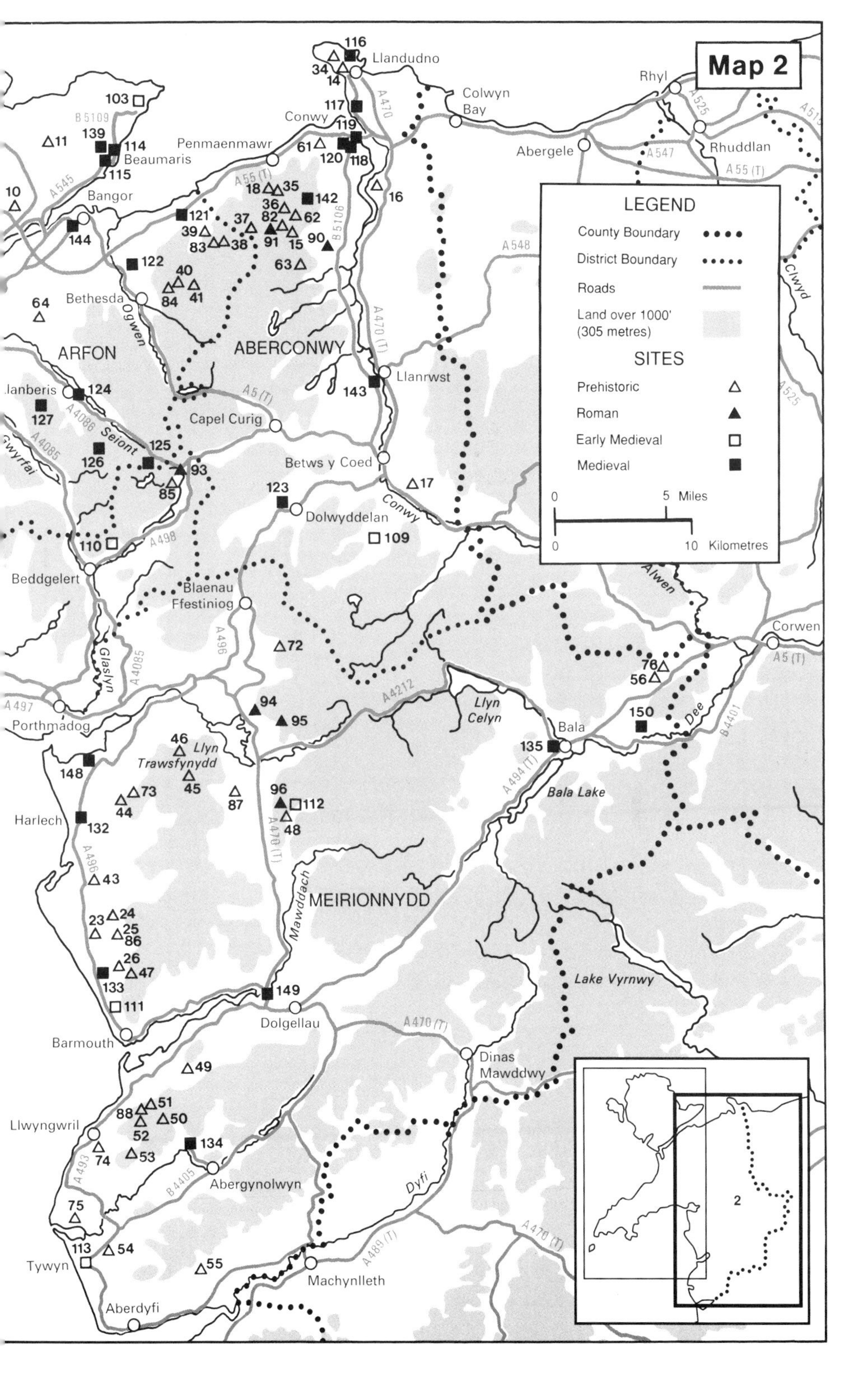

Map 2
LEGEND
County Boundary
District Boundary
Roads
Land over 1000' (305 metres)
SITES
Prehistoric
Roman
Early Medieval
Medieval
0 5 Miles
0 10 Kilometres
Llandudno
Colwyn Bay
Rhyl
Rhuddlan
Abergele
Conwy
Penmaenmawr
Beaumaris
Bangor
Bethesda
ARFON
ABERCONWY
MEIRIONNYDD
Llanrwst
Capel Curig
Betws y Coed
Dolwyddelan
Beddgelert
Blaenau Ffestiniog
Porthmadog
Harlech
Barmouth
Dolgellau
Llwyngwril
Abergynolwyn
Tywyn
Aberdyfi
Machynlleth
Dinas Mawddwy
Bala
Bala Lake
Corwen
Llyn Celyn
Llyn Trawsfynydd
Lake Vyrnwy
Conwy
Ogwen
Seiont
Gwyrfai
Glaslyn
Mawddach
Dyfi
Dee
Alwen
Clwyd
A470
A525
A547
A55 (T)
A548
A545
B5109
B5106
A470 (T)
A5 (T)
A4086
A4085
A498
A496
A497
A4212
A494 (T)
B4401
A493
B4405
A489 (T)